O C E A
D1034744
Vredenburgh
R. Marawina
Boucou
Gado Saby
R. Cottica
Barbacoeba
Casepoere
Devil's Harwar
R. Perica
R. Comewina
The Cordon Path
Jerusalem
Wana Creek
Cormoetibo Creek
Soribo
Bottle Creek
The Hope
Fauconberg
Claas Creek
Cassivinica Creek
Cupy
R. Cottica
La Rochelle
Patamaca Creek
Clarenbeek
R. Marawina
R. Comewina
N A M
Pininica Creek
Jocka Creek
Mapany Creek
Comewina Creek
Settlements of the Ouca Negroes
Tempaty Creek
Magdenberg
C A Y E N N E
Scale of Miles
0 10 20 30 40 50

A family of negro slaves

EXPEDITION TO SURINAM

being the narrative of a five years expedition
against the revolted negroes of Surinam in Guiana
on the wild coast of South America
from the year 1772 to 1777
elucidating that country and describing its productions
with an account of Indians of Guiana
and negroes of Guinea
by CAPTAIN JOHN STEDMAN
newly edited and abridged
by CHRISTOPHER BRYANT
and illustrated with engravings
selected from the earliest edition
themselves made after drawings by the author

The Folio Society · London · 1963

PRINTED IN GREAT BRITAIN
Printed and bound by Richard Clay & Co, Ltd, Bungay
Set in 'Monotype' Plantin 11 *point leaded* 1 *point*
Gravure illustrations by D. H. Greaves Ltd, Scarborough

ILLUSTRATIONS

INTRODUCTION

ALTHOUGH it was Columbus, when discovering Trinidad in 1498, who first made known the existence of Guiana, little attempt was made to explore the country until rumours began to percolate back to Europe, nearly a hundred years later, that here was to be found the fabulous city of El Dorado. The lust for gold spurred many people, Sir Walter Raleigh among them, to set out on often disastrous expeditions, but when the rumours turned out to be without foundation, no scope remained for the romantic adventurer and development was left to the widening searches of the trading companies.

The first trading posts were set up during the early part of the seventeenth century by the British and the Dutch, the former, rather paradoxically, establishing themselves in Surinam, and the latter in what was later to become British Guiana. The first permanent colony in Surinam was founded by Lord Willoughby, Earl of Parham (Paramaribo was not named after him) in 1652, and it was the large number of English Jews who came with him who formed the settlement at Jews' Savannah. Under Willoughby, who was made governor of all the British possessions in the Caribbean, the colony flourished, but shortly after his death, during the Second Anglo–Dutch War, Surinam was captured by the Dutch under Abraham Crijnssen. By the Treaty of Breda, which ended the war in 1667, this conquest was acknowledged and the colony formally ceded to the Dutch. In the meantime, however, so long did news take to travel from Europe to the Americas, a British fleet had recaptured Surinam, and it was only after a considerable amount of difficulty that the new British governor would agree to accede to the conditions of the treaty.

Surinam now belonged to Zeeland, but, unable to meet the costs of administration, Zeeland sold it in 1682 to the Dutch West India Company. The financial drain, however, still proved too great for any one organization to bear on its own and, within a few months, the Chartered Society of Surinam was formed, in which the Dutch West India Company retained a third interest and sold a third each to the City of Amsterdam and to Cornelis van Aerssens, lord of Sommelsdijk. It was Sommelsdijk who, at his own expense, became the first governor, who laid the foundations of organized government, and who first set about the subjugation of the Indian tribes. From the early days the colonists had drawn slave labour from among the natives and tribal retaliation had been an increasingly dangerous threat to the safety of the settlements. As a result of Sommelsdijk's activity, the tribes were pacified, their liberty and possessions guaranteed, and it was not the natives who were the source of future unrest. Slavery was now confined to negroes imported from Africa, but the traffic was considerable; as long as the slaves were kept under the control of their masters all was well, but as the number who succeeded in escaping and taking refuge in the jungle increased, and as they managed to gain access to arms, so they became a new and even more serious menace.

The situation started to become acute in 1712. Just over twenty years earlier, the colonists had driven off one French attack on Surinam, but this time a new attack, led by Admiral Cassard, met with far greater success. Although he failed to reduce Paramaribo, his forces committed such depredations among the plantations that the settlers, for fear of losing both their lives and their livelihood, forced the governor to surrender. Cassard, however, was less interested in conquest than he was in ransom, and the amount that he was able to extort in ransom money almost bankrupted the colony. But in many ways this was not the most serious consequence of the French attack. While the soldiers plundered and the planters fled, the negro slaves suddenly found a chance to gain their freedom, coupled with an opportunity to plunder and to arm themselves. They, in turn, were now capable of forays on outlying plantations, and the threat of insurrection became a daily part of the planters' lives.

By 1772 the position had become so serious that the Dutch Government was forced to take positive action and, on the orders of the States-General, an expeditionary force was sent out from Holland for the specific purpose of crushing the slave revolts. One of the officers on this expedition was an Englishman, Captain J. G. Stedman, and his account not only of the expedition itself but also of the prevailing conditions throughout the colony, is both an immensely human document and an authoritative source for the period.

When Stedman, together with the remnants of the expeditionary force, returned to Holland in 1777, the threat of organized insurrection had been finally dispelled. But the history of the Guianas themselves continued to be stormy. The outbreak of the American War of Independence saw a marked deterioration in Anglo-Dutch relations, for the sympathies of the latter were wholly on the American side. For some time the conflict was contained within continuous and fruitless negotiation, but, on 20 December 1780, it led to an open declaration of war. Surinam proved able to defend itself, but Demerara, Berbice and Essequebo (three separate colonies which were consolidated in 1831 to form British Guiana) were captured by the British forces. Peace was signed in 1784, but immediately afterwards the Dutch

West India Company was dissolved and its possessions came under the direct control of the States-General in Holland. With the outbreak of the Napoleonic Wars in 1803, the conflict was again resumed and Surinam itself was forced to surrender to the British in 1804. Only with the Peace of Paris in 1814 did the long years of warfare finally come to an end; Surinam was restored to Holland and the colonies took on the boundaries, minor disputes excepted, that they have retained to the present day.

The final end to slavery was, however, still some way off. In the years following the termination of the slave trade in 1821 there was considerable unrest among the existing slaves throughout the whole of the Caribbean area. But even the British colonies, who were the first to take action, did not emancipate their slaves until 1834; the French followed their example in 1848, but it was 1863 before the Dutch also fell into line. Over the preceding three centuries more than ten million slaves had been imported into the Americas alive; few places now remained where slavery was condoned.

John Gabriel Stedman, the eldest of five children, was born in Holland in 1744. Although, as he himself says, his ambition was to enter the British Navy, family misfortunes forced him to abandon this idea and, in 1760, he accepted an ensign's commission in General John Stuart's regiment in the Scots Brigade, then in the pay of the Dutch. He was promoted lieutenant in 1771, a rank he was allowed to retain when he volunteered to join the expeditionary force to Surinam in 1772. The five years that he spent in the Guianas, and the journal that was the fruit of his experiences, mark the highlights of his career. After he returned to Holland he rejoined Stuart's regiment and was shortly afterwards promoted to captain. When war between England and Holland broke out, however, the Scots Brigade was disbanded and Stedman returned to England. The brigade was afterwards reformed, and in 1793 Stedman was promoted to major. Three years later he was appointed, as a lieutenant-colonel, to the command of a regiment in garrison at Gibraltar, but when he was in London just prior to embarking he suffered severe injuries in an accident and was, as a result, unable to take up his post. He therefore retired to Tiverton, where he died the following year.

Throughout his journal Stedman shows every sign of having been genuinely and steadfastly devoted to his mulatto 'wife' Joanna and seems sincerely to have mourned her death in 1782. None the less, some years before this, in fact very shortly after he returned to Holland, he married Adriana Wiertz van Coehorn, a grand-daughter of the famous engineer. By her he had three sons, two of whom were killed while on active service, while the third died at sea on his way home after serving for forty years in India. He also had two daughters—the second of whom was christened Maria Joanna!

In his will Stedman gave instructions that he was to be buried by the side of Bamfylde Moore Carew, the king of the gipsies who had been born near Tiverton and who had died there about 1770. Possibly Stedman felt that their wanderings had made them kindred spirits; certainly there seems to be no nearer connection between them. In the event his instructions were not carried out and the two men lie at opposite sides of the church.

The full title of Stedman's book is *Narrative of a Five Years' Expedition against the Revolted Negroes of Surinam, in Guiana, on the Wild Coast of South America, from the year 1772 to 1777: elucidating the History of that Country, and describing its Productions, viz. Quadrupeds, Birds, Fishes, Reptiles, Trees, Shrubs, Fruits and Roots; with an Account of the Indians of Guiana and Negroes of Guinea.* This was first published in 1796, illustrated with a large number of engravings by many different artists (including, rather surprisingly, William Blake), all based on the author's own drawings. A second edition appeared in 1806 and was reprinted in 1813. A romance entitled *Joanna* and based on Stedman's narrative was also produced in 1824.

This edition is based on the first, but most of the author's notes on the flora and fauna of Guiana have been omitted as being really of interest only to the specialist. The early history of the colony has been condensed in the first part of this Introduction, the spelling of proper names has been made consistent, and punctuation has been modernized.

C.B.

EXPEDITION TO SURINAM

1

THE exploring of foreign countries having of late years, and particularly since the recent discoveries of the immortal Captain Cook, so generally been the object of persons both in private and public situations, and the histories of their labours and pursuits being so interesting to the curiosity of the public, I have ventured to offer such observations as I have had an opportunity of making in a very singular part of the globe, on which few Englishmen have been thrown, either by accident or curiosity.

As the nature, however, of these transactions can only be understood by a reference to the occasion which called me thither, I feel myself under the necessity of still premising a few words upon that subject.

Every part of the world where domestic slavery is established, may be occasionally liable to insurrection and disquiet, more especially where the slaves constitute the majority of the inhabitants; but the colony of Surinam, in Dutch Guiana, has been peculiarly unfortunate in this respect. Whether from the shelter which is afforded to the fugitives by the immense forests which overspread the most considerable part of this country, or whether the government of this settlement be radically defective, it is a certain fact that its European settlers are constantly exposed to the most violent ravages, and the most desperate outrage. Of these circumstances this is not however the place for a minute detail. Let it suffice therefore for the present only to observe that these repeated revolts and insurrections demanded at length the most vigorous measures for the restoration of a general peace; and that the accounts transmitted to Holland, in the year 1772, that a considerable body of armed people of this description had assembled in the forests and become extremely formidable to the colony, determined their High Mightinesses the States of the United Provinces to send out a sufficient maritime force to oppose the insurgents and, if possible, to quell the insurrection.

The British navy had ever been my choice and ambition, in which I was well recommended; but the small hopes of preferment I had naturally to expect in time of peace, and my paternal estate being lost just after my birth by accidental misfortunes, induced me to relinquish the hopes of advancement in the sea service, and to accept an ensign's commission, presented me without purchase, in one of the Scots brigade regiments in the pay of Holland, where Sir Joseph York at that period was ambassador from the British court. Before this nobleman I had the honour to take the usual oaths of abjuration and allegiance to my King and Country, as registered at the British war-office. This point I have also thought it right to premise, as a duty owing to myself, to show the world in general that it was necessity not choice that compelled me to enter into a *foreign* service, though perhaps a more ancient and distinguished corps does not exist than the above brigade has proved to be, both in this island and on the continent, for above two hundred years.

At the time of the above insurrection I was Lieutenant in the Honourable General John Stuart's regiment, when, impressed by the hopes of traversing the sea, my favourite element, and in some measure gratifying my curiosity in exploring a part of the world not generally known—still more by the prospect of that preferment which might be consequent on so dangerous an expedition—I instantly solicited admission into a corps of volunteers which was preparing to sail for Guiana, and had the honour, by his Serene Highness William V. Prince of Orange, to be advanced to the rank of Captain by brevet,* under Colonel Louis Henry Fourgeoud, a Swiss gentleman from the Alpine Mountains, who was appointed our commander-in-chief.

Having taken the oaths of fidelity on the 12th of November to the new corps, and prepared what was necessary for the voyage, I bade farewell to my old regiment, and immediately sailed to the island of Texel where several of our gentlemen were already assembled, and where, on going ashore, I nearly perished by the boat's shipping a sea and sinking in the surf.

The island of Wieringen was however the spot of general rendezvous. Colonel Fourgeoud arriving here on the 7th of December, the volunteers were all assembled, to the number of five hundred fine young men; and on the morning of the 8th we were formed into seven companies and embodied as a regiment of marines. Besides the *Boreas* and *Westellingwerf* men-of-war, commanded by Captains Van de Velde and Crass, three new frigate-built transports were put in commission, carrying ensign, jack, and pennant, and armed with from ten to sixteen guns, as sloops of war. On board these vessels we embarked the same afternoon under a general salute.

Our departure was not however immediately consequent on our embarkation. We lay wind-bound in the Texel roads for many days, during which time one of our young officers, a Mr Hesseling, was unfortunately seized with the small-pox. This gentleman, in order to prevent his infecting the ship's company, was ordered on shore to a

* Each officer was permitted to re-enter his former regiment, if he survived the expedition, and returned to Europe, a vacancy being there preserved for him during his absence.

town on the land's end, called the Helder, where I conducted him in a pinnace, and where we left him behind us. But on my return, the surgeon declaring he saw the symptoms of the same disorder on myself, I was also immediately ordered to the island of Texel. Having passed a most anxious quarantine in this place, I had the good fortune however to escape the loathsome malady, and to the doctor's surprise appeared once more on board perfectly well, just before the signal gun was fired for the fleet to weigh anchor. This circumstance cannot but induce me to wish that those in particular who are destined for a military or a naval life would avail themselves of the art of inoculation, in order to avoid a painful anxiety to themselves, and a most dangerous infection to their fellow-creatures.

On Christmas day our small fleet put to sea, at eight o'clock a.m. with a fresh breeze from east-north-east in company with above one hundred vessels bound for different parts of the globe, and the most beautiful clear weather. Having safely got without the soundings and saluted each other with nine guns, we kept our course down channel and soon passed the North Foreland, the Isle of Wight, and Portland Point; but here the *Westellingwerf*, having sprung a leak, was obliged to part company, and run into Plymouth for repair.

The wind now freshened as we approached the Bay of Biscay, where the mate of the vessel directed my particular attention to a kind of sea-swallow, commonly distinguished by the name of the *Storm-bird*, from its supposed property of foretelling an impending tempest. The colour of this bird is a very deep blue approaching to black, and enlivened by some variegated tints; its size is about that of a large martin or swallow; it is web-footed, the bill is very long and sharp, and the wings of an extraordinary length, which enable it to fly very fast and for a considerable time, skimming with incredible velocity around the horizon. It subsists entirely upon fish, which is probably the cause of its being sensible of the first indications of whatever may prevent its usual supply of food. It then flies along with extreme swiftness, in order to avoid the storm, but if overtaken by it, drops its wings and floats upon the surface of the waves.

On the following day, January 2nd, 1773, the predictions of the storm-bird were verified: a heavy gale sprung up from north-north-east by which, off Cape Finisterre, the *Boreas* and *Vigilance* were separated from us. We kept our course during the night with double reefed top-sails, and all the hatches laid, which made our men in general very sick. Here I ought not to forget that by way of experiment we had flung the hammocks *athwart* ships, and not as usual fore and aft. This method we found however to be both so roomy and convenient, that it has been since adopted by several other vessels.

On the morning of the 4th we spied a stout ship to windward in the offing, bearing straight down upon us. Conjecturing she might be an Algerine pirate from the African coast, and now but two ships out of five, we prepared to engage her; she however soon proved to be the *Boreas* man-of-war, which had parted company on the 2nd. From this date the men were daily exercised at the great guns, and by firing at a target suspended from the yard-arm.

On the 14th, in the morning-watch, we passed the Tropic, when the usual ceremony of ducking the fresh-water sailors was ransomed by tipping the foremast men with some silver. About this time the *Boreas* most unluckily lost one of her best seamen, the boatswain's mate who, his hand slipping in the wet, pitched from the fore-yard-arm into the sea. His presence of mind in calling to the captain, as he floated alongside, 'Be not alarmed for me, sir,' in the confidence of meeting with relief, attracted peculiar compassion, and even caused some murmuring as no assistance was offered him; in consequence, after swimming a considerable time within view, the unfortunate young man went to the bottom.

We now were got in the tract of the trade winds, which blowing continually east, and the weather becoming from day to day more temperate, made the voyage exceedingly pleasant—more so because of the many dolphins or dorados, which seem to take peculiar delight in sporting around the vessels. The real dolphin, which is of the cetaceous kind, was anciently celebrated in poetic story on account of its philanthropy and other supposed virtues: but to the dorado or dolphin of the moderns, this character is far from being applicable, for this fish is extremely voracious and destructive, and is known to follow the ships and exhibit his sports and gambols, not from attachment to man kind, but from the more selfish motive of procuring food, particularly on the eve of an approaching storm, of which he appears perfectly sensible.

Our progress was now daily marked by increasing warm weather, which released me from the confinement of a disagreeable cabin crowded with officers, most of whom had never been to sea, and enabled me to pursue my favourite amusements, whether of reading above deck, or exercise in the rigging. Thus circumstanced I, on the 17th, had the happiness of rendering a most important service to one of our young officers, a Mr Dumoulin, who by a sudden roll of the vessel was actually thrown over the gunwale. At that moment happening to stand without-board in the main-chains, I fortunately grasped hold of him in his fall, which saved him, as he could not swim, from inevitable death.

The entrance into warmer regions gave occasion to an observation perhaps not generally known, which (though uncouth) must be of great importance to sailors; namely, that between the Tropics, while vermin may remain in the head, none can possibly continue to exist in the bedding, clothes, linen, etc.

The two following days it blew very fresh, and heavy seas washed over the vessel. While helping to put a reef in the main-top-sail for a little exercise, I lost every one of my keys, which dropped from the yard-arm into the sea. This trifling accident I should never have related, had it not proved a very great inconvenience, by debarring me from coming at my private property, particularly since the whole ship's company, officers included, lived on salt provision alone, a pig and a couple of lean sheep excepted, whose legs had been broken by the rolling and pitching of the vessel. This manner of living on salt-beef, pork and peas, like common sailors, was introduced by our commander-in-chief, in order to inure us (he said) to such food as we were likely to be alone supplied with in the woods of Surinam; and from the *generous* motive of regaling his American friends with European refreshments, such as live sheep, hogs, fowls, ducks, bacon hams, bullocks, tongues, preserved vegetables, pickles, spices, etc. all of which were provided by the town of Amsterdam in profusion. But good intentions do not always meet with their rewards, since the worms, without anyone's permission, laid hold of the greatest part of the dead stock for themselves, and were, for a punishment, together with their plunder, thrown overboard into the ocean. Let me add, that instead of plate, our meals were frequently served up in small wooden tubs of not the most cleanly appearance, and only once a day; which negligence, however, I am willing to impute to Monsieur Laurant, the colonel's French valet-de-chambre. In short, the scurvy and other loathsome disorders began to make their appearance; dejection and low-spirits took place throughout the ship, while I complained *aloud*, and from that moment dates the *good-will* which Colonel Fourgeoud manifested towards me in particular, as will be seen throughout the expedition. It is with pain that I relate this passage—but no consideration shall prevent me from bringing to light particular foibles, as it will ever give me the greatest pleasure to render virtue conspicuous.

Becoming extremely low-spirited towards the close of our voyage, I now had recourse to daily sea-bathing, and to a cheering glass of claret, two ankers of which had been provided for each officer, independently of his own stock. These means proved efficacious, and I found myself in a few days perfectly recovered from my complaint. On the 30th the weather became hazy, when the ships brought-to and hove the lead in thirteen fathom foul water. The following day we passed several large black rocks to windward, called the Constables, and cast anchor near the Euripice, or Devil's Islands, off the coast of South America. The Euripice Islands are situated about twenty-four miles from the French settlement of Cayenne, and consist of a ridge of small uninhabited and very dangerous rocks for shipping. Here the current runs constantly from the south-east to the north-west at the rate of sixty English miles in twenty-four hours: consequently every vessel which happens to pass the mouth of the river Surinam must make a considerable circuit in order to regain the possibility of entering that river.

While we remained in this situation, we observed the narwhal, or sea-unicorn, and one or two large turtles, floating past the ship's side. The former of these is a large fish, and very distinguishable by a long spiral excrescence on its nose, like a tapering twisted rope. The one we saw at this time (though some are said to be forty or fifty) appeared but six or eight feet in length, and its horn about four. This weapon is dreadfully offensive to many fishes, especially to the whale, and when polished (either in hardness or whiteness) is considered not to be inferior to ivory.

The turtles are divided into two species, and are generally distinguished in Surinam by the names of *calapee* or green turtle, and *carett*. The former of these sometimes weighs four hundred pounds, and has a flattish shell; but the carett is inferior both in size and quality, except with respect to its shell, which is more valuable, and of a more convex form. Both the calapee and carett deposit their eggs, which are very excellent food, in the sand, where they are hatched by the heat of the sun. The manner of taking these animals is by turning them on their backs with a hand-spike when they are discovered on shore, and leaving them in this situation till a convenient opportunity occurs for carrying them away. Such is the heaviness of their structure, or so languid are their powers, that they are utterly unable to turn themselves, and effect their escape. They are publicly exposed for sale by the butchers in Surinam, like the shambles meat in the European markets, and are esteemed the most delicate food between the months of February and May.

On the morning of the 1st of February we now once more went under way, and kept course inshore till the evening, when we came to an anchor off the mouth of the River Marawina. This river has occasioned the loss of many ships, by seamen fatally mistaking it for the river Surinam, to which its entry bears indeed a very great resemblance. What renders the first so dangerous, are the numerous rocks, small islands and quicksands with which it is crowded; besides it is so shallow at high-water mark (and even with spring-tides) that all ships of any considerable burthen immediately run aground, and go to pieces.

On the 2nd, having got our anchor a-peak by daybreak, we again set sail, keeping course along the coast. Having doubled Braam's

Flagellation of a female slave

Point with a light breeze, under top and top-gallant sails, we finally entered the beautiful river Surinam, and at three o'clock, p.m. dropped anchor before the new fortress called Amsterdam. Here we were extremely happy to meet with our friends in the *Vigilance*, which vessel (as I have mentioned) had parted company with us in a gale of wind on the 2nd of January, off Cape Finisterre, and arrived two days before us in this river.

Our ships crews now were in the highest flow of spirits, seeing themselves surrounded by the most delightful verdure, while the river seemed alive by the many boats and barges passing and re-passing to see us, and by groups of naked boys and girls promiscuously playing and flouncing, like so many tritons and mermaids, in the water. The scene was new to all, and nothing was heard but music, singing, and cheering on deck, as well as in the rigging, from the ideas of happiness which each individual now promised himself in this luxuriant flourishing spot, while between decks the heat was becoming insupportable. But how miserably these poor fellows were mistaken in their reckoning shall soon be seen.

I must indeed acknowledge that nothing could equal the delicious sensations with which we seemed intoxicated by the fragrance of the lemons, limes, oranges, and flowers, wafted over from the adjoining plantations that line the banks of all the rivers in this ever-blooming settlement, and of which charming fruit large clusters were sent on board our ships by Colonel de Ponchera of the colonial troops. This gentleman, being the commandant of Fort Amsterdam, also saluted the vessels with nine guns from the batteries, while with an equal number we returned him the compliment from the ships. A long-boat, with one of our captains, was afterwards dispatched to Paramaribo to announce to the governor the arrival of the troops in the colony.

During our stay in this place the companies frequently walked on shore, and I accompanied them in their excursions; but the pleasure I had flattered myself with, from exchanging the confinement of a ship for the liberty of ranging over a delicious country, was damped by the first object which presented itself after my landing. This was a young female slave, whose only covering was a rag tied round her loins, which, like her skin, was lacerated in several places by the stroke of the whip. The crime which had been committed by this miserable victim of tyranny, was the non-performance of a task to which she was apparently unequal, for which she was sentenced to receive two hundred lashes, and to drag, during some months, a chain several yards in length, one end of which was locked round her ankle, and to the other was affixed a weight of at least a hundred pounds.

The grass in this part of the country was very long and coarse, and afforded a harbour to two species of very disagreeable insects, termed *pattat* and *sorapat* lice by the colonists, which settled on every part of our persons. The former of these is so small as to be scarcely visible; the latter is something larger, and formed like a crab, and both agree in adhering closely to the skin, and occasioning an intolerable itching. These insects abound most during the rainy season, when the best means of avoiding their attacks is supposed to be by walking bare-foot, as they are believed to fasten more easily, and consequently in greater numbers, upon the clothes, whence however they very speedily find their way to the skin. We did not get rid of our disagree-able companions till our return to the ship, when we washed the affected parts with the juice of limes or lemons, which considerably alleviated our troublesome sensations.

On the 3rd of March we received a visit from several officers of the Society, or West India Company's troops, accompanied by a number of other gentlemen, to welcome our arrival in the colony. Nor were they satisfied with paying us merely a compliment in words, but re-galed us with a large quantity of excellent fruits and other refresh-ments. They came in very elegant barges or tent-boats, adorned with flags, and attended by small bands of music. The vessels were rowed by six or eight negroes, who were entirely without clothes, except a small stripe of check or other linen cloth, which was passed between their thighs, and fastened before and behind to a thin cotton string tied round their loins. As the colonists generally make choice of their handsomest slaves for this office, and to attend them at table, the rowers, who were healthy, young, and vigorous, looked extremely well, and their being naked gave us a full opportunity of observing their skin, which was shining, and nearly as black as ebony. This scene was however contrasted by the arrival of two canoes filled with emaciated starving wretches, who clamorously solicited relief from the soldiers, and were ready to fight for the possession of a bone.

The day following our commander-in-chief was visited by a Mr Rynsdorp, who introduced to him two black soldiers, manumitted slaves, who composed part of a corps of three hundred which had been lately formed. These men were exhibited by Mr Rynsdorp as speci-mens of that valiant body which but a short time before had most gallantly distinguished itself by the protection it had afforded to the colony.

While we still remained at anchor before the fortress Amsterdam, I received a polite invitation from one Mr Lolkens—a planter to whom I had been recommended—to accept the use of his house and table on our arrival at Paramaribo, the capital of the colony.

On the 8th we once more went under way and, after the usual cere-monies on both sides on leaving the fortress, sailed up the river

Surinam with drums beating, colours flying, and a guard of marines drawn up on the quarter-deck of each vessel. Having at length reached Paramaribo, we finally came to anchor within pistol-shot of the shore, receiving a salute of eleven guns from the citadel Zelandia, which was returned by all the ships of our small fleet.

After being confined nearly the whole of sixty-three days within the limits of a small vessel, and upon an element to which few of the troops had been accustomed, it would not be easy to describe the pleasure we experienced on finding ourselves once more on land, and surrounded by a thousand agreeable circumstances.

The town appeared uncommonly neat and pleasing, the shipping extremely beautiful, the adjacent woods adorned with the most luxuriant verdure, the air perfumed with the utmost fragrance, and the whole scene gilded by the rays of an unclouded sun. We did not however take leave of our wooden habitation at this time, but the next day were formally disembarked with a general appearance of rejoicing, all the ships in the roads being in full dress and the guns keeping up an incessant fire till the whole of the troops were landed.

All the inhabitants of Paramaribo were collected to behold this splendid scene, nor were the expectations they had formed disappointed. The corps consisted of nearly five hundred young men (for we had been so fortunate as only to lose one during the voyage), the oldest of whom was scarcely more than thirty, and the whole party neatly clothed in their new uniforms and in caps ornamented with twigs of orange-blossom. We paraded on a large green plain between the town and the citadel, opposite to the Governor's palace, but during the course of the ceremonies several soldiers fainted from the excessive heat. The troops then marched into quarters prepared for their reception, whilst the officers were regaled with a dinner by the Governor, which would have derived a considerable relish from its succeeding the salt provisions to which we had so long been confined, had any constrast been necessary to heighten our opinion of its elegance. But the choicest delicacies of America and Europe were united in this repast, and served up in silver. A great variety of the richest wines were poured out with profusion; the dessert was composed of the most delicious fruits, and the company were attended by a considerable number of extremely handsome negro and mulatto maids, all naked from the waist upwards, according to the custom of the country, but the other parts of their persons arrayed in the finest India chintzes, and the whole adorned with golden chains, medals, beads, bracelets and sweet-smelling flowers.

After partaking of this superb entertainment till about seven o'clock, I set out in search of the house of Mr Lolkens, the hospitable gentleman who had so obligingly invited me to make it my own. I soon discovered the place, but my reception was so ludicrous that I cannot forbear relating the particulars. On knocking at the door, it was opened by a young female negro, of a masculine appearance, whose whole dress consisted of a single petticoat, and who held a lighted tobacco-pipe in one hand and a burning candle in the other, which she brought close to my face, in order to reconnoitre me. I enquired if her master was at home, to which she replied, but in a language totally unintelligible to me. I then mentioned his name, on which she burst into an immoderate fit of laughter, displaying two rows of very beautiful teeth; at the same time, laying hold of the breast-buttons of my coat, she made me a signal to follow her. I was much at a loss how to act, but went in, and was ushered by the girl into a very neat apartment, whither she brought some excellent fruit and a bottle of Madeira wine, which she placed upon the table. She then, in the best manner she was able, informed me that her *masera*, with the rest of his family, was gone to spend a few days at his plantation, and that she was left behind to receive an English Captain, whom she supposed to be me. I signified that I was and filled her out a tumbler of wine, which I had the utmost difficulty to persuade her to accept, for such is the degrading light in which these unhappy beings are considered that it is accounted a high degree of presumption in them to eat or drink in the presence of a European. I contrived for some time to carry on something like a conversation with this woman, but was soon glad to put an end to it by recurring to my bottle.

Tired with the employments of the day, I longed for some rest, and made a signal to my attendant that I wanted to sleep: but my motion was strangely misconstrued, for she immediately seized me by the neck and imprinted on my lips a most ardent kiss. Heartily provoked at this unexpected and (from one of her colour) unwelcome salutation, I disentangled myself from her embraces and angrily flung into the apartment allotted for my place of rest. But here I was again pursued by my black tormentor who, in opposition to all I could say, insisted upon pulling off my shoes and stockings, and in a moment disencumbered me of that part of my apparel. I was extremely chagrined at her conduct, though this is an office commonly performed by the slaves in Surinam to all ranks and sexes without exception. Nor ought anyone to conceive that this apparently extraordinary conduct resulted from any peculiarity of disposition in the girl; her behaviour was only such as would have been practised by the generality of female negro slaves, and will be found, by all who visit the West India settlements, to be characteristic of the whole dark sisterhood.

Finding in the morning that my friend the planter was not returned,

I took leave of his mansion and very hospitable servant, and after visiting the soldiers in their new abodes, was conducted by the quartermaster to a neat habitation appropriated to my use. I found the house entirely unfurnished, though not destitute of inhabitants, for, leaving my Captain's commission, which was of parchment, in the window the first night, I had the mortification to find in the morning that it was devoured by the rats.

Having taken possession of my habitation, my next wish was to furnish it properly, but all cares of this nature were rendered unnecessary by the generous hospitality of the inhabitants. The ladies supplied me with tables, chairs, glasses, and even plate and china, in great abundance; and the gentlemen loaded me with presents of Madeira wine, porter, cyder, rum and sugar, besides a quantity of the most exquisite fruits. Among the latter I was particularly struck with the shaddock and awara; the former of these, which is of a very agreeable flavour between a sweet and an acid, is produced from a tree supposed to be transplanted from the coast of Guinea by a Captain Shaddock, whose name it still retains throughout the English West India islands, but is called pompelmoose in Surinam. This fruit appears to be of the orange species, but is as large as the head of a child of eight or ten years old; the skin is extremely thick, of a bitterish taste, and a pale yellow or citron colour.

The *awara*, which is less remarkable for the excellence of its flavour than its beautiful appearance, grows upon a species of palm-tree, and is of an oval form, about the size of an Orlean plum, and of a rich deep orange colour, nearly approaching to red. It is much esteemed by the negroes, who exercise their ingenuity in forming rings out of the stones, which they decorate with cyphers, initial letters and other devices, then dispose of them to the Europeans, who mount them in gold. These stones are large, extremely hard, and as black as jet or ebony, but the pulp which surrounds them is very thin.

This day, on examining into the state of our remaining live stock, such as hogs, sheep, ducks, geese, fowls, and turkeys, we found them nearly as many in number as when we first sailed from Holland. These were all sent to the colonel's poultry-yard at the headquarters, while we had the additional mortification of seeing about sixty large kegs with preserved vegetables, etc. and just as many fine Westphalia hams (being perfectly rotten) thrown into the river Surinam to feed the sharks.

I now observed, on the second morning after our landing, that my face, my breast and hands were entirely spotted over like the skin of a leopard, occasioned by myriads of gnats or mosquitoes, which flying in clouds, had kept me company during the night, though the fatigue from my voyage and the oppressive heat of the climate had sunk me into so profound a sleep that I was insensible of their stings till I perceived the effects. These insects are inconceivably numerous here during the rainy season, and particularly on the banks of creeks or rivers. None are secured from their attacks, but they peculiarly infest strangers in preference to the natives, and wherever they insert their proboscis and remain unmolested, they suck the blood till they are scarcely able to fly. Every puncture they make is succeeded by a large blotch, or rather tumour, accompanied with an itching which is almost intolerable. The presence of the mosquitoes is indicated by their buzzing noise, which alone is sufficient to make one sweat, and which is so very disagreeable to those who have suffered from their stings as to have obtained for them the name of the *Devil's Trumpeters.* They are indeed inconceivably troublesome in every respect. The candles are no sooner lighted in an evening than they are stuck full of them; all kinds of food and drink are exposed to their disagreeable visits, from which even the mouth and eyes are not exempted.

The best cure for their stings is an application of the juice of lemons or limes, mixed with water, which is also a tolerable preservative against their attacks. Immediately before shutting the windows the inhabitants commonly burn tobacco in their apartments, the smoke of which occasions the insects to fly about the room; the negro girls unreservedly throw off their petticoats, the whole of their covering, and running naked about the chamber, chase the gnats therewith out at the windows, or destroy them. The more delicate or luxurious among the natives still employ their slaves in fanning them during the whole night, excepting such as have green gauze doors to their beds or pavilions; but the generality of the people in Surinam sleep in roomy cotton hammocks, which are covered with a very large thin sheet suspended from a tight line immediately over them, something like the awning of a ship. This serves in some measure to keep off these troublesome insects, and the want of one had exposed me to be thus stung all over.

On the morning of the 22nd, an elderly negro-woman, with a black girl about fourteen, entering my apartment, it would be difficult to express my astonishment when she gravely presented me her daughter to become what she was pleased to term my wife. I had so little gallantry, however, as to reject the offer with a loud laugh; but at the same time accompanied the refusal with a small but welcome present, with which they appeared perfectly satisfied, and departed with every possible demonstration of gratitude and respect. The girls here, who voluntarily enter into these connections, are sometimes mulattoes, sometimes Indians, and often negroes. They all exult in the circumstance of living with a European, whom in general they serve with the utmost tenderness and fidelity, and tacitly reprove those numerous *fair-ones* who break through ties more sacred and solemn. Young women of this description cannot indeed be married, or connected in any other way, as most of them are born or trained up in a state of slavery; and so little is the practice condemned, that while they continue faithful and constant to the partner by whom they are chosen, they are countenanced and encouraged by their nearest relations and friends, who call this a lawful marriage; nay, even the clergy avail themselves of this custom without restraint. Many of the sable-coloured beauties will however follow their own *penchant* without any restraint whatever, refusing with contempt the golden bribes of some, while on others they bestow their favours for a dram or a broken tobacco-pipe, if not for nothing.

The hospitality I had experienced on our first arrival in the colony was not confined to that time only: I had a general invitation to visit, besides His Excellency the Governor, and Colonel Texier, the commandant, in more than twenty respectable families, whenever it suited my convenience. So, though the officers of our corps had formed a regimental mess, I had seldom the honour of their company. One gentleman, a Mr Kennedy, in particular, carried his politeness so far as not only to offer me the use of his carriage, saddle-horses and table, but even to present me with a fine negro boy, named Quaco, to carry my umbrella as long as I remained in Surinam. The other gentlemen of the regiment also met with great civilities, and the whole colony seemed anxious to testify their respect by vying with each other in a constant round of festivity. Balls, concerts, card-assemblies, and every species of amusement in their power, were constantly contrived for our entertainment. The spirit of conviviality next reached on board the men-of-war, where we entertained the ladies with cold suppers and dancing upon the quarter-deck, under an awning, till six in the morning, generally concluding the frolic by a cavalcade or an airing in their carriages. This constant routine of dissipation, which was rendered still more pernicious by the enervating effects of an intensely hot climate where one is in a perpetual state of perspiration, already threatened to become fatal to two or three of our officers. Warned by their example, I retired from all public companies, sensible that by such means I could alone preserve my health in a country which has such a tendency to debilitate the human frame that a European, however cautious to avoid excesses, has always reason to apprehend its dreadful effects.

Dissipation and luxury appear to be congenial to the inhabitants of this climate, and great numbers must annually fall victims to their very destructive influence. Their fatal consequences are indeed too visible in the men, who have indulged themselves in intemperance and other sensual gratifications, and who appear withered and enervated in the extreme: nor do the generality of the Creole females exhibit a more alluring appearance; they are languid, their complexions are sallow, and the skin even of the young ladies is frequently shrivelled. This is however not the case with all, and I have been acquainted with some who, preserving a glow of health and freshness in their lovely countenance, were entitled to contend for the prize of beauty with the fairest European. But, alas! the numbers of this last description are so small that the colonists in their amours most usually prefer the Indian negro and mulatto girls, particularly on account of their remarkable cleanliness, health, and vivacity. For the excesses of the husbands in this respect, and the marked neglect which they meet from them, the Creole ladies most commonly, at a very early period, appear in mourning weeds, with the agreeable privilege however of making another choice in the hopes of a better partner; nor are they long without another mate. Such indeed is the superior longevity of the fair females of Surinam, compared to that of the males (owing chiefly, as I said, to their excesses of all sorts), that I have frequently known wives who have buried four husbands, but never met a man in this country who had survived two wives.

The ladies do not, however, always bear with the most becoming patience the slights and insults they thus meet with, in the expectation of a sudden release, but mostly persecute their successful sable rivals (even on suspicion) with implacable hatred and the most unrelenting barbarity, while they chastise their partners not only with a shew of ineffable contempt, but with giving in public the most unequivocal marks of preference towards those gentlemen who newly arrive from Europe. This occasioned the trite proverb and observation in the colony, that the tropical ladies and the mosquitoes have an instinctive preference for a newly-landed European. This partiality is indeed so very extreme, and the proofs of it so very apparent and nauseous, that some command of temper is necessary to prevent the disgust which such behaviour must naturally excite, particularly where the object is not very inviting; nay, it was even publicly reported at Paramaribo, that two of these tropical amazons had fought a duel for the sake of one of our officers.

I must now mention a word or two of the governor and Colonel Fourgeoud. Notwithstanding the polite reception our whole corps had met with ever since we first landed in the colony, it was evident to perceive the mutual coolness which subsisted between the governor and our commander-in-chief. The latter indeed gave the first public cause of animosity, on the very day of our debarkation, by drawing up his regiment with their backs towards the governor's palace.

It is easy to conceive that the disgust which so early and so reciprocally manifested itself between the above two gentlemen, who were both of them our commanders but totally independent of each other, could not but make our stay at Paramaribo extremely disagreeable to all the officers in our regiment, as well as those of the Society corps. The consequence was that, having resided but a few weeks in the colony, it was thought proper by the governor to acquaint Colonel Fourgeoud, that, 'as the rebel negroes seemed no further disposed to disturb the tranquillity of the settlement, its own troops and the corps of black rangers were deemed sufficient for its defence; Colonel Fourgeoud, with his marines, being therefore no longer wanted, was at liberty to return to Europe whenever he thought proper.'

Various were the feelings of pleasure and reluctance with which our gentlemen received this news. Preparations were, however, made for our departure, but in a few days these were again suspended by the inhabitants, who clamorously insisted on our staying.

2

THE discovery of Guiana, by some called the *Wild Coast*, has been long (though with uncertainty) attributed to the Spanish commander Vasco Nunes, who, in the year 1504, after discovering Cuba to be an island, landed on the continent of South America, penetrated as far as between the rivers Oroonoko and Amazon, and comprehended that country in the extensive tract of land, to which, in contradiction to Cuba and the adjacent islands, he gave the name of *Terra Firma*.

Its boundaries are marked by the rivers Viapary or Oroonoko on the north-west and by the Maranon or river Amazon on the south-east. The north-east is washed by the Atlantic Ocean; and the river Negris, or Black River, terminates its extent on the south-west so forming it into a kind of island, and separating it from New Grenada, Peru, and the Brazils.

Though situated, like Guinea, under the Torrid Zone, the heats in Guiana are much more supportable than those on that part of the African coast. The scorching rays of the sun are in Guiana daily tempered by cooling breezes from the sea, while in Guinea the intense heat is increased by the wind blowing continually over the land, and in its passage traversing numerous sandy deserts. The easterly or trade winds, which generally blow between the Tropics, are extremely refreshing to the coast of Guiana between the hours of eight or ten in the morning and six o'clock in the evening when they cease to operate, and a zephyr is scarcely ever heard to whisper during the night. These winds are succeeded by thick fogs and vapours exhaled from the earth, which render the nights in this country not only very chilly, but extremely damp and unhealthy. The length of the days and nights in Guiana never varies much more than forty minutes during the course of the year, as the sun always rises about six in the morning, and sets at the same hour in the evening.

The rainy and dry seasons which divide the year, as cold and warm weather divide it in Europe, may be termed the winter and summer of this country. There is however one remarkable difference between the European seasons and those in Guiana, which is, that Guiana has annually two winters and two summers, which are distinguished from each other by the appellation of the *greater* and the *smaller*, not because the rains are less violent in the two latter seasons, or the heat less intense, but from an opinion which has prevailed that their period of duration is but about half as long as that of the former. This distinction however appears to be more imaginary than real, as far as respects the rainy seasons; for as these downfalls of water only take place when the sun is vertical, which it is near the line twice a year and for an equal portion of time, the continuance of the rains will probably be equal in both seasons.

The continuance of the rains during the time when the sun is vertical in this climate, is necessary to the existence of animal and vegetable life, which without these seasonable refreshments must languish and expire under the fervid influence of its rays. Changes [of season] are always accompanied by tremendous claps of thunder, and very vivid flashes of lightning, which continue during several weeks and are frequently fatal both to the cattle and inhabitants of this country.

Some parts of Guiana present a barren and mountainous aspect, but in general the soil is abundantly fruitful, the earth during the whole of the year adorned with continual verdure, the trees loaded at the same time with blossoms and ripe fruit, and the whole presenting to the view the delightful union of spring and summer. This general appearance of fertility, particularly in Surinam, may be ascribed not only to the rains and warmth in this climate, but also to its low and marshy situation, which prevents the intense heats from destroying vegetation, and from the extreme richness of the soil, particularly in those parts which are cultivated by European industry. It must indeed be confessed that such situations are far from being favourable to health; but the spirit of gain is a very powerful principle, and the certainty of present profit will generally be considered as a weighty counterpoise to those evils which, if ever encountered, appear at a considerable distance and, as they are sometimes escaped, may be always esteemed as uncertain.

The uncultivated parts of Guiana are covered with immense forests, rocks, and mountains—some of the latter enriched with a great variety of mineral substances—and the whole country is intersected by very deep marshes or swamps, and by extensive heaths or savannas. The stream along the coast flows continually towards the north-west; and the whole shore is rendered almost inaccessible from its being covered with dangerous banks, quicksands, bogs and rocks, with prodigious bushes and a large quantity of brushwood, which are so closely interwoven as to be impenetrable.

From the earliest remembrance some fugitive negroes have taken refuge in the woods of Surinam; but these were of very small consideration till about the year 1726, or 1728, when their hostile numbers were much increased, and they had acquired lances and firelocks, which they had pillaged from the estates. By the accession of these arms, in addition to their usual weapons, bows and arrows, they were enabled to commit continual outrages and depredations upon the coffee and sugar plantations, as well from a spirit of revenge for the inhuman treatment which they had formerly received from their masters, as with a view of carrying away plunder, and principally gunpowder and ball, hatchets etc. in order to provide for their future subsistence and defence.

These negroes were in general settled in the upper parts of the river Copename and Seramica, from the latter of which they take the name of the Seramica rebels, in distinction from the other gangs which have since revolted.

Several detachments of military and plantation people were sent against them, but were of very small effect in reducing them to obedience by promises, or extirpating them by force of arms.

In 1730, a most shocking and barbarous execution of eleven of the unhappy negro captives was resolved upon, in the expectation that it might terrify their companions and induce them to submit. One man was hanged alive upon a gibbet by an iron hook stuck through his ribs; two others were chained to stakes and burnt to death by a slow fire. Six women were broken alive upon the rack, and two girls were decapitated. Such was their resolution under these tortures, that they endured them without even uttering a sigh.

This inhuman massacre produced an effect very contrary to what had been expected. Indeed it so much enraged the Seramica rebels, that for several years they became dreadful to the colonists who, no longer being able to support the expenses and fatigues of sallying out against them in the woods—in addition to the great losses which they so frequently sustained by their invasions, of which they lived in continual terror—at last resolved to treat for peace with their sable enemies.

Governor Mauricius, who was at this period at the head of the colony, now sent out a strong detachment to the rebel settlement at the Seramica river, for the purpose of effecting, if possible, a peace so ardently desired. This detachment, after some skirmishing with the straggling rebel parties, at last arrived at their headquarters, where they demanded and obtained a parley. A treaty of peace, consisting of ten or twelve articles, was actually concluded between the different parties in the year 1749. The chief of the Seramica rebels was a Creole negro called Captain Adoe, who upon this occasion received from the governor, as a present, a fine large cane with a silver pummel, on which were engraven the arms of Surinam as a mark of their independence. This was a preliminary to the other presents that were to be sent out the year following as stipulated by treaty, particularly arms and ammunition, on the performance of which the peace was to be finally concluded. Adoe presented in return a handsome bow, with a complete case of arrows, which had been manufactured by his own hands, as a token that during that time all enmity should cease on his side.

This affair gave great satisfaction to many and indeed to most of the inhabitants of Surinam, who now flattered themselves that their effects were perfectly secure; others, however, regarded this treaty as a very hazardous resource, and even as a step to the inevitable ruin of the colony.

I must confess indeed, that, notwithstanding the good intentions of Governor Mauricius, nothing appears to be more dangerous than making a forced friendship with people who, by the most abject slavery and ill usage, are provoked to break their chains and shake off their yoke in pursuit of revenge and liberty, and who, by the trust which is placed in them, have it in their power to become from day to day more formidable.

The insurrection having risen to such a height, the colonists ought perhaps to have continued to oppose it, while they were possessed of the power of opposition, not indeed from a motive of cruelty, but for the political good of so fine a settlement.

If it appeared that cruelty and ill treatment had driven these poor creatures to these extremities, policy, not less than humanity, ought to have dictated to the colonists a different conduct in future; but it may be asked whether it is possible to keep the African negroes in habits of obedience and industry without the strictest and often the severest discipline?—No. But I ask again, Why is it necessary to inflict such inhuman tortures, according to the humour and caprice of an unfeeling master, or a still more unprincipled overseer? Why should their reasonable complaints be never heard by a magistrate who has it in his power to redress them? Is it because this magistrate is a planter, and that he is interested in the arbitrary government of this unhappy race?—This is too evident.—It would, however, be great injustice if I were not to bear witness that I have not unfrequently seen the plantation slaves treated with the utmost humanity, where the hand of the master was seldom lifted, but to caress them, and where the eye of the slave sparkled with gratitude and affection.

Let us now proceed, and see what were the fruits of making peace with the Seramica rebels.

In 1750, which was the year after, the promised presents were dispatched to Captain Adoe; but the detachment that carried them were attacked on their march, and the whole of the corps murdered on the spot by a desperate negro, called Zam Zam, who not having been consulted concerning the treaty of peace, had afterwards put himself at the head of a strong party and now carried off the whole stock of the detachment, consisting of arms, ammunition, checked linens, canvas cloth, hatchets, saws, and other carpenter's tools—besides salt beef, pork, spirits, etc.—and kept them as his own private property. Adoe, on the other hand, not receiving the presents at the time he expected, too hastily concluded he was only to be amused with expectation till a reinforcement of troops should arrive from Europe to subdue him, and renewed his incursions. By this accident therefore the peace was immediately broken; cruelties and ravages increased more than before, and death and destruction once more raged throughout the colony.

In 1751, this settlement was in the utmost distress and confusion, and, in compliance with a request of the inhabitants presented to the States General, Baron Spoke was sent to Surinam, with six hundred fresh troops drafted from the different regiments in the Dutch service, and on their arrival the members of the court were ordered to send Governor Mauricius to Europe, to account for his proceedings. He never returned to the colony, and, in 1753 asked for and obtained his dismission, after having been honourably acquitted. Baron Spoke, who during the absence of Mauricius was appointed to officiate as governor, found everything in the greatest disorder, disunion having even arisen between the inhabitants and their rulers, to which it was highly necessary to apply the speediest means of redress. This application was indeed made by the Baron, but he died the year after, and a general distraction again took place.

In 1757, the aspect of affairs daily becoming worse (during the administration of a Mr Cromelyn, who now was governor of this colony), a new revolt broke out in the Tempaty Creek among the negroes, owing to the treatment which they received from their masters. This fresh insurrection indeed soon became of the most serious consequence. The new rebels joined themselves to sixteen hundred of the old fugitive negroes already settled in eight different villages near Tempaty Creek, and after repeated battles and skirmishes, the enemy being mostly well armed and in their resistance generally successful, the colonists saw themselves once more reduced to sue for peace with their own slaves, as they had done in the year 1749 with the rebels of Seramica.

The first thing proposed by the colonists was a parley, which was agreed to by the rebels who not only desired, but absolutely insisted, that the Dutch should send them yearly, among a great variety of other articles, a quantity of good fire-arms and ammunition, as specified in a long list, expressed in broken English, by a negro whose name was Boston, and who was one of their captains.

Governor Cromelyn next sent two commissioners, Mr Sober and Mr Abercrombie, who marched through the woods, escorted by a few military, to carry some presents to the rebels previous to the ratification of the peace, for which they now were commissioned finally to treat.

At the arrival of the above gentlemen in the rebel camp, at the Jocka Creek, about fifteen miles east of the Tempaty Creek, they were introduced to a very handsome negro, called Araby, who was their chief. He received them very politely and, taking them by the hand, desired they would sit down by his side upon the green. At the same time he assured them they need not be under any apprehensions of evil since, from their coming in so good a cause, not one intended, or would even dare to hurt them.

When the above-mentioned Boston, however, perceived that they had brought a parcel of trinkets, such as knives, scissors, combs and small looking-glasses, and had forgotten the principal articles in question—gunpowder, fire-arms, and ammunition—he resolutely approached the commissioners and demanded, in a thundering voice, whether the Europeans imagined that the negroes could live on combs and looking-glasses. He added that one of each was quite sufficient to let them all see their faces, while a single gallon of *mansancy*, gunpowder, would have been accepted as a proof of their confidence; but since that had been omitted, he should never consent to their return to their countrymen till every article of the list should be dispatched to them, and consequently the treaty fulfilled.

This expostulation occasioned the interference of a negro captain, called Quacoo, who declared that these gentlemen were only the messengers of their governor and court; and as they could not be answerable for their master's proceedings, they should certainly return to the settlement without injury or insult, and no person, not even he, Captain Boston, should dare to oppose them.

The chief of the rebels then ordered silence, and desired Mr Abercrombie to make up a list himself of such articles as he, Araby, should specify. When that gentleman had done so, and promised to deliver, the rebels not only gave him and his companions leave peaceably to return with it to town, but allowed their governor and court a whole year to deliberate whether they were to choose peace or war, unanimously swearing that during that interval all animosity should cease on their side. After this, having entertained them in the best manner their situation in the woods afforded, they wished them a happy journey to Paramaribo.

One of the rebel officers, on this occasion, represented to the commissioners how deplorable it was that the Europeans, who pretended to be a civilized nation, should be so much the occasion of their own ruin by their inhuman cruelties towards their slaves. 'We desire you,' continued the negro, 'to tell your governor and your court, that in case they want to raise no new gangs of rebels, they ought to take care that the planters keep a more watchful eye over their own property, and do not trust them so frequently to the hands of drunken managers and overseers, who by wrongfully and severely chastising the negroes, debauching their wives and children, neglecting the sick, etc. are the ruin of the colony, and wilfully drive to the woods such numbers of stout active people, who by their sweat earn your subsistence, without whose hands your colony must drop to nothing, and to whom at last, in this disgraceful manner, you are glad to come and sue for friendship.'

Mr Abercrombie now begged that he might be accompanied by one or two of their principal officers to Paramaribo, where he promised they should be well treated. But the chief, Araby, answered him with a smile, that it was time enough a year after, when the peace should be thoroughly concluded; that then even his youngest son should be at their service, to receive his education among them, while for his subsistence, and even for that of his dependants, he should take the sole care upon himself, without ever giving the Christians the trouble.

After this, the commissioners left the rebels, and the whole detachment arrived safe at Paramaribo.

The year of deliberation being ended, the governor and court sent out two fresh commissioners to the negro camp to bring the so much wished-for peace to a thorough conclusion. After much debate, and many ceremonies on both sides, it was at last finally agreed upon. Presents were promised to be sent by the Christians, agreeable to the wishes of the negroes; these last, as a proof of their affection to the Europeans, insisted that each of the commissioners should, during their remaining stay in the rebel camp, take for his constant companion one of their handsomest young women. They treated them also liberally with game, fish, fruit and the choicest productions of the forest, and entertained them, without intermission, with music, dancing and repeated volleys.

At the return of the commissioners, the stipulated presents were sent to the negroes at the Jocka Creek, under the care of Mr Mayer, escorted by six hundred men, soldiers and slaves. The pusillanimity of this gentleman, however, nearly undid the whole business, for he departed from his orders and delivered all the presents to the rebels without receiving the hostages in return. Fortunately Araby kept his word, and sent down four of his best officers as pledges to Paramaribo. By this the peace was perfectly accomplished, and a treaty of twelve or fourteen articles was signed by the white commissioners, and sixteen of Araby's black captains, in 1761. The ceremony took place on the plantation Ouca, in the river Surinam, where all the parties met, this being the spot of rendezvous appointed for the purpose, after four different embassies had been sent from the Europeans to the negroes.

Signing this treaty alone, however, was still not considered as sufficient by the rebel chief Araby and his people. They immediately bound themselves by an oath, and insisted on the commissioners doing the same after the manner which is practised by themselves, not trusting entirely, they alleged, to that made use of by the Christians, which they had seen them too frequently violate. It must indeed be confessed that the negroes themselves are uncommonly tenacious of these solemn engagements, as I never heard of an instance, during all the time I resided in the colony, of one of them violating his oath.

The solemnity made use of on this day, consisted in each party's letting a few drops of blood with a lancet or penknife from the arm, into a calabash or cup of clear spring water, in which were also mixed a few particles of dry earth. Of this all present were obliged to drink, without exception, and they call it drinking each other's blood, having first shed a few drops upon the ground by way of libation. Their gadoman or priest, with up-cast eyes and outstretched arms, took heaven and earth to witness, and with a most audible voice and in a most awful manner invoked the curse of the Almighty on those who should first break through this sacred treaty made between them, from that moment forward to all eternity. To this solemn imprecation the multitude answered *Da so!* which signifies in their language *Amen.*

The solemnity being ended, the chief Araby and each of his captains (to be distinguished from the inferior negroes, as the Seramican chief Adoe had been before in 1749) was presented with a fine large cane and silver pummel, on which was also engraved the arms of the colony.

The above-mentioned negroes are called Oucas, after the name of the plantation where the peace articles were signed, and by that name they are since distinguished from those of Seramica, whom I have already described.

This same year peace was also a second time concluded with the Seramica rebels, who were at that time commanded by a negro called Wille, instead of their former chief Adoe, who was dead. But this second peace was unfortunately broken by a rebel captain, called Muzinga, who had received none of the presents. They had in fact been again intercepted and captured on their way to the chief Wille, as they had been formerly on their way to the chief Adoe, by the very same enterprising and rapacious plunderer Zam Zam, with this difference only, that none of the detachment that were sent with them were now murdered, as on the preceding occasion, nor even one single person injured.

Upon this supposed breach of faith, captain Muzinga fought most desperately against the colonists; he gave battle face to face, and beat back, at close quarters, above one hundred and fifty of their best troops, killing numbers, and carrying off all their baggage and ammunition.

Soon after this, however, when the real cause of Muzinga's discontent was known, means were found and adopted to pacify this gallant warrior, by making him receive and share the presents sent out by the colonists, on an equal footing with his brother heroes, when peace was a third and last time concluded in 1762, between the Seramica rebels and the colony. This, as well as that with the Ouca negroes, has providentially been kept sacred and inviolable to this day. By their exertions in the field they thus obtained their freedom.

The hostages and chief officers of both the above-mentioned negro cohorts, on their arrival at Paramaribo, were entertained at the governor's own table, having previously paraded in state through the town, accompanied by his excellency in his own private carriage.

By their capitulation to the Dutch, the above Ouca and Seramica rebels must yearly receive, as I have mentioned, a quantity of arms and ammunition from the colony, for which the Europeans have received in return the negroes' promises to be their faithful allies, to deliver up all their deserters, for which they are to receive proper premiums, never to appear armed at Paramaribo above five or six at a time, and also to keep their settlement at a proper distance from the town and plantations: the Seramica negroes at the river Seramica, and those of the Ouca negroes at the Jocka Creek, near the river Marawina, where one or two white men, called post-holders, were to reside among them, in the quality of envoys.

Both these tribes were supposed, at the period I speak of, to amount in all to three thousand, and but a few years after, by those that were sent to visit their settlements (including wives and children) they were computed to be not less than fifteen or twenty thousand. They are already become overbearing and even insolent, brandishing their silver-headed canes in defiance of the inhabitants, and forcing from them liquors, and very often money, and reminding them how cruelly their ancestors had murdered their parents and their husbands.

From these circumstances, and their numbers increasing from day to day, I must conclude, that should the peace be ever broken, these new allies will become the most dreadful foes that ever the colony of Surinam can have to contend with.

During the time of an insurrection in 1761 among the negro slaves in the colony of Berbice, where they had not been treated so cruelly as in other colonies, not only was a regiment of marines, commanded by Colonel de Salse, sent over from Holland to that settlement, but troops were also dispatched from the neighbouring colonies in order to subdue the revolt. In this design they soon succeeded, since the woods in that part, being of small extent, are easily penetrated, which prevents the rebels from forming settlements. From the same cause they will not serve to conceal them from their pursuers. The consequence was, that after numbers had been shot dead, and others taken prisoners, the rest were forced to surrender at discretion and implore for mercy, or they must have been starved to death for want of subsistence.

During these troubles, it happened that one officer and about seventy men, sent from the colony of Surinam, had been posted on the banks of the river Corrantine. This detachment, together with a party of Indians, who are natural enemies to the negroes, but friends to the Europeans, had one day beaten the rebels in a skirmish, killed several of them, and retaken about the value of twenty or thirty pounds sterling in effects, which the negroes had pillaged from the neighbouring estates. The officer who commanded this detachment having, however, unwarrantably distributed this booty among the Indians alone, without giving a share to his soldiers, disgusted them so much that they revolted and, deserting their commander, took their march for the river Oroonoko through the woods, in hopes of soon falling in with Spanish settlements and being relieved. But how miserably were these deluded men mistaken and disappointed in their desperate undertaking, by meeting the rebels or bush negroes on the second or third day of their march! These, notwithstanding the solemn protestations of the soldiers that they were come without any evil intention towards them, and their intreaties to let them pass by unmolested, were suspected of being sent out to spy and betray them; the negroes therefore insisted that they should lay down their arms at mercy, which the deserters having complied with, the rebels immediately dressed them in one rank. Then having picked out ten or twelve to assist them in attending the sick and wounded, repairing their arms, and trying to make gunpowder (in which however they miscarried), they condemned all the others to death, which was instantly put in execution, and above fifty of those unfortunate men were one by one shot dead upon the spot.

It may well be supposed, that those who were saved alive by the negroes must have spun out a very melancholy existence among them, and indeed most of them died within very few months after by ill treatment, hardships, and want; and when the rebels surrendered themselves to the Europeans at discretion, the few remaining miserable wretches that were still found alive, were directly loaded with irons, and sent back from the colony of Berbice to Surinam, where three of them were executed in the town of Paramaribo, one being hanged, and two broken alive upon the rack. One of these miserable wretches was a Frenchman, called Renauld, who seemed to have imbibed the sentiments of the negroes by his residence among them. With a truly heroic spirit he comforted his accomplice, a German, and, tied down by his side, exhorted him to preserve his courage, while his own bones were being broken by the executioner with an iron bar.

The ring-leading negroes were roasted alive by half dozens in a shocking manner, being chained to stakes in the midst of surrounding flames, and expired without uttering a groan or a sigh.

3

THE colony now seemed in a prosperous and flourishing state, since the concluding of the treaty with the Seramica and Ouca negroes, and everything exhibited an aspect of peace and good order. The inhabitants believed their persons and effects in perfect security, so that nothing was thought of but mirth and dissipation, which was soon extended to lavishness and profusion. Surinam resembled, indeed, a large and beautiful garden, stocked with everything that nature and art could produce to make the life of man both comfortable to himself, and useful to society: all the luxuries, as well as the necessaries of life, abounded; every sense was apparently intoxicated with enjoyment; and, to use the figurative language of a sacred book, Surinam was a land that flowed with milk and honey.

But this delusive felicity lasted not long. The planter, too earnest to become immediately opulent, never once considered the wretchedness of the slave. While drunkenness, luxury, and riot became predominant in the one party, the misery of the other proportionably increased; nor did the destruction that so lately threatened them seem to have the smallest influence on their minds. At the same time the successful example of the Seramica and Ouca negroes served to stimulate the other slaves to revolt, and from these complicated causes the colony was again plunged into its former abyss of difficulties. The most beautiful estates in the settlement, called plantations, were once more seen, some blazing in flames and others laid in ashes, while the reeking and mangled bodies of their inhabitants were scattered along the banks of the river Cottica, with their throats cut, and their effects pillaged by their own negroes, who all fled to the woods, men, women, and children, without exception.

These new revolters were now distinguished by the name of the Cottica Rebels, from the spot on which their hostilities commenced. Their numbers augmenting from day to day, they soon became as formidable to the settlement as the Seramica and Ouca negroes had formerly been, and in 1772 they had nearly given the finishing blow to Surinam. At that period all was horror and consternation—nothing but a general massacre was expected by the majority of the inhabitants, who fled from their estates and crowded to the town of Paramaribo for protection. In this situation of affairs, the inhabitants were obliged to have recourse to the dangerous resolution of forming a regiment of manumitted slaves to fight against their own countrymen. When we consider the treatment which was so generally exercised against the slaves of this settlement, it must surprise the reader to be told that this hazardous resolution had providentially the desired effect. These brave men performed wonders above expectation, in conjunction with the Colonial or Society troops whose strength and numbers alone were no longer thought sufficient to defend this settlement. But not to rely absolutely on such precarious assistance, the society of Surinam made application to His Serene Highness the Prince of Orange for a regular regiment, and our corps was in consequence dispatched in the matter which has been already related. As, however, the events which preceded our arrival were of the utmost importance, I shall endeavour to lay before my readers the most authentic information I was able to obtain.

The regular troops from Europe that belong to the Society of Surinam, were intended to be twelve hundred men when complete, divided into two battalions, paid partly by the Society, and partly by the inhabitants: but they can never produce that number in the field, for many reasons—such as their either dying on their passage, while they are seasoning to the climate, or during their dangerous and fatiguing duty in the woods and swamps. Besides this number, a reinforcement of three hundred more was now sent them from the town of Amsterdam, but of these poor wretches scarcely fifty were landed fit for service. The remainder, owing to the inhumanity of their leader, participated in a fate little better than that of the poor African negroes in the vessel of the inhuman captain who, in 1787, threw 132 living slaves into the sea to perish. The unhappy creatures were starved and tormented by unnecessary severity, and his lieutenant, unable to continue a witness of the tyrannical punishments he inflicted, leapt from the cabin window, and terminated his existence.

The military in Surinam are composed of several very good and experienced officers, and well inured to the service, but for their private men I cannot say much; they are, in fact, little better than the outcasts of all nations. They are of all ages, shapes, and sizes, and seem by chance wafted together from all the different corners of the globe. Notwithstanding this, however, it has often been found that they behave well in action, and have on many different occasions, by their bravery, been of infinite service to this settlement.

Here is also a small corps of artillery, being part of the twelve hundred, which I must acknowledge to be a very fine company in all respects. As for what they please to call their militia, they are, a few gentlemen excepted who command them, so strange a collection of ill-disciplined rabble, that they can scarcely be mentioned as fighting men.

With respect to the new-raised corps of manumitted slaves, though in number they amounted but to three hundred, they indeed proved ultimately of as much service to the colony as all the others put together.* These men were all volunteers, and in general stout, able young fellows, selected from the different plantations, the owners of whom received for them their full value in money. None were accepted but those who were reputed to be of unexceptionable character. It must, however, be observed, that what we Europeans call a good character, was, by the Africans, looked on as detestable, particularly by those born in the woods, whose only crime consisted in revenging the wrongs done to their forefathers. I have been an ocular witness to astonishing proofs of the fidelity of these enfranchised slaves to the Europeans, and their valour against the rebel negroes.

Their chief leaders are three or four white men, called Conductors, to whom they pay the strictest obedience: one or two of these attend them when they set out on any enterprise of consequence. Every ten privates have one captain, who commands them in the forest by the different sounding of his horn—as the boatswain commands the seaman by his call, or as the cavalry of Europe are directed by the sound of the trumpets in the field—by which they advance, attack, retreat, spread, etc. They are armed only with a firelock and sabre, but of both weapons they understand the management in the most masterly manner. They generally go naked, in preference, in the woods, excepting trousers and a scarlet cap, the emblem of liberty, on which is their number, and which, together with their parole or watchword, which is *orange*, distinguishes them from the rebels in any action, to prevent disagreeable mistakes. They have, indeed, of late years, been farther distinguished by green uniforms.

I have already stated, that the newly revolted rebels, called Cotticas, were just preparing to give the finishing blow to Surinam, and I shall now proceed to relate how this catastrophe was prevented.

These negroes, being commanded by a desperate fellow named Baron, had erected a strong settlement between the river Cottica and the sea coast, whence they sallied forth to commit their depredations on the plantations.

I have called this settlement strong, because, like an island, it was entirely surrounded by a broad unfordable marsh or swamp, which prevented all communication, except by private paths under water, known only to the rebels, and before which Baron had placed loaded swivels which he had plundered from the neighbouring estates. It

* Blood-hounds were also proposed, to discover and attack the rebel negroes in the woods, but never adopted, from the difficulty of their proper training.

was moreover fenced and enclosed on every side by several thousand strong pallisadoes, and was on the whole no contemptible fortification. To this spot Baron gave the name of *Boucou* or *Mouldered*, intimating that it should perish in dust rather than it should be taken by or surrendered to the Europeans. He even presumed to suppose that it would never be discovered.

After many marches and counter-marches, however, this nest of desperadoes was at last discovered by the vigilance and perseverance of the Society troops and the black soldiers or rangers, by which name I shall for the future distinguish them, their service being chiefly like that of the rangers in Virginia, who were sent out against the Cherokee Indians. Another settlement of the rebels was, indeed, well known to exist in that corner of the colony known by the name of the Leashore, and situated between the rivers Surinam and Seramica; but here the situation, by marshes, quagmires, mud and water, is such that it fortifies them from any attempts of the Europeans. Nay, they are even indiscoverable by negroes, so thick and impenetrable is the forest on that spot, and so choked with thorns, briars and every species of underwood.

From these coverts they sally forth in small parties, during the night, to rob the gardens and fields surrounding Paramaribo, and carry off the young women. In this wilderness a young officer, Lieutenant Freidrecy, was lost two or three days and nights, as he went out on a shooting party, and would probably never have been heard of had not the governor, by ordering a gun to be fired at intervals, given a signal for him to find his way back, and thus restored him once more to his friends.

As soon as it was determined that the rebels commanded by Baron, at Boucou, should be besieged and rooted out, a strong detachment of white and black troops were sent against them, under the command of the brave Captain Myland, who was to head the first, and Lieutenant Freidrecy, a spirited young officer who, with the conductors, was to lead the latter. The detachment, on their arrival at the marsh, however, were obliged to encamp on its borders, not being able to pass through it on account of its unfordable depth.

On the discovery of the troops, the bold negro Baron immediately planted a white flag within their view, which he meant not as a token of peace, but of defiance; an incessant firing instantly took place on both sides, but with very little effect.

It was then projected to throw a fascine bridge over the marsh, by the troops; but this plan, after several weeks had been spent in the attempt and a number of men shot dead while employed upon it, was of necessity laid aside. Thus every hope of passing through the marsh into the fortress being frustrated, and the food and ammunition being considerably lessened, added to the loss of many men, affairs at length arrived at such a crisis, that the siege must have been broken up, and the remaining troops must have marched back to Paramaribo, had not the rangers, by their indefatigable efforts and (however strange to think) implacable enmity against the rebels, found out and discovered to the Europeans the under-water paths of communication to Boucou, several being shot and drowned in the execution of this important service.

On this intelligence, Captain Myland with the regulars, forded the swamp on one side, and instantly making a feint attack on the fortress, drew Baron with all the rebels, as was expected, to its defence. Meanwhile Lieutenant Freidrecy, with the rangers, having crossed the swamp on the other side, embraced the opportunity of leaping, with his black party, over the palisadoes, sword in hand, without opposition.

A most terrible carnage at this time ensued, while several prisoners were made on both sides, and the fortress of Boucou was taken; but Baron, with the greatest number of the rebels, escaped into the woods, having first found means, however, to cut the throats of ten or twelve of the rangers, who had lost their way in the marsh, and whom he seized as they stuck fast in the swamp. Cutting off the ears, nose and lips of one of them, he left him alive in this condition to return to his friends, with whom however the miserable man soon expired.

This Baron had formerly been the negro slave of a Mr Dahlbergh, a Swede, who on account of his abilities had advanced him to the rank of a favourite, had taught him to read and write, and bred him a mason; he had also been with his master in Holland, and had been promised his manumission on his return to the colony. But Mr Dahlbergh breaking his word with regard to his liberty and selling him to a Jew, Baron obstinately refused to work, in consequence of which he was publicly flogged under the gallows. This usage the negro so violently resented, that from that moment he vowed revenge against all Europeans without exception and fled to the woods where, putting himself at the head of the rebels, his name became dreadful, particularly to his former master Dahlbergh, as he solemnly swore that he should never die in peace till he had washed his hands in the tyrant's blood.

To those who know how greatly mankind are affected by self-interest, it will not appear so extraordinary, as it may to a superficial observer, that these black rangers should so inveterately engage against their friends and countrymen. What will not men do to be emancipated from so deplorable a state of subjection. And this emancipation was obtained upon more certain and advantageous grounds by the consent of the Europeans, than if they had absconded into the woods. Having thus once engaged in this service, it is evident they must be considered by the other party as apostates and traitors of the blackest dye; they must be convinced that defeat must not only expose them to death, but to the severest tortures. They were therefore fighting for something more than liberty and life: success was to bring them the most solid advantages, miscarriage was to plunge them in the severest misery.

The taking of Boucou was now greatly spoken of, and deemed a very severe blow to the rebels; both the regulars and the rangers, indeed, behaved with unprecedented intrepidity and courage. Captain Myland's gallant conduct was most highly acknowledged, while Lieutenant Fredericy was presented by the Surinam Society with a beautiful sabre, a fusee, and a brace of pistols, mounted in silver, and ornamented with emblems expressive of his merit; besides which, he obtained the rank of captain. It must be confessed, that on this occasion the whole detachment, white and black, without exception, justly met with the fullest marks of approbation for their spirited behaviour. In this state were the public affairs of Surinam when, in 1773, our fleet dropped anchor before the town of Paramaribo.

4

HAVING already stated that, from our arrival till February 27th, we seemed to be landed in Guiana for little more than idle dissipation, I shall now proceed from the same date, which was about the commencement of the rainy season when our mirth and conviviality still continued, to present to the reader, as a contrast to the preceding scenes of horror, a description of the beautiful mulatto maid Joanna. This charming young woman I first saw at the house of a Mr Demelly, secretary to the court of policy, where I daily breakfasted and with whose lady, Joanna, but fifteen years of age, was a very remarkable favourite. Rather taller than the middle size, she was possessed of the most elegant shape that nature can exhibit, moving her well-formed limbs with more than common gracefulness. Her face was full of native modesty, and the most distinguished sweetness; her eyes, as black as ebony, were large and full of expression, bespeaking the goodness of her heart; with cheeks through which glowed, in spite of the darkness of her complexion, a beautiful tinge of vermillion, when gazed upon. Her nose was perfectly well formed, rather small; her lips a little prominent, which, when she spoke, discovered two regular rows of teeth, as white as mountain snow; her hair was a dark brown inclining to black, forming a beautiful globe of small ringlets, ornamented with flowers and gold spangles. Round her neck, her arms, and her ankles, she wore gold chains, rings and medals: while a shawl of India muslin, the end of which was negligently thrown over her polished shoulders, gracefully covered part of her lovely bosom, a petticoat of rich chintz alone completed her apparel. Bare-headed and bare-footed, she shone with double lustre, as she carried in her delicate hand a beaver hat, the crown trimmed round with silver. The figure and appearance of this charming creature could not but attract my particular attention, as they did indeed that of all who beheld her, and induced me to enquire from Mrs Demelly, with much surprise, who she was that appeared to be so much distinguished above all others of her species in the colony.

'She is, Sir,' replied this lady, 'the daughter of a respectable gentleman, named Kruythoff, who had, besides this girl, four children by a black woman, called Cery, the property of a Mr D. B. on his estate called Fauconberg, in the upper part of the river Comewina.

'Some few years since Mr Kruythoff made the offer of above one thousand pounds sterling to Mr D. B. to obtain manumission for his offspring; this being inhumanly refused, it had such an effect on his spirits, that he became frantic, and died in that melancholy state soon after, leaving in slavery, at the discretion of a tyrant, two boys and three fine girls, of which the one now before us is the eldest.*

'The gold medals which seem to surprise you, are the gifts which her faithful mother, who is a most deserving woman towards her children and of some consequence among her cast, received from her father (whom she ever attended with exemplary affection) just before he expired.

'Mr. D. B. however, met with his just reward: for having since driven all his best carpenter negroes to the woods by his injustice and severity, he was ruined and obliged to fly the colony, leaving his estate and stock to the disposal of his creditors. One of the above unhappy deserters, a samboe,† has by his industry been the protector of Cery and her children. His name is Jolycoeur, and he is now the first of Baron's captains, whom you may have a chance of meeting in the rebel camp, breathing revenge against the Christians.

'Mrs D. B. is still in Surinam, being arrested for her husband's debts, till Fauconberg shall be sold by execution to pay them. This lady now lodges at my house, where the unfortunate Joanna attends her, whom she treats with peculiar tenderness and distinction.'

Having thanked Mrs Demelly for her account of Joanna, in whose eye glittered the precious pearl of sympathy, I took my leave and went to my lodging in a state of sadness and stupefaction. However trifling, and like the style of romance, this relation may appear to some, it is nevertheless a genuine account, and on that score I flatter myself may not entirely be uninteresting to others.

When reflecting on the state of slavery altogether, while my ears were stunned with the clang of the whip and the dismal yells of the wretched negroes on whom it was exercised from morning till night, and considering that this might one day be the fate of the unfortunate mulatto I have been describing should she chance to fall into the hands of a tyrannical master or mistress, I could not help execrating the barbarity of Mr D. B. for having withheld her from a fond parent, who by bestowing on her a decent education and some accomplishments, would probably have produced, in this forsaken plant now exposed to every rude blast without protection, an ornament to civilized society.

I became melancholy with these reflections, and in order to

* In Surinam all such children go with their mothers; that is, if she is in slavery, her offspring are her master's property, should their father be a prince, unless he obtains them by purchase.

† A *samboe* is between a mulatto and a negro.

counterbalance, though in a very small degree, the general calamity of the miserable slaves who surrounded me, I began to take more delight in the prattling of my poor negro boy Quaco, than in all the fashionable conversation of the polite inhabitants of this colony. But my spirits were depressed, and in the space of twenty-four hours I was very ill indeed, when a cordial, a few preserved tamarinds, and a basket of fine oranges, were sent by an unknown person. This first contributed to my relief, and losing about twelve ounces of blood, I recovered so far that on the fifth I was able, for change of air, to accompany a Captain Macneyl, who gave me a pressing invitation to his beautiful coffee plantation, called Sporkesgift, in the Matapaca Creek.

We set out from Paramaribo for Sporkesgift, in a tent-boat or barge, rowed by eight of the best negroes belonging to Mr Macneyl's estate—everybody, as I have already mentioned, travelling by water in this colony.

These barges I cannot better describe than by comparing them with those that accompany what is usually styled the Lord Mayor's Show on the river Thames. They are, however, somewhat less, though some are very little inferior in magnificence, and are often decorated with gilded flags, filled with musicians, and abound in every convenience. They are sometimes rowed by ten and even by twelve oars, and being lightly built, sweep along with astonishing celerity. The rowers never stop, from the moment they set out till the company is landed at the place of destination but continue, the tide serving or not, to tug night and day, sometimes for twenty-four hours together, singing a chorus all the time to keep up their spirits. When their labour is over, their naked bodies still dripping with sweat, like post-horses, they headlong, one and all, plunge into the river to refresh themselves.

We now passed a number of fine plantations, but I could not help taking particular notice of the Cacao estate, called Alkmaar, situated on the right side in rowing up the river Comewina, which is no less conspicuous for its beauty than for the goodness of its proprietor, the invaluable lady the widow Godefroy, whose humanity and friendship must always be remembered by me with gratitude.

At our arrival on the estate Sporkesgift, I had the pleasure to be the spectator of an instance of justice which afforded me the greatest satisfaction.

The scene consisted in Mr Macneyl's turning the overseer out of his service, and ordering him to depart from the plantation in an inferior boat, called a *ponkee*,* to Paramaribo, or wherever he thought proper. The cause of his disgrace was having, by bad usage and

* A *ponkee* is a flat-bottomed boat of four or six oars, something like a square-toed shoe: sometimes it has a tilt, and sometimes not.

cruelty, caused the death of three or four negroes. His departure was made completely joyful to all the slaves, by an holiday, which was spent in festivity, by dancing and clapping hands on a green before the dwelling-house windows.

The overseer's sentence was the more ignominious and galling, as at the time of receiving it a negro foot-boy, who was buckling his shoes, was ordered back, and he was desired to buckle them himself. The spirited conduct of this planter, the joy of his negroes, the salubrity of the country air, and the hospitable manner in which we were entertained at his estate, had such an effect on my constitution and my spirits, that on the ninth I returned, if not recovered at least greatly benefited, to Paramaribo. But I should be guilty of partiality, did I not relate one instance, which throws a shade over the humanity even of my friend Macneyl.

Having observed a handsome young negro walk very lamely while the others were capering and dancing, I enquired into the cause of his crippled appearance. I was informed by this gentleman, that the negro having repeatedly run away from his work, he had been obliged to hamstring him, which operation is performed by cutting through the large tendon above one of the heels. However severe this instance of despotism may appear, it is nothing when compared with some barbarities which the task I have undertaken will oblige me, at the expense of my feelings, to relate.

On our return to the town of Paramaribo, the only news that occurred consisted in a few shocking executions; also that the *Boreas* man-of-war, Captain Van-de-Velde, had sailed for Holland, and that Colonel Fourgeoud had on the eighth, the Prince of Orange's anniversary, entertained a large company with a ball *en militaire*, in the officers' guard-room. The music on this occasion consisted of two fiddlers only, who had the conscience to make the colonel pay one hundred and twenty Dutch florins for rosin and catgut.

About this time I was attacked by a distemper called the *prickly heat*, by the colonists *rootvont*. It begins by the skin taking a colour like scarlet (occasioned by a number of small pimples), and itching inconceivably; under the garters, or any place where the circulation is impeded, the itching is almost insupportable.

With this pest all new-comers from Europe are soon infected; the cure is to bathe the parts with the juice of limes and water, as for the bites of gnats or mosquitoes. The prickly heat is supposed to be a prognostic of good health by the inhabitants, and I have reason to think this true, since from that period my health and spirits were perfectly re-established, and I was once more as happy as Paramaribo could make me.

At this time Colonel Fourgeoud set out with a barge to inspect the situation of the rivers Comewina and Cottica, in case the actual service of our troops should soon be wanted; at his departure he was saluted by the guns from Fort Zelandia, and by those of the ships in the roads. This compliment I acknowledge astonished me, after the coolness which took place, and was now rooted, between this gentleman and the governor of the colony.

As we were still in a state of inaction, I made another excursion, with a Mr Charles Ryndorp, who rowed me in his barge to five beautiful coffee estates, and one sugar plantation, in the Mattapaca, Paramarica, and Werapa Creeks, the description of which I must defer to another occasion. On one of which, called Schovnort, I was the witness to a scene of barbarity which I cannot help relating.

The victim of this cruelty was a fine old negro slave who, having been as he thought undeservedly sentenced to receive some hundred lashes by the lacerating whips of two negro drivers, in the midst of the execution pulled out a knife, which, after having made a fruitless thrust at his persecutor the overseer, he plunged up to the haft in his own bowels, repeating the blow till he dropped down at the tyrant's feet. For this crime he was, being first recovered, condemned to be chained to the furnace which distils the *kill-devil*,* there to keep in the intense heat of a perpetual fire night and day, being blistered all over, till he should expire by infirmity or old age, of the latter of which however he had but little chance. He showed me his wounds with a smile of contempt, which I returned with a sigh and a small donation: nor shall I ever forget the miserable man, who, like Cerberus, was loaded with irons and chained to everlasting torment. As for everything else I observed in this little tour, I must acknowledge it to be elegant and splendid, and my reception hospitable beyond my expectation: but these Elysian fields could not dissipate the gloom which the infernal furnace had left upon my mind.

Of the coffee estates, that of Mr Sims, called Limeshope, was the most magnificent, and may be deemed with justice one of the richest in the colony. We now once more, on the sixth of April, returned safe to Paramaribo, where we found the *Westerlingwerf* man-of-war, Captain Crass, which had arrived from Plymouth in thirty-seven days, into which port he had put to stop a leak, having parted company with us, as already mentioned, off Portland, at the end of December 1772. This day, dining at the house of my friend, Mr Lolkens, to whom I had been, as I have said, recommended by letters, I was an eye witness of the unpardonable contempt with which negro slaves are

* *Kill-devil* is a species of rum which is distilled from the scum and dregs of sugar cauldrons. This is much drunk in this colony, and the only spirits allowed the negroes; many Europeans also, from a point of economy, make use of it, to whom it proves no better than a slow but fatal poison.

treated in this colony. His son, a boy not more than ten years old, when sitting at table, gave a slap in the face to a grey-headed black woman, who by accident touched his powdered hair as she was serving in a dish of kerry. I could not help blaming his father for overlooking the action, but he told me, with a smile, that the child should no longer offend me, as he was next day to sail for Holland for education. To this I answered that I thought it almost too late. At the same moment a sailor passing by, broke the head of a negro with a bludgeon, for not having saluted him with his hat. Such is the state of slavery, at least in this Dutch settlement!

About this time, Colonel Fourgeoud made a second excursion, and now departed with a barge, to explore the banks and situation of the river Surinam, as he had before done those of Rio Comewina and Rio Cottica.

At this time died Captain Barends, one of the masters of the transports, which were still kept in commission in case they should be wanted for our return to Europe. Five or six sailors belonging to the merchant ships, were now buried every day, whose lamentable fate I cannot pass by unnoticed. They are actually used worse than the negroes in this scorching climate, where, besides rowing large flat-bottomed barges up and down the rivers, day and night, for coffee, sugar, etc. and being exposed to the burning sun and heavy rains, and besides stowing the above commodities in a hold as hot as an oven they are obliged to row every upstart planter to his estate at a call, which saves the gentleman so many negroes, and for which they receive in return nothing—many times not so much as a mouthful of meat and drink. They palliate hunger and thirst by begging from the slaves a few bananas or plantains, eating oranges and drinking water, which in a little time relieves them from every complaint, by shipping them off to eternity. In every part of the colony they are no better treated, but, like horses, they must (having unloaded the vessels) drag the commodities to the distant storehouses, being bathed in sweat, and bullied with bad language, sometimes with blows. A few negroes are ordered to attend, but not to work, by the direction of their masters, which many would willingly do to relieve the drooping sailors, to whom this usage must be exceedingly disheartening and galling. The planters even employ those men to paint their houses, clean their sash-windows, and do numberless other menial services, for which a seaman was never intended. All this is done to save the work of their negroes; while by this usage thousands are swept to the grave, who in the line of their profession alone might have lived for many years. Nor dare the West India Captains to refuse their men, without incurring the displeasure of the planters, and seeing their ships rot in the harbour without a loading. Nay, I have heard a sailor fervently wish he had

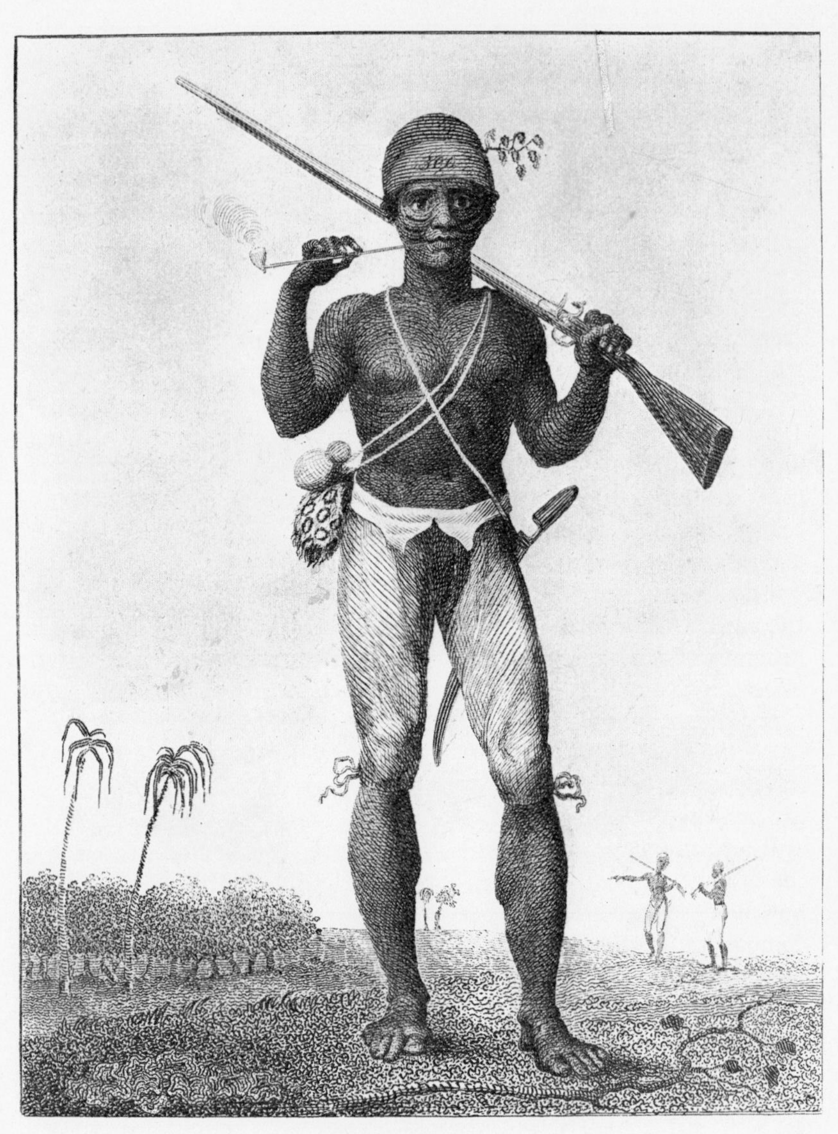

A free negro ranger

been born a negro, and beg to be employed among them in cultivating a coffee plantation.

I now took an early opportunity to enquire of Mrs Demelly what was become of the amiable Joanna. I was informed that her lady, Mrs D. B. had escaped to Holland on board the *Boreas* man-of-war, under the protection of Captain Van-de-Velde, and that her young mulatto was now at the house of her aunt, a free woman, whence she expected hourly to be sent up to the estate Fauconberg, friendless, and at the mercy of some unprincipled overseer appointed by the creditors, who had now taken possession of the plantation and stock, till the whole should be sold to pay the several sums due to them by Mr D. B. Good God! I flew to the spot in search of poor Joanna: I found her bathed in tears. She gave me such a look—ah! such a look! From that moment I determined to be her protector against every insult, and persevered, as shall be seen in the sequel. Here, reader, let my youth, blended with extreme sensibility, plead my excuse; yet assuredly my feelings will be forgiven me.

I next ran to the house of my friend Lolkens, who happened to be the administrator of Fauconberg estate; and asking his assistance, I intimated to him my strange determination of purchasing and educating Joanna.

Having recovered from his surprise, after gazing at me silently for some time, an interview at once was proposed, and the beauteous slave, accompanied by a female relation, was produced trembling in my presence.

It now proved to be she who had privately sent me the cordial and the oranges in March, when I was nearly expiring, and which she now modestly acknowledged 'was in gratitude for my expressions of compassion respecting her sad situation'; with singular delicacy, however, she rejected every proposal of becoming mine upon any terms. She was conscious, she said, 'that in such a state should I soon return to Europe, she must either be parted from me for ever, or accompany me to a part of the world where the inferiority of her condition must prove greatly to the disadvantage of both herself and her benefactor, and thus in either case be miserable'. Joanna firmly persisting in these sentiments, she was immediately permitted to withdraw, and return to the house of her aunt; while I could only intreat of Mr Lolkens his generous protection for her, and that she might at least for some time be separated from the other slaves, and continue at Paramaribo; and in this request his humanity was induced to indulge me.

On the 30th the news arrived that the rangers, having discovered a rebel village, had attacked it and carried off three prisoners, leaving four others dead upon the spot, whose right hands, chopped off and barbecued or smoke-dried, they had sent to the governor of Paramaribo as a proof of their valour and fidelity.

On receiving this intelligence, Colonel Fourgeoud immediately left the river Surinam, where he still was, and on the first of May returned to town, in expectation of his regiment being employed on actual service. But there the business ended and we still, to our utter astonishment, were allowed to linger away our time, each agreeably to his own peculiar fancy. On the 4th of May, the rangers however were reviewed in the Fort Zelandia, at which ceremony I was present, and must confess that this corps of black soldiers had a truly manly appearance: warriors whose determined and open aspect could not but give me the satisfaction of a soldier in beholding them. They here once more received the thanks of the governor for their manly behaviour and faithful conduct, particularly at the taking of Boucon; besides which, they were entertained with a rural feast, at the public expense, at Paramaribo, to which were also invited their families; and at which feast several respectable people of both sexes made their appearance with pleasure, to witness the happiness of their sable friends, the day being spent in mirth and conviviality, without the least disturbance, nay even with decorum and propriety, to the great satisfaction of the inhabitants.

The *Westerlingwerf*, Captain Crass, now left the river also, bound for Holland, but first for the colony of Demerary. Thus both ships of war having sailed without us, there was some reason to suppose we were soon to be employed on actual service. There were many motives, indeed, for wishing either that this might be the case, or that we might speedily be permitted to return to Europe. Not only our officers, but our privates, began to feel the debilitating effects of the climate, and many of that continued debauchery so common in all ranks in this settlement. As hard labour and bad treatment constantly killed the poor sailors, so now our common soldiers fell the victims of idleness and licentiousness, and died frequently six or seven in a day; whence it is evident to demonstration, that all excesses, of whatever kind, are mortal to Europeans in the climate of Guiana.

But men will give lessons which they do not themselves observe. Thus, notwithstanding my former resolution of living retired, I again relapsed into the vortex of dissipation. I became a member of a drinking club, I partook of all polite and impolite amusements, and plunged into every extravagance without exception. I did not, however, escape without the punishment I deserved. I was seized suddenly with a dreadful fever; and such was its violence, that in a few days I was no more expected to recover. In this situation I lay in my hammock until the 17th, with only a soldier and my black boy to attend me, and without any other friend. Sickness being universal among the newcomers to this country, and every one of our corps having so much to do to take care of themselves, neglect was an inevitable consequence, even among the nearest acquaintance. This, however, is a censure which does not apply to the inhabitants, who perhaps are the most hospitable people on the globe to Europeans. These philanthropists not only supply the sick with a variety of cordials at the same time, but crowd their apartments with innumerable condolers, who from morning till night continue prescribing, insisting, bewailing, and lamenting, friend and stranger without exception; and this lasts until the patient becomes delirious and expires. Such must inevitably have been my case, between the two extremes of neglect and importunity, had it not been for the happy intervention of poor Joanna, who one morning entered my apartment, to my unspeakable joy and surprise, accompanied by one of her sisters. She informed me that she was acquainted with my forlorn situation; that if I still entertained for her the same good opinion, her only request was, that she might wait upon me till I should be recovered. I indeed gratefully accepted her offer, and by her unremitting care and attention had the good fortune so far to regain my health and spirits, as to be able, in a few days after, to take an airing in Mr Kennedy's carriage.

Till this time I had chiefly been Joanna's friend, but now I began to feel I was her captive. I renewed my wild proposals of purchasing, educating, and transporting her to Europe; which, though offered with the most perfect sincerity, were, by her, rejected once more, with this humble declaration:

'I am born a low contemptible slave. Were you to treat me with too much attention, you must degrade yourself with all your friends and relations, while the purchase of my freedom you will find expensive, difficult, and apparently impossible. Yet though a slave, I have a soul, I hope, not inferior to that of a European, and blush not to avow the regard I retain for you, who have distinguished me so much above all others of my unhappy birth. You have, Sir, pitied me, and now, independent of every other thought, I shall have pride in throwing myself at your feet, till fate shall part us or my conduct becomes such as to give you cause to banish me from your presence.'

This she uttered with a downcast look, and tears dropping on her heaving bosom, while she held her companion by the hand.

From that instant this excellent creature was mine; nor had I ever after cause to repent of the step I had taken, as will more particularly appear in the course of this narrative.

I cannot omit to record, that having purchased for her presents to the value of twenty guineas, I was the next day greatly astonished to see all my gold returned upon my table, the charming Joanna having carried every article back to the merchants, who cheerfully returned her the money.

'Your generous intentions alone, Sir (she said), were sufficient: but allow me to tell you, that I cannot help considering any superfluous expense on my account as a diminution of that good opinion which I hope you have, and will ever entertain, of my disinterested disposition.'

Such was the language of a slave, who had simple nature only for her instructor, the purity of whose sentiments stood in need of no comment, and these I was now determined to improve by every care.

In the evening I visited Mr Demelly, who, with his lady, congratulated me on my recovery from sickness. At the same time, however strange it may appear to many readers, they, with a smile, wished me joy of what, with their usual good humour, they were pleased to call my conquest. One of the ladies in company assured me that while it was perhaps censured by some, it was applauded by many, and she believed in her heart it was envied by all. A decent wedding, at which many of our respectable friends made their appearance, and at which I was as happy as any bridegroom ever was, concluded the ceremony.

5

On the 21st of May our Lieutenant Colonel Lantman died, and a number of our officers lay sick.

Instead of gaiety and dissipation, disease and mortality now began to rage among us, and the devastation increased from day to day among the private men in a most alarming proportion. The remains of the deceased officer were interred with military honours in the centre of the fortress Zelandia, where all criminals are imprisoned and all field officers buried. At this place I was not a little shocked to see the captive rebel negroes and others clanking their chains, and roasting plantains and yams upon the sepulchres of the dead; they presented to my imagination, the image of a number of diabolical fiends in the shape of African slaves, tormenting the souls of their European persecutors. From these gloomy mansions of despair, on this day, seven captive negroes were selected, who being led by a few soldiers to the place of execution, which is in the savannah where the sailors and soldiers are interred, six were hanged and one broken alive upon the rack with an iron bar; besides which a white man was scourged before the court house by the public executioner, who is in this country always a black. The circumstance which led me to take particular notice of this affair, was the shameful injustice of showing a partiality to the European, who ought to have been better informed, by letting him escape with only a slight corporal punishment, while the poor uneducated African for the same crime—stealing money out of the Town Hall—lost his life under the most excruciating torments, which he supported without heaving a sigh or making a complaint. One of his companions, with the rope about his neck and just on the point of being turned off, uttered a laugh of contempt at the magistrates who attended the execution. I ought not in this place to omit that the negro who flogged the white man inflicted the punishment with the greatest marks of commiseration. These transactions almost induced me to decide between the Europeans and Africans in this colony, that the first were the greater barbarians of the two.

Having testified how much I was hurt at the cruelty of the above execution, and surprised at the intrepidity with which the negroes bore their punishment, a decent looking man stepped up to me, 'Sir (said he), you are but a newcomer from Europe, and know very little about the African slaves, or you would testify both less feeling and surprise. Not long ago, I saw a black man suspended alive from a gallows by the ribs, between which, with a knife, was first made an incision, and then clinched an iron hook with a chain; in this manner he kept alive three days, hanging with his head and feet downwards, and catching with his tongue the drops of water (it being in the rainy season) that were flowing down his bloated breast. Notwithstanding all this he never complained, and even upbraided a negro for crying while he was flogged below the gallows, by calling out to him—You man?—*Da cay fasy*? Are you a man? you behave like a boy. Shortly after which he was knocked on the head by the commiserating sentry, who stood over him, with the butt end of his musket. Another negro, I have seen quartered alive. After four strong horses had been fastened to his legs and arms, and iron sprigs had been driven home underneath every one of his nails on hands and feet, he first asked a dram, and then bid them pull away, without a groan. But what afforded us the greatest entertainment, were the fellow's jokes, by desiring the executioner to drink before him, in case there should chance to be poison in the glass, and bidding him take care of his horses, lest any of them should happen to strike backwards. As for old men being broken upon the rack, and young women roasted alive chained to stakes, there can be nothing more common in this colony.' I was petrified at the inhuman detail, and breaking away with execrations from this diabolical scene of laceration, made the best of my way home to my own lodgings.

On the 24th, having received a supply of provisions from Holland, and absolutely doing no service in the colony, it was universally resolved that we should proceed home; our regiment, notwithstanding its being partly paid by the United Provinces, still being exceedingly chargeable to the Society and the inhabitants, who, in conjunction, paid all other expenses. Thus, in the hopes of sailing in the middle of June, the transports were ordered a second time to wood, water, and make all other necessary preparations.

I must say nothing of what I felt on this occasion. I continued, however, not long in this state of suspense, for the following day intelligence being brought that a plantation was demolished and the overseers murdered by the rebels, our stay was prolonged a second time, at the request of the governor himself and inhabitants. In consequence, the three transports, which had since February the 9th been kept waiting at a great expense, were finally put out of commission and the provisions stowed at the headquarters in a temporary storehouse erected for that purpose.

The minds of the people began now to be quieted, finding at last that the troops were in earnest preparing for actual service, a circumstance greatly, indeed, to be lamented as to the occasion, but certainly much better for the colony, than to let the regiment linger away an idle life at Paramaribo.

Thus our warlike preparations for some days proceeded, and our marines appeared in excellent spirits, when again, on the 7th of June, to our unutterable surprise, we were for the third time officially acquainted that, things seeming quiet and presuming that tranquillity was at last re-established, the colony of Surinam had no farther occasion for our services. These fluctuating councils did not fail to produce much discontent among the military, as well as the inhabitants, and cabals were formed which threatened to break out into a civil contest.

Some charged the governor with being jealous of the unlimited power which was vested in Colonel Fourgeoud, who was also by many others blamed as abusing that power, and as not treating the governor with that civility which he might have evinced without lessening his own consequence. Thus, while one party acknowledged us to be the bulwark of the settlement by keeping the rebels in awe, the opposition hesitated not to call us the locusts of Egypt who were come to devour the fruits of the colony.

Without entering into the merits of the question, it is sufficient to say that our life was rendered very uncomfortable, and a great number of us could not help thinking that between the two parties we were but ill treated. This same day, while at dinner on board a Dutch vessel in the roads, the company were alarmed by the most tremendous claps of thunder I ever heard in my life. On our side of the continent, several negroes and cattle were killed by lightning; while, on the other side, nearly at the same time, the city of Guatimala, in Old Mexico, was swallowed up by an earthquake, by which eight thousand families are said to have instantly perished.

On the 11th, the ships, being taken again into commission, were ordered with all possible expedition to prepare for our final departure, and everyone was making himself ready for the voyage.

Being thus apparently disengaged from military service, I received a polite invitation from a Mr Campbell, who was lodged with a Mr Kerry at my friend Kennedy's, to accompany him on a visit to the island of Tobago, where I might recruit my debilitated health and dejected spirits. His plan was to return with me by the Leeward Islands to Europe. It was, indeed, to me a most agreeable offer, all things considered, and I should certainly with pleasure have accepted it, had not my application to Colonel Fourgeoud been prevented by a fresh alarm, which was received on the 15th. The substance of this was no less, than that an officer of the Society troops had been shot dead by the rebels, and his whole party, consisting of about thirty men, entirely cut to pieces. So alarming a piece of intelligence could not fail to throw the whole colony once more into the utmost confusion and consternation. The above gentleman, whose name was Lepper, and only a lieutenant, was in a great measure the cause of this misfortune, by his impetuosity and intrepidity totally unregulated by temper or conduct;* but as this censure in general terms may appear severe, it becomes in some degree incumbent on me to relate the particulars.

The period when this unhappy event took place, was that which, in the language of the colony, is termed the short-day season. During this, Mr Lepper having been informed that between the rivers Patamaca and Upper Cormoetibo, a village of negroes had been discovered by the rangers some time before, he determined with his small party, which was only a detachment from the Patamaca post, to sally through the woods and attack them. But the rebels being apprized of his intentions by their spies, which they constantly employ, immediately marched out to receive him; in his way they laid themselves in ambush, near the borders of a deep marsh, through which the soldiers were to pass to the rebel settlement. No sooner had the unfortunate men got into the swamp and up to their arm-pits, than their black enemies rushed out from under cover, and shot them dead at their leisure in the water, while they were unable to return the fire more than once, their situation preventing them from re-loading their muskets. Their gallant commander, being imprudently distinguished by a gold-laced hat, was shot through the head in the first onset. The few that scrambled out of the marsh upon the banks were immediately put to death in the most barbarous manner, except five or six, who were taken prisoners and carried alive to the settlement of the rebels. The melancholy fate of these unfortunate men, I shall, in a proper place, describe, as I had it since from those that were eye-witnesses of it.

The intelligence had scarcely reached Paramaribo, than the whole town was in a tumult; some parties were so vehement that they were ready to tear the governor and council to pieces, for having dismissed Colonel Fourgeoud with his regiment, while others ingenuously declared, that if we were intended for no further use than we had hitherto been, our company might without regret be dispensed with. All this could not but be exceedingly galling to our officers, who wished nothing more than to be employed on actual service for the advantage of the colony. On the other side, most bitter lampoons were spread through the town against the governor and his council; libels of such a black and inflammatory nature that no less than a thousand gold

* This gentleman formerly belonged to the life-guards in Holland, from which he fled, after thrusting his antagonist through the heart with his sword in a duel.

ducats were offered as a reward for the discovery of their author, with a promise of concealing the name of the informer if he required it: but the whole was to no purpose, and neither author nor informer made their appearance. The general clamour however still continuing, the governor and council were forced a third time to petition us to remain in Surinam, and to protect the distracted colony. To this petition we once more condescended to listen, and the ships were actually a third time put out of commission.

We, however, still continued doing nothing, to the unspeakable surprise of every person concerned. The only part on duty, hitherto, had consisted of a subaltern's guard at the headquarters, to protect the chief, his colours, his storehouses, pigs and poultry—which guard regularly mounted every day at half past four o'clock—and another on board the transports, until the provisions had been stowed on shore in the magazines. This, a few field-days excepted, when the soldiers were drilled for pomp alone in a burning sun till they fainted, comprehended the whole of our military manoeuvres. But I perceive the reader is already impatient for some information respecting these two extraordinary men, who, from their inveteracy and opposition to each other, as well as from other causes, were the authors of these unaccountable and fluctuating proceedings; and the outlines of these two characters may perhaps assist in unravelling the mystery.

As the ingredients of flattery or fear make but a small part of that man's composition who presumes to give them, and who pretends perfectly to have known both, the reader may depend on having them painted in their true original colours, however strong the shades.

Governor Nepveu was said to be rather a man of sense than of learning, and was wholly indebted to his art and address for having risen to his present dignity from sweeping the hall of the court-house. By the same means he was enabled, from nothing, to accumulate a fortune, by some computed at no less than eight thousand pounds sterling annually, and to command respect from all ranks of people, no person ever daring to attack him but at a distance. His deportment was affable, but ironical, without ever losing the command of his temper, which gave him the appearance of a man of fashion, and rendered his influence almost unbounded. He was generally known by the appellation of Reynard, and was most certainly a fox of too much artifice to be run down by all the hounds in the colony.

Colonel Fourgeoud was almost exactly the reverse of this portrait. He was impetuous, passionate, self-sufficient, and revengeful: he was not cruel to individuals, but was a tyrant to the generality, and caused the death of hundreds by his sordid avarice and oppression. With all this he was partial, ungrateful, and confused; but a most indefatigable man in bearing hardships and in braving dangers, not exceeded by Columbus himself, which, like a true buccaneer, he sustained with the most heroic courage, patience, and perseverance. Though unconquerably harsh and severe to his officers, he was however not wanting in affability to the private soldiers. He had read, but had no education to assist him in digesting what he read. In short, few men could talk better, but on most occasions few could act worse.

Such were the characters of our commanders, while the opposition of two such men to each other could not fail to produce unhappiness to the troops, and operated as a sufficient cause for the fluctuating state of political affairs in this dejected colony.

On the 21st died Mr Renard, one of our best surgeons, who was buried the same afternoon, a process quite necessary in this hot country where putrefaction so instantaneously takes place, and more especially when the patient dies of a putrid fever, which is in this country extremely frequent. This dreadful disease first appears by bilious vomiting, lowness of spirits and a yellowish cast of the countenance and eyes; and unless proper remedies be immediately applied, the distemper becomes fatal, and certain death in a few days is the consequence.

It was, indeed, lamentable to observe the state to which we were already reduced from a corps of the finest, healthiest young men that ever sailed from Europe, with blooming fresh complexions now changed to the sallow colour of a drum-head. It was no alleviation of the calamity to reflect that all this waste of life and health had been hitherto to no purpose. Though some persons chose to report that the whole was no more than a political scheme to have another regiment added to the war-establishment in Holland, others gave this but very little credit.

Of the hospitality of the country at least we could not complain, since this was actually one of the principal sources of our misfortunes, and we were likely in a few months to be caressed to death by the civilities of the men and the kindness of the ladies.

On the 27th of June, the gentleman-like Lieutenant-Colonel Baron de Gersdorph died, much regretted indeed by every person; while the grim King of Terrors, conscientiously beginning at the head of the corps with the field officers, could not fail to afford some consolation to the inferior gentry who succeeded to their places, by the appointment of Colonel Fourgeoud, the commander-in-chief, who himself exhibited as yet no symptoms of mortality. Major Becquer was now made lieutenant-colonel, and a Captain Rockaph advanced to the rank of major.

The European animals that live in this country are no less debilitated and diminutive than the human species. The oxen, for instance, are very small, and their beef not near so delicate as it is in Europe, owing probably to their perpetual perspiration and the coarseness of the grass on which they feed, which is not so good as that of the salt marshes in Somersetshire. On the banks of the Oroonoko the oxen run wild, and are sold by the Spaniards for two dollars per head. A single piece of ready-roasted beef is often sent from Europe to Guiana as a most valuable and delicate present. The manner of preserving the meat for this long voyage, when roasted, is by putting it in a block-tin box or cannister, then filling up the empty space with gravy or dripping till it is perfectly covered over, after which the box must be made fast and soldered round about, so that neither air nor water can penetrate: by this means I was told it may be with safety carried round the globe.

The sheep in this country are so small that, when skinned, they seem not larger than young lambs in Whitechapel market; they have no horns nor wool, but straight hair, and are to a European but very indifferent eating—the more so, since all beef, mutton, etc. must be consumed the same day that it is killed, which causes it to eat tough, while keeping it longer exposes it to putrefaction. Neither of these animals are natural to Guiana: the breed has been imported from the Old Continent. So also was the breed of the hog, but with far better success, for these animals, in my opinion, thrive better in South America than in Europe. The hogs here are large, fat, good, and plentiful; as in England, they feed on almost everything that is eatable, and on the estates are often fattened with green pineapples, a fruit which grows spontaneously in this climate, and of which they are exceedingly fond. As for the poultry, nothing can thrive better; the common fowls are here as good and as plenty as in any country, but smaller, and their eggs differ in shape, being more sharp-pointed. The turkeys are very fine, and so are the geese, but the ducks are excellent, being of the large Muscovy species, with crimson pearls betwixt the beak and the head: these are here juicy, fat, and in great plenty.

After the various delays we had experienced, the reader will be surprised to learn that the hour of action at last arrived, and all the officers and men were ordered to be ready at a minute's warning to set out on actual service, though our little corps was already melted down from five hundred and thirty able men to about three-fourths of that number by death and sickness, the hospital being crowded by invalids of every kind. The loss of so large a proportion of men was supplied in a manner that will appear extraordinary to a European.

There were two negroes, one called Okera, the other Gowsary, two desperadoes, who had both been rebel captains in the colony of Berbice, and who, for taking Atta their chief, and delivering him to the governor of that settlement, had received their pardon. By these two men the most inhuman murders had been committed on the Europeans in the year 1762, when the revolt took place in the above colony. These were now admitted as private soldiers in our regiment, and were Colonel Fourgeoud's greatest favourites.

It is a painful circumstance that the narrative of my travels must so frequently prove the record of cruelty and barbarity; but once for all I must declare that I state these facts merely in the hope that it may, in some mode or other, operate for their future prevention. Before my departure, I was informed of a most shocking instance of depravity, which had just occurred. A Jewess, impelled by a groundless jealousy (for such her husband made it appear), put an end to the life of a young and beautiful Quadroon girl, by the infernal means of plunging into her body a red-hot poker. But what is most incredible, and what indeed will scarcely be believed in a civilized country, is that for this most diabolical crime the murderess was only banished to the Jew Savannah, a village which I shall afterwards describe, and condemned in a trifling fine to the fiscal or town clerk of the colony.

Another young negro woman, having her ankles chained so close together that she could scarcely move her feet, was knocked down with a cane by a Jew, and beaten till the blood streamed out of her head, her arms, and her naked sides. So accustomed, indeed, are the people of this country to tyranny and insolence, that a third Israelite had the impudence to strike one of my soldiers for having made water against his garden fence. On this miscreant I took revenge for the whole fraternity, by wresting the offending weapon out of his hand, which I instantly broke into a thousand pieces on his guilty naked pate.

I nevertheless was just enough to flog another man out of the regiment for picking a Jew's pocket and, to their credit be it mentioned, so jealous are the Dutch soldiers of what they call a point of honour, that were a thief to be known and kept in the ranks, the whole regiment would lay down their arms. This etiquette is of great utility, and would be no bad practice to be introduced into some other armies where a thief is too often accounted as good as another if he is so fortunate as to be six feet high.

We now seriously prepared for victory or death on board the wooden walls of the Colony, consisting of half a dozen crazy old sugar barges, such as are used by the colliers in the Thames, only roofed over with boards, which gave them the appearance of so many coffins. How well they deserved this name, I am afraid will too soon appear by the number of men they buried.

On the first of July were dispatched for the river Comewina, one captain, two subalterns, one sergeant, two corporals and eighteen men. This same day we also dispatched another barge with two subalterns, one sergeant, one corporal, and fourteen men, commanded by Lieutenant Count Randwyck, to the river Pirica. In the evening, having entertained some select friends in my house, I bade farewell to my Joanna, to whose care I left my all, and herself to the protection of her mother and aunt, with my directions for putting her to school until my return. After this, I at last marched on board, with four subalterns, two sergeants, three corporals and thirty-two men under my command, to be divided into two barges, and bound for the upper part of the river Cottica.

The above barges were all armed with swivels, blunderbusses, etc. and provided with allowance for one month: their orders were (that which went to the Jews Savannah excepted) to cruise up and down the upper parts of the rivers. Each barge had a pilot and was rowed by negro slaves, ten of which were on board of each for the purpose, which made my complement, including my black boy Quaco, exactly sixty-five, thirty-five of which embarked with myself. With this ship's company was I now stowed in my hen-coop; on board of my lieutenant's barge the crew consisted of twenty-nine only, and consequently they were less crowded.

I must take notice that from our first landing in Surinam till this time our private men were paid in silver coin, which the captains had proposed to exchange for card money at the rate of ten per cent gain for them; by this the poor fellows would have benefited between two and three hundred pounds sterling per annum, to buy refreshment. But Colonel Fourgeoud insisted they should continue to receive their little pittance in coin, which in small sums was of no more value than paper; this I thought unaccountably hard, since it was hurting the whole, without profit to one single individual. One thing more I must remark, which is, that all the officers who were now proceeding upon duty continued to pay at the mess, which cost each captain at the rate of forty pounds. For this, in his barge, he was to receive provisions at the rate of ten pounds (thus he lost thirty pounds), and these provisions were salt beef, pork and pease, on an equal footing with the private soldiers, a few bottles of wine excepted. But certainly some greater indulgence was due, and I must say necessary, to officers who were going to be stationed where absolutely no kind of refreshment was to be had, being surrounded by the most horrid and impenetrable woods, beyond the hearing of a cannon-shot from any port or plantation whatever. This was not the case with the other barges, who were stationed in the midst of peace and plenty, being within view of the most beautiful estates. We were indeed pitied by all ranks without exception who, foreseeing our approaching calamities, crowded my barge with the best commodities they had to present, which they insisted upon my accepting.

6

On the third of July, 1773, at four o'clock in the morning, the fleet cast off from their moorings, and with the ebb tide rowed down as far as the fortress New Amsterdam, where, being wind and tide bound, we dropped anchor off the battery.

It may not be improper, in this place, to describe the dress of our marines, which was blue turned up with scarlet, short jackets, and leather caps. They carried a musket, sabre, and pistols; a large wallet or knapsack across one shoulder, and their hammocks slung over the other. While in the woods, they wore trousers and check shirts, with short linen frocks, as most adapted to the climate.

Having first reviewed both my ship's companies, *viz.* four subalterns, two sergeants, three corporals, thirty-two privates, two pilots, twenty negroes, and my black boy Quaco, and having placed the arms, consisting of blunderbusses, swivels, etc., stowed the luggage, and slung the hammocks, I perused my orders. These were to cruise up and down Rio Cottica, between the Society posts, La Rochel at Patamaca, and Slans Welveren above the last plantation, to prevent the rebels from crossing the river, to seize or kill them if possible, and to protect the estates from their invasions: in all which operations I was to be assisted, if necessary, by the troops of the Society on the above posts, with whom I was also to deliberate on the proper signals to be given in case of an alarm.

On the fourth of July, in the morning, we weighed anchor and, having doubled the Cape, rowed with the flood till we arrived before Elizabeth's Hope, a beautiful coffee plantation, where the proprietor, Mr Klynhams, inviting us on shore, showed us every civility in his power and loaded my barge with refreshing fruits, vegetables, etc. He told us that he pitied our situation from his heart, and foretold the miseries we were going to encounter, the rainy season being just at hand, or indeed having already commenced with frequent showers, accompanied by loud claps of thunder. 'As for the enemy,' said he, 'you may depend on not seeing one single soul of them; they know better than to make their appearance openly, while they may have a chance of seeing you from under cover. Thus, Sir, take care to be upon your guard—but the climate, the climate will murder you all. However,' continued he, 'this shows the zeal of your commander, who will rather see you killed, than see you eat the bread of idleness at Paramaribo.' This pleasant harangue he accompanied with a squeeze of the hand. We then took our leave, while the beautiful Mrs Dutry, his daughter, shed tears at our departure. This evening we anchored before the Matapaca Creek.

I here created my two barges men-of-war, and named them the *Charon* and the *Cerberus*, by which names I shall distinguish them during the rest of the voyage, though the *Sudden Death* and *Wilful Murder* were much more applicable, as will be seen. We now continued rowing up the river Cottica, having passed, since we entered Rio Comewina, some most enchantingly beautiful estates of coffee and sugar, which line the banks of both these rivers, at the distance of one or two miles from each other.

My crew having walked and dressed their dinner ashore on the plantation l'Avanture, we anchored, on the evening of the 5th, before Rio Pirica.

On the following day we rowed still further up the river Cottica, and went on shore on the estate Alia. At all the above plantations we were most hospitably received, but we met with fewer plantations as the river grew narrower.

On the 7th we continued our course, and having walked ashore on the estate Bockkestyne, the last plantation up the river Cottica on the right except one or two small estates in Patamaca, at night we cast anchor at the mouth of Coopman's Creek. This day the *Charon* was on fire, but happily it was soon extinguished.

On the 8th, we again kept rowing upwards, and at eleven o'clock a.m. cast anchor off the fort Slans Welveren, which was guarded by the troops of the Society. Here I stepped on shore, with my officers, to wait on Captain Orzinga, the commander, and delivered three of my sick men into his hospital, where I beheld such a spectacle of misery and wretchedness as baffles all imagination. This place was formerly called Devil's Harwar, on account of its intolerable unhealthiness—a name by which alone I shall again distinguish it, as much more suitable than that of Slans Welveren, which signifies the welfare of the nation.

Here I saw a few of the wounded wretches who had escaped from the engagement in which Lieutenant Lepper, with so many men, had been killed, and one of them told me the particulars of his own miraculous escape. 'I was shot, Sir,' said he, 'with a musket-bullet in my breast; to resist or escape being impossible, I threw myself, as the only means left me to save my life, down among the mortally wounded and the dead, without moving hand or foot. Here in the evening the rebel chief, surveying his conquest, ordered one of his captains to begin instantly to cut off the heads of the slain in order to carry them home to their village, as trophies of their victory: this captain, having already chopped off that of Lieutenant Lepper and one or two more,

A private marine of Colonel Fourgeoud's Corps

said to his friend, *Sonde go sleeby, caba mekewe liby den tara dogo tay tamara*—The sun is just going to sleep, we must leave those other dogs till tomorrow. Upon saying which (continued the soldier) as I lay on my bleeding breast, with my face resting on my left arm, he, dropping his hatchet into my shoulder, made the fatal wound you see, of which I shall perhaps no more recover. I, however, lay quite still. They went away, carrying along with them the mangled heads of my comrades, and five or six prisoners alive, with their hands tied behind their backs, of whom I have never since heard. When all was quiet and it was very dark, I found means, on my hands and feet, to creep out from among the carnage, and get under cover in the forest, where I met another of our soldiers who was less wounded than myself. Together, after ten days wandering, in torment and despair, without bandages, not knowing which way to proceed, and only one single loaf of black bread for our subsistence, we at last arrived emaciated at the military post of Patamaca, our putrefied wounds full of live worms.'

I gave the miserable creature half-a-crown and, having agreed with Captain Orzinga upon the signals, we left this pest-house and, stepping on board my man-of-war, rowed up till we arrived before a creek called Barbacoba, where we once more came to an anchor.

On the following day we continued to row farther up the river, till we came before the Cormoetibo Creek, where we moored the fleet, as being my head station by Colonel Fourgeoud's command. Here we saw nothing but water, wood and clouds; no trace of humanity, and consequently the place had a most dismal, solitary appearance.

On the 10th I detached the *Cerberus* to her station, Upper Patamaca; for this place she rowed immediately with a long list of paroles, according to my orders, but they were never of any service.

We now tried to cook the victuals on board; our furnace was a large tub filled with earth, and we succeeded, at the expense of having almost scalded one of my men to death, and at the hazard of setting the barge once more on fire. As we had no surgeon along with us, this office fell to my lot and, by the help of a small chest of medicines, I performed so well, that in a few days the scalded marine recovered.

To prevent, however, a similar accident again, I sought an opening in the creek above-named, which having found not very far from the mouth, I ordered my negroes to build a shed, and my men to dress their victuals below it, placing sentinels around them to prevent a surprise, and in the evening we returned to our station. This cooking we continued to perform every day until the fourteenth, when we rowed down to Barbacoba.

Here we built another shed on the 15th, for the same purpose; and then, the rain already beating through my decks, we rowed down to

Devil's Harwar for repair, where I put one of my negroes sick in the hospital.

On the 16th, I got my deck caulked and payed, and sent an account of our arrival to Colonel Fourgeoud.

On the 17th, we returned to Cormoetibo Creek, having lost an anchor among the roots of the mangrove-trees that on both sides line the banks of all the rivers in the colony. These trees are of two species, the red and the white, but the former is that of which I now speak: the most remarkable property of this tree is that from its extended branches, and even its trunk, descend thousands of ligneous shoots, like the ropes of a ship, which dropping to the earth, take root and again re-ascend, forming for a great circumference an impenetrable thicket, while, like so many props, they keep the tree steady in all weathers. The white mangrove is found mostly in places more distant from the water.

This evening my sentinel, when it was very dark, called out that he saw a negro, with a lighted tobacco-pipe, cross the Cormoetibo Creek in a canoe. We lost no time in leaping out of our hammocks, but were not a little mortified when one of my slaves declared it was no more than a fire-fly on the wing—which actually was the case.

These insects are above an inch long, with a round patch under the belly, of a transparent greenish colour, which in the dark gives a light like a candle: its eyes are also very luminous, and by the light of a couple of these flies one may see very well to read small print.

On the 18th, having nothing else to do, I shot a bird, which is here called a *tigri-fowlo*, or tiger-bird, but which I take to be of the heron species; it is about the size of a heron, but of a reddish colour, covered over with regular black spots, from which it has derived its name: on the head, which is small, it has a roundish black spot, and its eyes are a beautiful yellow.

By a water-patrol from the *Cerberus* I received intelligence this evening, that the men began to be sickly; and on the following day I was informed, that on the spot where we had dressed our victuals in the Cormoetibo Creek, and which is on the rebel side of the river, a strong detachment had lately been murdered by the enemy. I therefore ordered the shed to be burnt to the ground, and the meat to be dressed on board the barges. Here all the elements now seemed to unite in opposing us; the water pouring down like a deluge, the heavy rains forced themselves fore and aft into the vessel, where they set everything afloat; the air was infested with myriads of mosquitoes, which, from sun-set to sun-rising, constantly kept us company, prevented us from getting any sleep, and left us in the morning besmeared all over with blood and full of blotches. The smoke of the fire and tobacco, which we burnt to annoy them, was enough to choke us, and not a footstep of land could we find where we might cook our salt provisions in safety. To all this misery may be added that discord broke out between the marines and the negroes, with whom, as promises or threats had as yet no weight, I was obliged to have recourse to other means. I tied up the ringleaders of both parties and, after ordering the first to be well flogged and the latter to be horsewhipped for half an hour, after due suspense and expectation I pardoned them all without one lash. This had equally the effect of the punishment, and peace was perfectly re-established; but to prevent approaching disease was totally out of my power.

We rowed down on the 20th, till we arrived before the Casepoere Creek, in hopes of meeting some relief, but were equally uncomfortable. So very thick were the mosquitoes now, that by clapping my two hands together, I have actually killed to the number of thirty-eight at one stroke.

I now had recourse to the advice of an old negro. 'Caramaca,' said I, 'what methods do you take to preserve your health?' 'Swim every day twice or thrice, Sir,' said he, 'in the river. This, *Masera*, not only serves for exercise where I cannot walk, but keeps my skin clean and cool; and the pores being open, I enjoy a free perspiration. Without this, by imperceptible filth, the pores are shut, the juices stagnate, and disease must inevitably follow.' Having recompensed the old gentleman with a dram, I instantly stripped and plunged headlong into the river. I had, however, no sooner taken this leap, than he called to me for God's sake to come on board; which having done with much astonishment, he reminded me of the alligators, as well as of a fish which is here called *pery*. 'Both these, Sir,' said he, 'are exceedingly dangerous, but by following my directions you will run no hazard. You may swim entirely naked, only take care that you constantly keep in motion; for the moment you are quiet, you run the risk of their snapping off a limb, or being dragged to the bottom.'

I acknowledge his account at first discouraged me from the plan of daily bathing for health; but finding by following his direction that the dangers he represented were to be avoided, I resolved to do so, and derived great benefit from the practice as long as I remained in the colony. This negro also advised me to walk bare-footed and thinly dressed. 'Now is the season, *Masera*,' said he, 'to use your feet to become hard, by walking on the smooth boards of the vessel; the time may come when you will be obliged to do so for want of shoes, in the midst of thorns and briers, as I have seen some others. Custom,' said he, '*Masera*, is second nature: our feet were all made alike. Do so as I advise you, and in the end you will thank old Caramaca. As for being thinly dressed,' continued the negro, 'a shirt and trousers is fully sufficient; this not only saves trouble and expense, but the body wants air as well as it does water, so bathe in both when you have the opportunity.' From that moment I followed his counsels, to which, besides being cleanly and cool, I in a great measure ascribe the preservation of my life. I now frequently thought on Paramaribo, where I enjoyed all the delicacies of life, while here I was forced to have recourse to many expedients much worse than any savage; yet should I not have repined had any person profited by our sufferings.

Having, on the 22nd, sent my sergeant and one man sick to the hospital at Devil's Harwar, we now rowed again to the head station before Cormoetibo Creek.

The 23rd, being the day appointed by Captain Orzinga and myself for the trial of the signals, at twelve o'clock precisely the whole number of blunderbusses and swivels were fired at Devil's Harwar on board the *Charon*, and on board the *Cerberus* still stationed at Patamaca; but it proved to be to no purpose, no person on board either of the vessels having been able to hear the report of the guns fired by the other. During this, however, I met with a small accident, by firing myself one of the blunderbusses, which I placed like a musket against my shoulder. I received such a stroke by its rebounding as threw me backward over a large hogshead of beef, and nearly dislocated my right arm. This, however, it seems was owing to my ignorance of the manner of using the blunderbuss, as I have since been informed that all such weapons ought to be fired under the hand, especially when heavy charged; then by swinging round the body suddenly, the force of the rebound is broken, and the effect scarcely sensible. I insert this only to show in what manner heavy loaded muscatoons ought always to be fired; especially since, without any aim, the execution from their wide mouth is almost equally fatal.

On the 26th, by a canoe that came down from Patamaca, I received intelligence that the *Cerberus* was in danger of being surprised by the enemy, who had been discovered hovering round about her; and the part of the river where she was moored being very narrow, I considered her situation as critical. I therefore immediately rowed the *Charon* up to the Pinneburgh Creek and, having manned the yawl as being the most expeditious, went myself, with six men, to their assistance, but was agreeably surprised at finding the whole to be a false alarm. In the evening we returned back to our station. In rowing down I was astonished at being hailed by a human voice, which begged me for God's sake to step on shore. This I did, with two of my men, and was accosted by a poor old negro woman, imploring me to afford her some assistance. It seems she was the property of a Jew, to whom belonged the spot of ground where I found her, and where the poor creature lived quite alone, in a hut not larger than a dog-kennel, surrounded by a wilderness, with only a few plantain-trees, yams, and cassava, for her support. She was no longer of use to work on the great estate, and was banished here only to support her master's right to the possession, since this spot had been ruined by the rebels. Having left with her a piece of salt beef, some barley, and a bottle of rum, I took my leave, when she offered me in return one of her cats. But this I could not accept, for by this token, I mean upon the information of the cats, my negro rowers firmly insisted that she must be a witch; which evinces that this superstition is not confined to Europe.

In this creek, the banks of which on both sides are covered with mangrove-trees, thorns, and briers, we found floating on the surface of the water a kind of large white nut, which seemed to have dropped of themselves by ripeness from the shell. They are sweet, crisp, and exceedingly good eating, but I neglected to inquire from what tree they had fallen. A kind of water shrub, called the *mocco-mocco*, is here also to be found in great quantities. It grows about six or eight feet high, thick at bottom, jointed and prickly all the way to the top, where it is very small, and divided into three or four large smooth oval leaves, which possess almost the quality of blistering by their violent adhesion to the skin.

As we approached the *Charon* in the evening, I found my sentinel fast asleep, which enraged me so much, that having quietly entered on board the barge, I fired my pistol close to his ear, just over his head, assuring him that I would the next time blow it through his brains: the whole crew flew to their arms, and the poor fellow nearly leaped into the water. But however it might be necessary to threaten in this manner, at a post where a surprise might be fatal, it would have been excessive cruelty to have executed it in such a situation, where the bite of the mosquitoes rendered it impossible to reckon upon sleep at stated times, and thus the interruption of it at one time made the approach of it unavoidable at another.

We now returned, on the 27th, to Cormoetibo Creek, where my negroes, having been ashore to cut wood for the furnace, brought on board a poor animal alive, with all its four feet chopped off with the bill-hook, and which lay still in the bottom of the canoe. Having freed it from its torment by a blow on the head, I was acquainted that this was the sloth, called *loyaree* or *heay* by the natives, on account of its plaintive voice. It is about the size of a small water-spaniel, with a round head something like that of a monkey, but its mouth is remarkably large; its hinder legs are much shorter than those before, to help it in climbing, being each armed with *three* very large and sharp claws, by which it holds its body on the boughs, but which, as being offensive weapons, my negroes had so cruelly chopped off; its eyes are languid, and its voice is squeaking, like that of a young cat. The greatest particularity of this creature, however, is that its motion is so very slow that it often takes two days to get up to the top of a moderate tree, from which it never descends while a leaf or a bud is remaining. It begins its devastation first at the top, to prevent its being starved in coming to the bottom, and then goes in quest of another, proceeding incredibly slow indeed while on the ground. Some say, that to avoid the pain of exercising its limbs, it forms itself into a ball and drops down from the branches: that may be true or not, but this I know to be a fact, that it cannot mend its pace.

Now came down from Patamaca, on the 28th, Lieutenant Stromer, the commander of the *Cerberus*, in a burning fever and scorched by the sun in an open canoe, drinking cold water from the river as his only relief. In this situation, a Jew soldier of the Society post La Rochelle, accompanied him, with the account that the rebels had, as had been first reported, actually passed the creek two days before, one mile above the last estate, marching from east to west. He at the same time delivered to me a negro woman, with a sucking infant, who had formerly been stolen by the rebels and had now found means to make her escape. From below I received also the news that Major Medlar had sent to town from the Jew Savannah two dried hands of the enemy, killed by the rangers; that an officer with ten men and some provisions were landed at Devil's Harwar, there to be under my command; and that one of my marines at that place was dead. The same dispatches brought an order for me to look out for a dry spot, and, if possible, to build a temporary storehouse.

I immediately detached my lieutenant, Mr Hamer, to take the command of the *Cerberus*, and having weighed anchor, rowed down till I arrived before the Casepoere Creek, where we passed such a night as no pen can describe. The sick groaned, the Jew prayed aloud, the soldiers swore, the negroes intreated, the women sang, the child squeaked, the fire smoked, the rains poured down, and the whole vessel stank to such a degree that I began to think myself but little better off than the unfortunate persons who were confined in the black hole at Calcutta. At six o'clock the next morning, however, the joyful sun broke through the clouds, and I dropped down with the *Charon* before Devil's Harwar.

On the 29th, I delivered my sick officer and five sick men, besides my other passengers, for whom I had done all that was in my power, but that was very little. Having stowed the newly-arrived provisions in a proper place, I once more returned to my dreadful station, where I came to an anchor on the first of August.

The following day, between the showers, we saw great numbers of monkeys, of which I shot one, and having had no fresh meat for a long time, I ordered it to be dressed, and ate it with a good appetite. We were at this time in a shocking situation, not only wanting refreshment; the men's clothes and hammocks were rotting from day to day, not only from their being almost constantly wet, but being also composed of the very worst materials sent from Holland.

On the third, I received the account that Lieutenant Stromer was dead at Devil's Harwar.

On the fourth, we dropped down before the place, to bury him directly, in the hope of doing it with decency, but we were disappointed; for having contrived to make a coffin of old boards, the corpse dropped through it before it reached the grave, and exhibited a shocking spectacle. We nevertheless found means to go through the rest of the interment with some decorum, having covered it over with a hammock by way of a pall; then fired three volleys with all the troops that had strength to carry arms. This being over, I regaled the officers with a glass of wine, and once more took a farewell of Devil's Harwar.

On the sixth, having first written to Colonel Fourgeoud to acquaint him that the rebels had passed above La Rochelle and that I had found a spot for a magazine at Barbacoeba, I informed him also of the death of my lieutenant, Mr Stromer, and recommended my sergeant, who had been an officer of hussars, for advancement.

To give the reader some idea of this spot called Devil's Harwar, I will here take the opportunity to describe it.

This place was formerly a plantation, but is now entirely occupied by the military, who keep here a post to defend the upper parts of the river Cottica. The soil is elevated and dry, which makes it the more remarkable that it should be so extremely unwholesome, yet such it certainly is: and here hundreds of soldiers have been buried.

The buildings on Devil's Harwar are all made of the *pina* or manicole-tree and consist of a dwelling-house for the commanding-officer, with four very good rooms; another for the subalterns; a good lodge for the private soldiers; and an hospital for the sick, which is large and roomy: but this is no more than is necessary, as it never is without inhabitants. There is also a powder and victualling magazine, proper kitchens and a bake-house, besides a well with fresh water. The Society troops feed a flock of sheep, pigs, and poultry at this place, for the use only of the hospital: here was also at this time a cow, which had been allotted for the rangers after Boucou was taken, but the feast had not been kept at this place. She had now a calf, and afforded milk for the officers to their tea, but for us poor fellows in the barges there was nothing at all of the kind.

The circumstance which renders Devil's Harwar so unhealthy, in my opinion, is the myriads of mosquitoes that prevent the people from rest, and the multitudes of *chigoes* or sand-fleas which abound in that station.

On the seventh, I arrived again at Cormoetibo Creek, where I resolved to make a landing on the south shore at all hazards—for my own soldiers to cook their beef and barley—concluding it as well to be shot by the enemy at once, as to be gradually consumed to death on board the *Charon*. It was, however, a difficult task to find the smallest spot for the purpose, the whole of that shore being so very marshy and overgrown with every kind of underwood that we could scarcely put our new project in execution; at last, my negroes having made a temporary kind of bridge, to step from the yawl upon a small speck of dry ground, and having formed a slight shed of manicole-leaves to keep off the rain, we found means to keep in a fire and were infinitely more comfortable than we were on board the *Charon*. Our danger in this situation, however, was certainly greater than in our former station, since an old rebel settlement was not very far away. Notwithstanding this village had been demolished, it was well known that the rebels still frequently visited the spot to pick up some of the yams and casadas (which the ground continued, in its uncultivated state, to produce) for a temporary subsistence. I was indeed almost absolutely convinced that the rebels, who had lately passed above La Rochelle in Patamaca, were at this moment encamped at the above spot, Pinneburgh, and ready to commit some depredations on the estates on the river Cottica or Pirica, if not to attack ourselves. On this account I always kept double sentinels round the landing-place, and gave orders that no men should be allowed to speak or make any kind of noise while on that spot, in order that we might hear the smallest rustling of a leaf, and so obviate our danger by vigilance and alacrity.

On the 8th my other officer Macdonald fell sick, but refused to be sent to Devil's Harwar, as he would not suffer me to be left quite by myself.

I have said that we had no surgeon, but carried with us a parcel of medicines, which consisted of emetics, cathartics and powders, of which I knew not the proper use. At their desire, however, I daily distributed them to the men, who, loading their stomachs with heavy salt provisions, and using no exercise, had sometimes occasion for art to assist nature. But these briny meals of pork and beef, Colonel Fourgeoud insisted were much more wholesome food in a tropical country than fresh provisions; for, by a most curious theory, he asserted that the latter corrupted in the stomach by the heat, whereas the others underwent a proper digestion. Unfortunately for us, there were but few on board either the *Cerberus* or the *Charon*, whose stomachs were in a state to digest such food. I had also some plaisters on board the barge, but these were soon expended by the running ulcers with which the whole crew was covered; and this was easily accounted for, since in this climate, where the air is impregnated with myriads of invisible animalcula, the smallest scratch immediately becomes a running sore. The best antidote and cure for such complaints in this country is lemon or lime acid, but this we had not. The next best mode of treatment is never to expose an open wound, or even the smallest scratch, to the air, but the instant they are received, to cover them with grey paper wetted with spirits, or any kind of moisture, so that it may stick to the skin. For my own part, no man could enjoy a better state of health than I continued to enjoy, wearing nothing but my long trousers, and checked shirt loose at the collar and turned up in the sleeves. Nay, even when the sun was not too hot, I stripped all together, and twice every day continued to plunge into the water: by these means I was always cool and clean. I also daily used a cheering glass of wine, having first hung it a few fathoms under water, which rendered it much more cool and pleasant.

This evening we heard the sound of a drum, which we could suppose to be no other than that of the rebels; nevertheless we determined to continue dressing our victuals ashore, still keeping on our guard, according to the advice of Mr Klynhams.

On the 9th Mr Macdonald was much worse; however, on seeing me receive a letter from Colonel Fourgeoud, he seemed to revive, as we all did, expecting now to be relieved from our horrid situation. But what was our mortification at reading that we were still to continue on this forlorn station! This letter was accompanied by a present of fish-hooks and tackle, to make up for the deficiency of other refreshments and, indeed, of salt provisions, which began daily to get both worse and less.

The receipt of such unwelcome intelligence made the whole crew declare they were sacrificed for no manner of purpose; while the negroes sighed, pronouncing the words, *Ah! poty backera!* Oh! poor Europeans! By the distribution however of a few tamarinds, oranges, lemons, and Madeira wine, which were by this opportunity sent me by my best friend at Paramaribo, I found means to impart, not only to my officers but also to my drooping soldiers, some relief. But this cheering sunshine could not last long: the day following we were as much distressed as ever, when I had once more recourse to the nimble inhabitants of the forest, and brought down two monkeys with my gun from the top of the mangroves, where they were sporting in flocks consisting of some hundreds.

On the 11th, I sent two men sick to the hospital, and the same evening we again heard the drums. On the following day, at noon, we were disturbed by a hurricane; the *Charon* broke loose from her anchors and was driven ashore, her upper works being terribly damaged by the stumps of trees that hung over the river, while the water from the clouds broke in upon us like a torrent, and I expected no less than a shipwreck.

On the 15th the other officer, Lieutenant Baron Owen, came down sick from the *Cerberus*, and at his request I ventured to send him down to Paramaribo. I now received another letter from Colonel Fourgeoud, with a little money for the men to purchase refreshments where nothing was to be met with: but not a word intimating that we were to be relieved.

On the 20th I received a report that the *Cerberus*, having only four private men left, had retired to the post at La Rochelle; and, on the 21st, I sent two of my men to her assistance, and ordered her back to her former station.

I now was myself at last attacked with a fever, and upon the whole felt myself in a truly distressed condition, deprived by sickness of my two only officers and my sergeant, my men upon the three stations (the two barges and Devil's Harwar together) melted down to fifteen from the number of forty-two, without a surgeon or refreshment, surrounded with a black forest, and exposed to the mercy of relentless enemies, who must be formidable indeed, should they be informed by any means of our defenceless situation. The remaining few were, with truth, declaring they were doomed to destruction, insomuch that they could with difficulty be prevented from mutiny and from proceeding down the river Cottica with the *Charon* against my orders.

For my own part, I was not altogether free from uneasiness. In fact, a few troops from all quarters ought to have marched against the enemy when they crossed the Patamaca Creek; that is, from La Rochelle, Devil's Harwar, and the river Pirica. Being assailed at once from three quarters, the rebels might have been, if not entirely routed, at least severely punished for their presumption, not to speak of the happy effect which such a check must have had in saving the lives and property of those victims who, after such incursions, are generally devoted to their rage.

On the 23rd I felt myself rather better, and between the fits of the fever shot a couple of large black monkeys to make some broth, to supply the want of fresh provisions. That monkeys, especially when young, are no bad food, may easily be accounted for, since they feed on nothing but fruits, nuts, eggs, young birds, etc. Indeed, in my opinion, all young quadrupeds are eatable: but when one compares those which are killed in the woods to those filthy and disgusting creatures that disgrace the streets, no wonder that they should disgust the least delicate stomach. As for the wild ones, I have eaten them boiled, roasted and stewed, and found their flesh white, juicy and good. That which I shot the second instant is what is called in Surinam *micoo*: it is nearly the size of a fox, and of a reddish grey colour, with a black head and very long tail. Those I killed on the tenth were indeed exceedingly beautiful, and much more delicate when dressed than the former: they are called the *keesee-keesee* by the inhabitants, are about the size of a rabbit, and most astonishingly nimble. The colour of their body is reddish, and the tail, which is long, is black at the extremity; but the fore-feet are orange colour. The head is very round, the face milk white, with a round black patch in the middle, in which are the mouth and the nostrils; and this disposition of the features give it the appearance of a mask: the eyes are black, and remarkably lively. These monkeys we saw daily pass along the sides of the river, skipping from tree to tree, but mostly about mid-day, and in very numerous bodies, regularly following each other like a little army, with their young ones on their backs, not unlike little knapsacks. Their manner of travelling is thus: the foremost walks to the extremity of a bough, from which it bounds to the extremity of one belonging to the next tree, often at a most astonishing distance, and with such wonderful activity and precision that it never once misses its aim: the others one by one, and even the females with their little ones on their backs, which stick fast to the mother, follow their leader, and perform the same leap with the greatest seeming facility and safety.

As I am speaking of the animals found in this part of the country, I must not omit the otters here, called *tavous*, which in the Cormoetibo Creek frequently attracted our attention by their disagreeable noise: as they are amphibious, they live mostly on fish. They are about three feet in length, grey-coloured, and all over spotted with white; their legs are short, they are web-footed and armed with five claws; the head is round, the nose beset with whiskers like a cat; the eyes are small and placed above the ears; the tail is very short. This animal moves awkwardly upon land, but in the rivers proceeds with great velocity.

Notwithstanding the favourable appearances of the preceding day, I was, on the 24th, exceedingly ill indeed, not being able to sit up in my hammock, under which the black boy Quaco now lay, crying for his master, and on the following day the poor lad himself fell sick; at the same time I was also obliged to send three men in a fever to Devil's Harwar. As misfortunes often crowd together, I received, at this fatal period, the melancholy account that the officer, Mr Owen, was also dead, having expired on his passage downwards at the estate Alica, where he was buried. My ensign, Mr Cottenburgh, who had since gone to Paramaribo, died next; and for myself no better was now to be expected. In the height of a burning fever I now lay, forsaken by all my officers and men, without a friend to comfort me, and without assistance of any kind, except what the poor remaining negro slaves could afford me by boiling a little water to make some tea. In this situation the reader may judge of the consolation which was afforded me the very evening when these accumulated misfortunes seemed to threaten our extinction, by the receipt of an order from the Colonel, to come down with both the barges to Devil's Harwar, where I was again to take post on shore and relieve Captain Orzinga of the Society service who, with his men was to proceed to La Rochelle in Patamaca, to strengthen the troops already there. Ill as I was, this had such a powerful effect on my spirits that I immediately ordered the *Cerberus* down to the mouth of the Cormoetibo Creek, where she joined me that evening.

On the 26th, we bid farewell to this destructive place and, having weighed anchor, rowed down as far as Barbacoeba, during which time a circumstance happened which will probably prove more entertaining than the repeated accounts of sickness and deaths.

As I was resting in my hammock, between the paroxysms of my fever, about half way between Cormoetibo and Barbacoeba, while the *Charon* was floating down, the sentinel called to me that he had seen and challenged something black and moving in the brushwood on the beach, which gave no answer but which, from its size, he concluded must be a man. I immediately dropped anchor and, having manned the canoe ill as I was, I stepped into it and rowed up to the place mentioned by the sentinel. Here we all stepped ashore to reconnoitre, as I suspected it to be no other than a rebel spy or a straggling party detached by the enemy. But one of my slaves, of the name of David, declared it was no negro but a large amphibious snake, which could not be far from the beach, and I might have an opportunity of shooting it if I pleased. To this, however, I had not the least inclination, from the uncommon size of the creature, from my weakness, and the difficulty of getting through the thicket, which seemed impenetrable to the water's edge. I therefore ordered all of them to return on board. The negro then asked me liberty to step forward and shoot it himself, assuring me it could not be at any great distance, and warranting me against all danger. This declaration inspired me with so much pride and emulation, that I determined to take his first advice and kill it myself, provided he would point it out to me and be responsible for the hazard by standing at my side—from which I swore that if he dared to move, I should level the piece at himself and blow out his own brains.

To this the negro cheerfully agreed and, having loaded my gun with a ball-cartridge, we proceeded, David cutting a path with a bill-hook, and a marine following with three more loaded firelocks to keep in readiness. We had not gone above twenty yards through mud and water, the negro looking every way with an uncommon degree of vivacity and attention, when starting behind me, he called out, 'Me see snakee!' and in effect there lay the animal, rolled up under the fallen leaves and rubbish of the trees, and so well covered that it was some time before I distinctly perceived the head of this monster, distant from me not above sixteen feet, moving its forked tongue, while its eyes, from their uncommon brightness, appeared to emit sparks of fire. I now, resting my piece upon a branch for the purpose of taking a surer aim, fired; but missing the head, the ball went through the body, when the animal struck round, and with such astonishing force as to cut away all the underwood around him with the facility of a scythe mowing grass, and by flouncing his tail, caused the mud and dirt to fly over our heads to a considerable distance. Of this proceeding however we were not torpid spectators, but took to our heels, and crowded into the canoe. The negro now intreated me to renew the charge, assuring me the snake would be quiet in a few minutes, and at any rate persisting in the assertion that he was neither able nor inclined to pursue us; an opinion he supported by walking before me till I should be ready to fire. And thus I again undertook to make the trial, especially as he said that his first starting backwards had only proceeded from a desire to make room for me. I now found the snake a little removed from his former station, but very quiet, with his head, as before, lying out among the fallen leaves, rotten bark, and old moss. I fired at it immediately, but with no better success than the other time: and now, being but slightly wounded, he sent up such a cloud of dust and dirt as I never saw but in a whirlwind, and made us once more suddenly retreat to our canoe, where now, being heartily tired of the exploit, I gave orders to row towards the barge. But David still intreating me to permit *him* to kill the animal, I was, by his persuasions, induced to make a third and last attempt, in company with him. Thus, having once more discovered the snake, we discharged both our pieces at once, and with this good effect, that he was now by one of us shot through the head. David, who was made completely happy by this successful conclusion, ran leaping with joy, and lost no time in bringing the boat-rope in order to drag him down to the canoe. But this again proved not a very easy undertaking, since the creature, notwithstanding its being mortally wounded, still continued to writhe and twist about in such a manner as rendered it dangerous for any person to approach him. The negro, however, having made a running noose on the rope, and after some fruitless attempts to make an approach, threw it over his head with much dexterity; and now, all taking hold of the rope, we dragged him to the beach, and tied him to the stern of the canoe to take him in tow. Being still alive, he kept swimming like an eel, and I, having no relish for such a ship-mate on board, whose length (notwithstanding to my astonishment all the negroes declared it to be but a young one come to about its half growth) I found upon measuring it to be twenty-two feet and some inches, and its thickness about that of my black boy Quaco, who might then be about twelve years old, and round whose waist I since measured the creature's skin.

Being arrived alongside of the *Charon*, the next consideration was how to dispose of this immense animal; it was at length determined to bring him on shore at Barbacoeba to have him skinned and take out the oil, etc. In order to effect this purpose, the negro David having climbed up a tree with the end of the rope, let it down over a strong forked bough, and the other negroes hoisted up the snake and suspended him from the tree. This done, David, with a sharp knife between his teeth, now left the tree and clung fast upon the monster which was still twisting, and began his operations by ripping it up, and stripping down the skin as he descended. Though I perceived that the animal was no longer able to do him any injury, I confess I could not without emotion see a man stark naked, black and bloody, clinging with arms and legs round the slimy and yet living monster. This labour, however, was not without its use, since he not only dexterously finished the operation, but provided me, besides the skin, with above four gallons of fine clarified fat, or rather oil, though there was wasted perhaps as much more. This I delivered to the surgeons at Devil's Harwar, for the use of the wounded men in the hospital, for which I received their hearty thanks, it being considered, particularly for bruises, a very excellent remedy. When I signified my surprise to see the snake still living, after he was deprived of his intestines and skin, Caramaca, the old negro, whether from experience or tradition, assured me he would not die till after sun-set. The negroes now cut him in slices, in order to dress and feast upon him (they all declaring that he was exceedingly good and wholesome), but to their great mortification I refused to give my concurrence, and we rowed down with the skin to Devil's Harwar.

Of this species several skins are preserved in the British and Mr Parkinson's Museums. This wonderful creature, which in the colony of Surinam is called *Aboma*, is called by Mr Westley *Lyboija*, and *Boa* in the British Encyclopedia. Its length, when full grown, is said to be sometimes forty feet, and more than four feet in circumference; its colour is a greenish black on the back, a fine brownish yellow on the sides, and a dirty white under the belly: the back and sides being spotted with irregular black rings, with a pure white in the middle. Its head is broad and flat, small in proportion to the body, with a large mouth, and a double row of teeth: it has two bright prominent eyes, is covered all over with scales—some about the size of a shilling—and under the body, near the tail, armed with two strong claws like cock-spurs, to help it in seizing its prey. It is an amphibious animal, that is, it delights in low and marshy places, where it lies coiled up like a rope, and concealed under moss, rotten timber, and dried leaves, to seize its prey by surprise, which from its immense bulk it is not active enough to pursue. When hungry, it will devour any animal that comes within its reach, and is indifferent whether it is a sloth, a wild boar, a stag, or even a tiger. Having twisted itself round by the help of its claws, so that the creature cannot escape, it breaks, by its irresistible force, every bone in the animal's body. It then covers it over with a kind of slime or slaver from its mouth, to make it slide, and at last gradually sucks it in, till it disappears. After this, the *aboma* cannot shift its situation, on account of the great knob or knot which the swallowed prey occasions in that part of the body where it rests till it is digested, for till then it would hinder the snake from sliding along the ground. During that time the *aboma* wants no other subsistence. I have been told of negroes being devoured by this animal, and am disposed to credit the account; for should they chance to come within its reach when hungry, it would as certainly seize them as any other animal. I do not apprehend that its flesh, which is very white and looks like that of fish, is in any respect pernicious to the stomach. I should have had no objection to the negroes eating it till it was consumed, had I not observed a kind of dissatisfaction among the remaining marines, who would not have been pleased with my giving the negroes the use of the kettle to boil it. The bite of this snake is said not to be venomous; nor do I believe it bites at all from any other impulse than hunger.

I shall only add, that having nailed its skin on the bottom of the canoe, and dried it in the sun, sprinkling it over with wood-ashes to prevent it from corruption, I sent it to a friend at Paramaribo, whence it was since sent to Holland as a curiosity.

7

On the 27th of August I relieved Captain Orzinga with his men, and took the command of Devil's Harwar, having been on board the *Charon* exactly fifty-six days, in the most wretched condition that can be described. But I hoped now to get the better of my complaint by the help of a few refreshments, such as milk, which could not be obtained in our former situation. The Society troops (above one hundred in number) being to set off next day with my empty barges to La Rochelle, in Patamaca, I reviewed my marines, when I found I had left out of five officers but two, who were both sick, the three others being dead. I had also only one sergeant, two corporals, and fifteen privates, out of fifty-four healthy men who embarked with me on the second day of last July. This army was not more than sufficient to defend the hospital (which was crowded with sick) the ammunition and victualling magazine etc., on a spot where lately had been kept three hundred soldiers, particularly while the enemy were certainly lurking not far off. In consideration of this, the Society Captain reinforced me with twenty of his men. The next evening he entertained me and my two subalterns with a supper of *fresh meat*, both roast and boiled, to our great comfort and surprise; but which, to my unspeakable mortification, proved to be the individual poor cow with her calf, on whom we had built all our hopes for a little relief. It appeared that one of his sentinels, as concerted between them, had shot it by a wilful mistake. Thus did Captain Orzinga, for the sake of a momentary gratification, deprive us all of that lasting comfort on which we had so much depended, and of which we had so much need, being altogether emaciated for want of wholesome and nutritive food.

On the morning of the 28th the Society troops rowed to Patamaca, when, examining the twenty soldiers they had left me, they proved to be the refuse of the whole, part with agues, wounds, ruptures and rotten limbs, and most of them next day were obliged to enter the hospital.

On the 29th, having bastinadoed my late pilot for stealing from the soldiers, I dispatched the information to Colonel Fourgeoud that I had taken post and, acquainting him with my weak situation, requested a proper reinforcement. In the evening two of my men died.

All things now being regulated and settled, I thanked Heaven in

The skinning of the aboma snake shot by Captain Stedman

the expectation of getting some rest, being still extremely weak; and with these cheering hopes retired at ten o'clock at night to my hammock. But this tranquillity was again of short duration, for having scarcely closed my eyes I was awaked by my sergeant and the following letter put into my hand, sent by an express from the captain of the militia in Cottica.

SIR,
This is to acquaint you, that the rebels have burnt three estates by your side, Suyingheyd, Peru, and L'Esperance, the ruins of which are still smoking; and that they have cut the throats of all the white inhabitants that fell in their way. As on their retreat they must pass close by where you are posted, be on your guard. I am in haste.

Your's etc.
(Signed) STOELEMAN

Conscious of my defenceless situation, I immediately started up, and the express who brought the letter having spread the news the moment of his landing, there was no necessity for beating to arms, since not only the few soldiers who were well, but the whole hospital burst out and several of them, in spite of my opposition, crawling on their hands and feet to their arms, dropped dead upon the spot. May I never behold such another scene of misery and distress! Lame, blind, sick, and wounded, in the hope of preserving a wretched existence, rushed upon certain death!

For my own part, I was in a very weakly condition indeed; however, we continued to lie all night on our arms, during which I pressed the messenger to stay, in order to add one to our miserable number, being determined to sell our lives as dearly as possible. But no enemy appearing in the morning, we buried the dead in their hammocks, not having a board to make a coffin on the whole post. In this situation I lost all patience, and had the audacity to write to my commander, that (beside what had happened) my last men stood upon the brink of the grave, from hardships and for want of being properly supported, the very waiters of the hospital having deserted on the moment of my arrival here, and gone to Paramaribo. Our whole number, indeed, was now melted down to twelve men who were to protect twelve buildings, and that with no more than two very small chests of ammunition, and no retreat for the sick, as the barges were gone to Patamaca, and the last canoe dispatched with my letter to Colonel Fourgeoud, for I had set adrift that belonging to the express, who was a bookkeeper of a neighbouring plantation, in order to prevent him or any other from making their escape. In this situation, I was now obliged to convert the slaves into soldiers: these I armed with a hatchet, not daring to trust them with a firelock. For this whole night we again watched under arms, and in the morning found two more of our little party dead on the ground.

I now began really to think we were all devoted to destruction, while the men, regardless of all order (self-preservation excepted) threw out the most bitter invectives against their persecutor, Fourgeoud, which I could not prevent; nor can I help remarking the generalship of the rebel negroes, who had kept lying quiet till the removal of the Society troops from Devil's Harwar, and seized the very first day of their departure, convinced of its being guarded only by my sick and emaciated soldiers, in order to commit their depredations on the Cottica estates. They well knew that my force was not sufficient to pursue them, nay, hardly to stand in my own defence: all this, however, was but according to my expectation. Had my strength been sufficient, they could never have escaped at least from being cut off in their retreat, especially if the troops in Rio Perica had acted conjointly with those in Cottica, by patrolling the path between the two rivers, across which the rebels were twice unavoidably obliged to pass.

On the 1st of September we waited once more till morning, and then buried another of my poor men. I cannot conceive how anyone was able to survive such a series of toil, in such a debilitated state and in a tropical climate; yet some did, though few. At length, being persuaded that the rebels must have passed the Cordon, without having thought proper to pay us a visit on their retreat, I determined to let the remaining few watch no longer, but permit them to die a natural death. At last, in the evening, when all was too late, there came down by water from the post La Rochelle to our assistance, one officer and ten men—I having had but nine left to do the duty at the time of their arrival.

On the 2nd another man died and I once more reviewed my forces, which now amounted exactly to seven marines, the few scarecrows of the Society excepted; however, the chance of being massacred by the rebels was at this time over, thanks alone to their pusillanimity, or rather their hurry!

I now received a letter from Colonel Fourgeoud, condoling with me on the loss of so many good officers, acquainting me that I was to be reinforced, and that on my recommendation my sergeant, Mr Cubanns, was appointed an ensign; which gave me pleasure, and took place at a very suitable time, since this day my poor Ensign Macdonald was sent down very sick to Paramaribo. I answered to all this, that I was obliged to him, adding that while I remained without reinforcement I could not be accountable for what consequences might happen, in a place where I was left to defend a whole river with none but sick people; and even these without sufficient ammunition, and hourly expiring for want of proper medicines or a surgeon to attend them, there being none here but one or two surgeon's mates belonging to the troops of the Society, who could do little more than occasionally draw blood, and cut off a beard or a corn.

On the 4th we buried another of my marines, and on the following day another died; and I had not one now remaining who was not ill, or who was not rendered unserviceable, by his feet being swelled with the insects called *chigoes*: these poor men were mostly Germans, who had been accustomed to a healthy climate in their own country. I began now to be reconciled to putting my last man under ground, and almost wishing to leap into the grave after him myself, when a barge arrived from Paramaribo with the proper reinforcement, ammunition, provisions, medicines, a surgeon, and an order from my chief to trace out the track of the rebels immediately, on the former path of communication called the Cordon between Cottica and Perica, and to write him the result of my discoveries; he intimated also that he intended to keep his magazines at Devil's Harwar, and that I was not to make use of the spot I had found out for that purpose at Barbacoeba Creek.

On the 6th I prepared to march myself, having recovered a little strength, on the grand project of discovery, and then placed the ammunition in the magazine.

As the manner of marching in this country is so very different from that in Europe, I shall, before we set out, endeavour briefly to describe the nature of these expeditions.

In the first place, in Surinam no such thing is practicable as three or even two ranks; thus there is no marching by divisions or platoons. The whole party being dressed in one rank, face to the right, and every man follows his leader, the negro slaves interspersed between the men, in order to guard their persons as well as what they carry; and this manner of marching is called Indian file. With a detachment of sixty men, consisting of one captain, two subalterns, two sergeants, four corporals, one surgeon, and fifty privates, twenty negro slaves at least ought to be employed, for the use of whom their masters are paid at the rate of two shillings sterling a day by the colony; and this is a much greater expense than waggons and horses would be, which in this country cannot be employed for military service.

The manner of interspersing them among the troops is as follows. The foremost are generally two negroes, with bill-hooks to cut a way so as to make a practicable path, with one corporal and two men to reconnoitre the front, and, in case of necessity, to give the alarm; and then one subaltern, six privates, and a corporal, form the van. Then follows, at some distance, the corps in two divisions; in the first, one captain, one corporal, twelve privates, one surgeon, and two negroes to carry the powder; in the second, is one sergeant and twelve privates; and then again follows, at some distance, the rear guard, consisting of one subaltern, one sergeant, one corporal, and eighteen privates, with sixteen negroes to carry the medicines, beef, bread, spades, axes, rum, etc.; the sick also are carried. The three last of all being one corporal and two men at a distance, to give the alarm in case of an attack, as the others had orders to do in the front.

Everything being ready, according to the above rules, for my small party, which consisted of myself, an officer of the Society, Mr Hertsbergh, one surgeon's mate, one guide, two sergeants, two corporals, forty privates, and only eight negro slaves to cut open the passage and carry the baggage, we faced to the right at six o'clock in the morning, and sallied forth into the woods, keeping our course directly for the Perica river. Having marched till about eleven o'clock on the Cordon, I discovered, as I had expected, the track of the rebels by the marks of their footsteps in the mud, by the broken bottles, plantain-shells, etc., and found that by appearance it bore towards Pinneburgh, already mentioned.

I had now indeed found the nest, but the birds were flown. We continued our march till eight o'clock, when we arrived at the Society post Scribo, in Perica, in a most shocking condition, having waded through water and mire above our hips, climbed over heaps of fallen trees, and crept underneath on our bellies. This, however, was not the worst, for our flesh was terribly mangled and torn by the thorns, and stung by the Patat lice, ants, and *wassy-wassy*, or wild bees. This last is an insect not larger than an English blue-bottle fly, and is of a black colour, quite different from our bees; they are never kept in hives, but swarm wild in the forest, where they build in hollow trees or between the branches. This little flying army is extremely formidable, pitching always by instinct on the eyes, lips, and hair, whence they cannot be dislodged; their stings generally cause a fever, and swell the parts so very much that they occasion blindness for several hours; their honey is of a dark-brown colour, and so is their wax, but gummy, being both of little value.

The worst of our sufferings, however, was the fatigue of marching in a burning sun, and the last two hours in total darkness, holding each other by the hand, and having left ten men behind, some with agues, some stung blind, and some with their feet full of chigoes. Being in the most hospitable manner received at Scribo by the commanding officer, I went to my hammock very ill of a fever.

On the following morning I felt myself better for my night's rest; but neither myself nor my men were able to march back, wherefore the other captain sent a small party of his soldiers to pick up the poor marines I had lost the day before, and of whom they brought with them seven, carried in hammocks tied to poles, each by two negroes, the other three having scrambled back to Devil's Harwar.

During our stay here I wrote a letter to Colonel Fourgeoud, couched in such terms as few people in their full senses would do to their commanders, *viz.* that I had found the path; that if I had had support in time I might have cut off the enemy's retreat, instead of finding their footsteps only; but that now all was too late, and the party all knocked up to no purpose. This letter, I have been since told, incensed him, as it is easy to suppose, in the highest degree. Being sufficiently refreshed to renew my march, we left Scribo on the 9th, at four o'clock in the morning, and at four o'clock arrived, after indescribable sufferings, at Devil's Harwar, covered over with mud and blood, and our legs and thighs cut and torn by the thorns and branches. Most of the men were without shoes and stockings of necessity, while I, who had gone this march in the same condition from choice, had absolutely suffered the least of the whole party, by having inured myself gradually to walk barefooted on the barges.

At Devil's Harwar, I now found Lieutenant Colonel Westerloo and a quarter-master arrived to take the command, his troops not being expected till the next day. I was by this circumstance, however, made exceedingly happy, hoping at last to meet with some relief; and having ceded him my written orders, the magazine, hospital, etc. I stripped and plunged into the river to wash myself and take a swim, by which (being before much over-heated) I found myself greatly refreshed, as well as by receiving a quantity of fine fruit, Jamaica rum, wine, and sugar, from Joanna. But how did my blood chill, when the quarter-master told me, as a secret, that my sergeant, one Fowler, having first got drunk with my wine, offered violence to this poor woman, and that he was to be at Devil's Harwar next day, when I should see the marks of her just resentment on his face!

The reader will, I trust, excuse my violence, when I tell him that I vowed immediate destruction to the villain and having ordered a negro to cut twelve bamboo canes, I retired like a person deprived of his senses, determined to punish him according to his supposed crime.

On the 10th there arrived two subalterns, with a second barge full of men, ammunition, medicine, and provisions, which having marched into quarters and stowed, I sent for the hapless Fowler, whose face being in three places wounded, I locked him up in a room, and, without asking one question, broke six of the bamboos over his head, till he escaped all bloody out at the window, and my resentment gradually abated. He certainly had suffered much, but nothing equal to what were my sensations at being still further informed that

Colonel Fourgeoud had seized all my effects and had sealed and locked them up in an empty storeroom in expectation of my decease, which, according to all appearances, might be looked for. My house was given to another, by which means I could not procure so much as a clean shirt to relieve me from my disgraceful tatters. Nevertheless, by the hope of going down myself, my spirits were supported. The other news, of more importance, was that the hero in person, with most of the troops, had at last left Paramaribo; that he had quartered them partly at Devil's Harwar, in Rio Cottica, the estate Bellaiz, in Rio Perica, and at the estates Charenbeck and Cravassibo in Rio Comewina, whence, conjunctly with the troops of the Society and the Rangers, he intended to move in quest of the rebels; that he had also ordered all the barges to be relieved at last, and their remaining troops to reinforce the above-mentioned posts, which I must remark was a very wise and well-planned regulation.

From Patamaca we were informed, that the rebels, on their repassing the river above La Rochelle, had again destroyed a small estate, and murdered its proprietor, a Mr Nyboor.

It was either about this time, or very shortly after, that an overseer escaped by the assistance of a negro boy, who, desiring him to leap into a canoe, and lie down flat upon his belly, leaped himself into the water, where, by swimming with one hand, and guiding the canoe with the other, he ferried his master safe over the creek Patamaca, through a shower of musket bullets, the rebels firing upon them all the while, but without execution. However, for this material piece of service, he was recompensed the week after with three hundred lashes by the same master, only for having forgotten to open one of the sluices or flood-gates. On this act of inhumanity I shall make no comment, but proceed to my own miserable situation. Having remonstrated with Lieutenant Colonel Westerloo on the state of my health, which disabled me from joining the corps on their march, I requested that I might be removed to Paramaribo for the chance of recovery; but this he peremptorily refused to allow me, by Colonel Fourgeoud's express command. The refusal of so reasonable a request made me almost distracted, and agitated my spirits so much, that on the morning of the 12th, determined to exchange my wretched existence one way or other, I insisted on being immediately removed, or wished for *death*, which the surgeons declared must be the consequence soon, if I was not permitted to go down. In the meanwhile I vowed that I should attribute my decease to their unprecedented barbarity. A consultation was now held on the subject, and at last, not without great difficulties, a boat was ordered to row me down to Paramaribo, but no white servant was permitted to attend me. Thus leaving the Lieutenant Colonel employed in fortifying Devil's Harwar with pallisadoes, where now also was a numerous garrison, I at noon walked to the water-side, supported by a negro, on whose shoulder I rested, till I at length stepped into the boat, followed by my black boy Quaco, and finally left the diabolical spot where I had buried so many brave fellows.

On the 14th, having rowed day and night, we arrived at the town at two o'clock in the morning, extremely ill indeed. Having no residence of my own, I was hospitably received at the house of a Mr De La Marre, a merchant. This gentleman not only received me, but immediately sent a servant for poor Joanna, who was at her mother's, and another for a physician to attend me, as my weak and hopeless condition now required every assistance that the town of Paramaribo could afford.

8

ON September 15th, I found myself in an elegant and well-furnished apartment, encouraged by the hopes given by the physician, caressed by my friends, and supported by the care and attention of my incomparable Mulatto.

A Captain Brant having at this time the command in Colonel Fourgeoud's absence, he sent, the morning after my arrival, my trunks and baggage which had been sealed up; but on looking into them, I found I had enemies at home as well as abroad, since most of my shirts, books, etc. were gnawed to dust by the blatta or cockroach, called *cakreluce* in Surinam: nay, even my shoes were destroyed, of which I had brought with me twelve pairs new from Europe, as they were extremely dear and bad in this country.

This insect, which is of the beetle kind, is here one inch and sometimes two inches long, oval, flat, and of a dark reddish colour. By getting through the locks of chests or boxes, it not only deposits its eggs there, but commits its ravages on linen, cloth, silk, or anything that comes in its way; by getting also into the victuals and drink of every kind, it renders them extremely loathsome, for it leaves the most nauseous smell, worse indeed than that of a bug. I think the only way to keep the boxes free from them is to place them on four empty wine bottles kept free from dust, which, by their smoothness, prevent the insects ascending to get through the keyholes, or even the smallest openings in the bottoms; but this precaution had been neglected by my good friend Colonel Fourgeoud. I found, however, linen sufficient for present use, and by the industry of Joanna I was soon provided with a new stock. None can conceive the comfort I felt in being properly dressed and shifted; my mental faculties were recruiting apace, and I felt with gratitude the blessing of a strong constitution; but poor Macdonald was still ill at Mr Kennedy's, who had humanely afforded him an asylum on his return from Devil's Harwar.

Having now time, I enquired concerning Fowler's conduct. To my infinite surprise, I was informed that he had indeed got drunk, as was reported to me, by which he had fallen among the bottles and cut his face, but that he never had attempted the smallest rudeness: so much indeed was his conduct the reverse of what had been reported, that his inebriety had proceeded from his resentment at seeing both me and Joanna ill treated, and my property transported away against his inclination. I was now extremely chagrined at my past conduct, and was gently reproved by the *cause* of it, to whom I promised to be Fowler's friend for ever after—and I kept my word.

My fever was now much abated, but I was infested with another disorder peculiar to this climate, the ring-worm. On the 26th I had a relapse, and was twice bled in one day. I was also this morning visited by poor Mr Henaman, a young volunteer I have not before mentioned, who looked like a ghost, and was left sick at Paramaribo to manage for himself.

On the 2nd of October I was a little better, and was exalted from living like a savage, to the temporary command of a few troops left at Paramaribo, Captain Brant being ordered to join Fourgeoud in Rio Comewina. The colours, regiment's cash, etc. were transmitted to my own lodging, and a sentinel placed before my door.

The first exercise I made of my power was to discharge the sour wine which had been bought for the sick officers as well as the men, whom I supplied from the money now in my possession with good wholesome claret; but I was sorry not to be able also to exchange the salt beef, pork, and pease, that were left at the hospital, for fresh provisions. This step was however particularly forbidden by the commander; while the butter, cheese, and tobacco were taken away—for which they got one quart of oil among ten—and their bread reduced to two pounds each man for a whole week. As to the officers, they were left to shift for themselves or submit to the same allowance, notwithstanding they kept on paying their quota to a regimental mess which now no longer existed.

On the 3rd, I took the air for the first time on horseback, in company with Mr Henaman, on a species of gravel that leads to the Wanica Path, which I have already mentioned as communicating with the river Seramica, and as the only passable road in the colony. This evening arrived sick, from the headquarters at the estate Cravassibo in Comewina, Colonel Texier, the commanding officer of the Society troops. This gentleman had intended to have marched conjunctly with Colonel Fourgeoud through the woods in quest of the rebels; but his constitution, already weak, not being able to support the regimen of the commander-in-chief, and to live only on salt provisions, had begun to flag from the beginning, till he was sent home to Paramaribo in this drooping condition.

On the sixth of October the fever had left me, and the ring-worms began to abate; but the misery and hardships which I had so lately undergone still had an effect upon my constitution, and enormous boils broke out on my left thigh, which entirely prevented me from walking. My physician, however, ordering me daily to take the air, I had an opportunity this day of waiting on His Excellency the Governor of the colony, by the help of my friend Kennedy's chaise; and as I returned homeward, I stopped the carriage at the water-side to behold a group of human beings, who had strongly attracted my attention. They were a drove of newly-imported negroes, men and women, with a few children, who were just landed from on board a Guinea ship that lay at anchor in the roads, to be sold for slaves. The whole party was such a set of scarcely animated automatons, such a resurrection of skin and bones as forcibly reminded me of the last trumpet. These objects appeared that moment to be risen from the grave, or escaped from Surgeon's Hall; and I confess I can give no better description of them, than by comparing them to walking skeletons covered over with a piece of tanned leather.

Before these wretches, in all about sixty in number, walked a sailor, and another followed behind with a bamboo-rattan; the one serving as a shepherd to lead them along, and the other as his dog to worry them occasionally, should anyone lag behind or wander away from the flock. At the same time, however, equity demands the acknowledgment that instead of all those horrid and dejected countenances which are described in pamphlets and newspapers, I perceived not one single downcast look among them all; and I must add that the punishment of the bamboo was inflicted with the utmost moderation by the sailor who brought up the rear.

From what I have learned by enquiry from persons well informed on the subject, it clearly appears that numbers of the negroes offered for sale have been taken in battles and made prisoners of war, while many others have been scandalously kidnapped, and some others transported for offences.

These groups of people are marched from every inland part to the factories erected by different nations upon the coast, where they are sold, or more properly speaking, bartered, like the other productions of their country, such as gold and elephants' teeth, to the Europeans, for bars of iron, fire-arms, carpenters' tools, chests, linens, hats, knives, glasses, tobacco, spirits, etc. Next they are embarked for exportation, during which time they feel all the pangs that mental or corporeal misery can inflict. Being torn from their country and dearest connections, stowed hundreds together in a dark stinking hold—the sexes being separated—the men are kept in chains to prevent an insurrection. In this manner are they floated over turbulent seas, not certain what is to be their destiny, and generally fed during the passage with horse-beans and oil for their whole subsistence. But these sufferings are often so far alleviated with better food by the more humane, that none or few of the cargo die during the passage, and the whole crew arrive healthy in the West Indies. I even remember one instance, where the captain, mate, and most of the sailors, having expired at sea, so that the remaining few could not work the ship without the negroes' assistance, yet these last having been well treated, helped at last to run the vessel on shore, by which means they not only saved many lives, but tamely and even cheerfully allowed themselves to be fetched and sold to any person who would please to buy them.

No sooner is a Guinea-ship arrived, than all the slaves are led upon deck, where they are refreshed with pure air, plantains, bananas, oranges, etc., properly cleaned and washed, and their hair shaved in different figures of stars or half-moons—which they generally do the one to the other (having no razors) by the help of a broken bottle and without soap. After this operation, one part of them is sent ashore for sale, decorated with pieces of cotton to serve as fig-leaves, while the others spend the day in dancing, hallooing, and clapping hands on board the vessel.

The next circumstance that takes place before the bargain is struck, is to cause the negroes for sale, one after another, to mount on a hogshead or a table, where they are visited by a surgeon, who obliges them to make all the different gestures, with arms and legs, of a Merry-Andrew upon the stage, to prove their soundness or unsoundness; after which they are adopted by the buyer, or rejected, as he finds them fit for his purpose, or otherwise. If he keeps them, the money is paid down, and the new-bought negroes are immediately branded on the breast or the thick part of the shoulder by a stamp made of silver with the initial letters of the new master's name. These hot letters, which are about the size of a sixpence, do not occasion that pain which might be imagined, and the blisters being rubbed directly with a little fresh butter, are perfectly well in the space of two or three days. No sooner is this ceremony over, and a new name given to the newly-bought slave, than he or she is delivered to an old one of the same sex, and sent to the estate, where each is properly kept clean by his guardian, instructed and well fed without working, for the space of six weeks. During this period, from living skeletons, they become plump and fat, with a beautiful clean skin, till it is disfigured by the inhuman flogging of some rascally proprietor, or rather his overseer.

Here I must leave them for some time, and continue my narrative. On the 10th, the surgeon having lanced my thigh, I scrambled out once more, to witness the selling of slaves to the best bidder. After what has been related, the reader may form some judgment of my surprise and confusion, when I found among them my inestimable Joanna—the sugar-estate Fauconberg, with its whole stock, being this day sold by an execution for the benefit of the creditors of its late possessor, Mr D. B., who had fled.

I now felt all the horrors of the damn'd. I bewailed again and again my unlucky fortune, that did not enable me to become her proprietor myself, and in my mind I continually painted her ensuing dreadful situation. I fancied I saw her tortured, insulted, and bowing under the weight of her chains, calling aloud, but in vain, for my assistance. I was miserable, and indeed nearly deprived of all my faculties, till restored by the assurances of my friend, Mr Lolkens, who providentially was appointed to continue administrator of the estate during the absence of its new possessors, Messrs Passelege and Son, at Amsterdam, who bought it and its dependants for only four thousand pounds.

No sooner was he confirmed in his appointment, than this disinterested and steady friend brought Joanna to my presence, and pledged himself that in every service which he could render to myself or her, and which he had now more in his power than ever, no efforts on his side should be wanting.

Being informed that Colonel Fourgeoud had left Cravassibo estate, and entered the woods just above the plantation Clarenbeck, on his way to the Wana Creek, to try if he could fall in with the rebels, I requested by a letter that I might join him there as soon as I should be recovered, and having shipped off for the last-mentioned estate medicines and such surgeons of ours as had been left at Paramaribo, I employed Mr Greber, the surgeon of the Society, on my own authority and at the regiment's expense, to attend the sick officers and soldiers, who were left in town, destitute of cash, and now without assistance. At the same time I also ordered to be purchased two more ankers of the best claret for their support. Thus was I determined properly to avail myself of my command, which at best could but last a few days longer.

This evening my friend De La Mara took his departure, with his twenty-five free mulattoes, for the river Surinam, he being a captain of the militia, and they being infinitely preferable to the European scarecrows.

I was so far recovered as to be able to ride out every morning, when the following ludicrous adventure happened to me on the road that leads to Wanica. In this place a Mr Van de Velde, boasting how fast his horse could gallop, proposed to me to run a race; to which I agreed, allowing him the start at twenty paces distance. The start indeed he had, but did not long retain his advantage, for my English horse passing him with the rapidity of a cannon-shot, his galloway sprung, rider and all, through a hedge of thick limes, and left poor Mr Van de Velde, not like Doctor Slop in the dirt, but like Absalom hanging among the branches.

On the 18th Ensign Mathew arrived sick from Devil's Harwar, one of the officers by whom I had been relieved; and the same day he was followed by his commander and friend, Colonel Westerloo, supported by two soldiers. I was at dinner with a Mr Day when I saw him pass by a miserable spectacle, and choosing to forget what had passed at Devil's Harwar, and in reality having a regard for this gentleman, I started up immediately and got him a coach in which I accompanied him to his lodgings. Having placed a sentinel before his chamber-door to keep out the rabble, I sent for a Doctor Van Dam, as well as a Doctor Rissam, an American, to attend him, forbidding all other communication, that of an old negro woman, his manservant and a black boy excepted, and by these means I apparently preserved his life.

On the 20th, Lieutenant Count de Randwyk came down also indisposed with Ensign Coene, and at last my poor old shipmate Lieutenant Hamer, who had been kept at Devil's Harwar near four months till, overcome by disease, he obtained leave to be transported to Paramaribo.

Being now perfectly recovered, I resolved to join Colonel Fourgeoud at the Wana Creek, without waiting his order, and to accompany him on his excursions through the forest: in consequence of which, having first cropped my hair as being more convenient in the woods as well as more cleanly, and provided myself with the necessary bush-equippage, I waited on the governor to ask his commands. He entertained me in a most polite manner, and told me that what I was now going to suffer would surpass what I had already undergone. I nevertheless persisted in wishing to go without waiting an order from the chief, and accordingly applied to the magistrates for a boat and the necessary negroes to transport me. This being promised for the succeeding day, I transferred the colours and regiment's cash, with the command of the remaining sick troops, to Lieutenant Meyer, the only healthy officer then at Paramaribo.

Indeed the colours, the cash, and the sick soldiers were nearly of equal use in Surinam, the first never having been displayed except at our landing, the second invisible to all except to Colonel Fourgeoud, and the third dying away one after another.

9

On the 25th of October, being ready to proceed upon my second campaign, I repaired to the water-side at six o'clock in the evening. Instead of a tent-boat, I found a greasy yawl, with a few drunken Dutch sailors, to row me to an estate in the river Comewina, whence they were going to bring their captain back to Paramaribo, and from which place I might, if I pleased, beg the rest of my passage upwards, or manage for myself in the best manner I was able. I had already one foot in the boat when, reflecting that I was going voluntarily on a hazardous expedition, without orders, and only from a desire to serve an ungrateful people, I repented and stepped back upon the shore where, positively declaring I would not move in their defence till I should be decently transported, should the whole colony be on fire, I was seconded by all the English and Americans in the town, and a general tumult took place. The Dutch exclaimed against the expense of a tent-boat which would cost them thirty shillings, when they could have the other for nothing; while the others declared they were a set of mean and parsimonious wretches, who deserved not the smallest protection from Colonel Fourgeoud's troops. A mob collected and a riot ensued at the water-side, before Mr Hardegen's tavern, while hats, wigs, bottles, and glasses, flew out at his windows. The magistrates were next sent for, but to no purpose, and the fighting continued in the street till ten o'clock at night, when I with my friends fairly kept the field, having knocked down several sailors, planters, Jews, and overseers, and lost one of my pistols, which I threw after the rabble in a passion. Nor would it have ended here, had not my friend Mr Kennedy, who was member of the Court of Policy, and two or three more gentlemen whom he brought with him, found means to appease the disputants, by declaring I had been very ill treated and should have a proper boat the next day.

Having now slept and refreshed myself a few hours, I was waited on by four American captains—Captain Timmons of the *Harmony*, Captain Lewis of the *Peggy*, Captain Bogard of the *Olive Branch*, and Captain Minet of the *America*—who insisted on my refusing any vessel whatever from the colony this time, and offering to send me up in one of their own boats, manned by their own sailors only, to which each would equally contribute. I can aver that, notwithstanding the threatening rupture between Great Britain and her Colonies, which seemed then upon the eve of breaking out into open violence, nothing could surpass the warm and cordial friendship which these gentlemen possessed, not only for me, but for every individual that bore a British name or had any connection with that island; they professed that they still retained the greatest regard for everything in Britain but its administration. I accepted their very polite proposal, and, having received a letter from Mr Kennedy, to be delivered to one of the militia captains (a Mr N. Reeder) in the river Comewina, with orders to send me farther up in a proper tent-boat, and arranged matters in such a manner at home that neither Colonel Fourgeoud nor the cockroaches could injure me, I shook hands with my mulatta, and at six in the evening repaired once more to the water-side, escorted by my English and American friends. There, having drank a bowl of punch, we separated. I then departed for my station, they having hoisted the colours on board all their vessels in the road, and at the boat's going off saluted me with three cheers, to my great satisfaction and the mortification of the gaping multitude by which we were surrounded. We soon rowed beyond the view of Paramaribo.

Being arrived at the fortress of New Amsterdam, we were obliged to stop for the return of the tide to row up the river Comewina. In this interval, I was genteelly entertained with a supper by the Society officers quartered there, but at twelve o'clock we got aboard and, having rowed all night, I breakfasted with Captain Macneyl, who was one of General Spork's captains in 1751. After this we once more set out, and arrived at the plantation Charlottenburgh, where I delivered Mr Kennedy's letter to Mr Reeder, who promised next morning to assist me. So much incensed was I at the usage I had met with at Paramaribo, and so well pleased with the English sailors, that I ordered the tars a dinner of twelve roasted ducks, and besides a guinea, gave them thirty-six bottles of claret, my whole stock. When the tide ebbed they took their leave, and rowed down to their vessels, as well pleased, and as drunk as wine or strong spirits could make them.

On the 30th I arrived at Devil's Harwar, and the succeeding day rowed up the Cormoetibo Creek. Having tied the boat to a tree which overspread it with thick branches, we quietly lay down to sleep during the night, myself and Quaco in the boat upon the benches, and the negroes under the seats, except those whom I ordered alternately to keep watch and awake me if they heard the least rustling in the woods, forbidding them all absolutely to speak or make any noise, lest the rebels, who were hovering on both sides of the Creek, might hear and surprise us. As for myself, who was the only white person among them all, I was confident I should not, in such a case, escape their fury. After these precautions, we all lay down and slept soundly from nine o'clock till about three in the morning, at which time Quaco and myself were both suddenly thrown down from our benches, by the boat all at once heeling upon one side, while all the negroes leaped overboard into the water. I instantly cocked my pistol, and jumping up, asked aloud what was the matter, positively determined to defend myself to the last extremity, rather than be taken alive by so relentless an enemy. For the space of a few seconds I obtained no answer, when the boat suddenly rectifying itself again (by the motion of which I was thrown off my feet) one of the swimming negroes called '*Masera, da wan sea-cow*,' and to my great happiness it proved to be no other than the manati, or sea-cow. By the account of the negroes it had slept under the boat, which, by the creature's awaking, had been lifted up and thrown upon one side, and again replaced when the manati made its escape from underneath it. I did not so much as see the creature, nor indeed hardly had the negro, owing to the darkness of the night which lasted some hours after; but during that time we had no farther inclination to rest. At last the sun's bright beams began to dart through the trees and gild the foliage; on which we cast off from our moorings, and continued rowing up Cormoetibo Creek (which was now very narrow) till near noon, when we discovered a smoke, and at last came to the mouth of the Wana Creek, the place of rendezvous. The troops, however, were not yet arrived, though opposite were encamped a few of the rangers, to guard the provisions that were waiting the arrival of Colonel Fourgeoud and his party.

On the third of November, one party of the troops being arrived, and encamped on the south-west side of the Cormoetibo Creek, about one mile above the mouth of the Wana Creek, I went with a couple of rangers to pay them a visit. Major Rughcop, the commanding officer, informed me that Colonel Fourgeoud had marched last from Patamaca in two columns, of which he led the one, while the other was hourly expected; and that the rest of the regiment was divided between the rivers Cottica, Perica, and Comewina, excepting those that were sick in the hospital at Paramaribo. I was now in excellent health and good spirits and, in the hopes of being reconciled to Fourgeoud by this voluntary proof of my zeal for the service, I returned to the rangers' camp to await his arrival. I was indeed well acquainted with his irreconcileable temper, and at the same time conscious of my own wild and ungovernable disposition when I thought myself ill treated; but soon forgot trifling injuries, and was now determined, by my active and affable behaviour, to make him my friend if possible.

At length the wished-for hour arrived; and being apprised of Colonel Fourgeoud's approach, I went half a mile from the camp to

View of the Hope

View of the Devil's Harwar

meet him, acquainting him that I was come *pour participer de la gloire*, and to serve under his immediate command, which he having answered with a bow, I returned it, and we marched together to the rangers' camp.

The occurrences in this march were the troops taking from the enemy three villages, particularly one called the Rice Country on account of the great quantity of rice which was found there, some ripe and some in full blossom, which we totally destroyed after putting the rebels to flight. These were commanded by one Bonny, a relentless mulatto, who was born in the forest and was quite unconnected with Baron's party, which had lately been driven from Boucou. We further learned that they had found seven human skulls stuck upon stakes, under which lay mouldering the bodies above ground and part of the garments, which proved them to be the remains of the unfortunate Lieutenant Lepper, with six of his unhappy men, most of whom being taken alive, had one by one been stripped naked by the rebel negroes at the arrival in their village, and (for the recreation of their wives and children) by Bonny's orders flogged to death. This information we got from a rebel woman who had been made a prisoner by Fourgeoud on his march through the above village, and whom we treated with every kindness.

This inhuman conduct in Bonny was directly opposite to that of Baron who, notwithstanding all his threats and menaces, it was well known had sent back to Paramaribo different soldiers whom he might have killed. He even assisted in concealing them from his enraged accomplices, and furnished them with provisions, perfectly sensible that they were not the cause of the disturbance. But not a ranger, as I have said before, that had the misfortune to fall into his hands could escape his ungovernable fury.

On further conversation, we found that the whole party, being nearly starved, had conjunctly called out for bread, as it was known that there was plenty in the boxes, but that it had been kept back three days, and rice served out in its stead. To suppress this kind of mutiny, the officers had rushed in among the men with cocked pistols and drawn swords, and indiscriminately laying hold of the first in their way, had unluckily seized a poor man named Shmidt whom, notwithstanding all the others averred to be innocent, they had, for an example to the rest, bastinadoed between two corporals, till the blood gushed out of his mouth like a fountain; and thus ended the revolt.

While I was now about noon resting in my hammock very contentedly, I was accosted by my friend Lieutenant Campbell, who acquainted me, with tears in his eyes, that the evening before Colonel Fourgeoud had given to the officers of the Surinam Society, not only of that brave and gallant corps the Scots Brigade in the Dutch service but of the British in general, the most unmerited character that could be invented. I immediately started up and, having got Campbell's information confirmed, went to Fourgeoud and asked him in public the cause of this unmanly slander. He replied, with a stare, that his observations only regarded my petticoat-trousers, which I wore for coolness and conveniency, as many British seamen do, and which he had never seen on the mountains of Switzerland. But as to the rest of what was said respecting us, he laid it totally to the charge of Mr Stoelman, captain of the Cottica militia, who was absent. Thus I could only answer by denouncing, in the severest terms, vengeance upon this assassin of our reputation, and after promising to transform my short trousers into long ones, we coolly separated.

An hour however after this, I received a sudden order to cross the Cormoetibo River, and be henceforth under the command of Major Rughcop, who was with his party or column at this time encamped on the south-side at the mouth of Wana Creek.

Being arrived in Major Rughcop's camp, and having got a couple of negroes to serve me, the next measure was to build a hut or, more properly speaking, a shed over my hammock, to keep me free from the rain and the sun, which was done within the space of one hour. Neither hammers nor nails, nor indeed any kind of carpenter's tools are required; a strong cutlass or bill-hook being all that is wanted. They are instantly raised, and form not only lasting, but the most delightful and convenient habitations, with even two stories, one above the other, if required. For these erections not more than two articles are wanting; the first the manicole, or pine-tree, and the second the nebees.

The manicole-tree, mostly found in marshy places, is about the thickness of a man's thigh, very straight, and grows to the height of from thirty to fifty feet from the ground. On the top the manicole-tree spreads in beautiful green boughs, with leaves hanging straight downwards like silk ribbons, which form a kind of umbrella. The manner of using it for building huts or cottages is by cutting the trunk in pieces of as many feet long as you wish to have the partition high; these pieces are next split into small boards the breadth of a man's hand, divested of their pithy substance, and then they are fit for immediate use. Having cut and prepared as many of these laths as you want to surround the dwelling, nothing remains but to lash them in a perpendicular position close to each other to two cross bars of the same tree fixed to the corner posts. The whole is cut and shaped with the bill-hook alone, and tied together by the nebees or *tay-tay*, which I think have derived their name from our verb *to tie*, since the English had possession of the colony. The nebees are a kind of ligneous rope of all sizes, both as to length and thickness, that grow in the woods and climb up along the trees in all directions: they are so plentiful and wonderfully dispersed that, like the ligneous cordage of the mangrove, they make the forest appear like a large fleet at anchor, killing many of the trees by mere compression, and entwining themselves with each other to the thickness of a ship's cable. These nebees are exceedingly tough, and may be used for mooring large vessels to the shore.

The roofing is done by the green boughs or branches of the same manicole-tree that made the walls, and in the following manner: each bough, which I can compare to nothing so well as to the shape of a feather, and which is as large as a man, must be spilt from the top to the bottom in two equal parts, and a number of these half boughs are tied together by their own verdure to form a bunch; you next take these bunches and tie them with nebees one above another upon the roof of your cottage, as thick as you please, and in such a manner that the verdure, which looks like the mane of a horse, hangs downwards. This covering, which at first is green but soon takes the colour of the English reed-thatching, is very beautiful, lasting and close, and finishes your house, as I have said, without the help of a hammer or nails; the doors and windows, tables, seats, etc. are made in the same manner, so are the enclosures for gardens, or other places for keeping cattle; and by this conveniency it is that the rebel negroes never want good houses which, if burnt to ashes one day, are again perfectly rebuilt the next, though they never rebuild them exactly in the places where they have once been discovered by Europeans.

When this temporary fabric is completely finished, it will not only keep dry both the inhabitants and their boxes, but (by the help of the nebees) fuzees, swords, pistols, etc. may be suspended from the rafters.

While we continued in this station, one morning, being returned from a patrol with twenty marines and twenty rangers, and sitting round a species of table to take some dinner with the other officers, I was rudely insulted by a Captain Meyland of the Society troops, who, as I said, with Lieutenant Fredericy, had taken Boucou, and who was Colonel Fourgeoud's countryman and friend. The affront consisted in Meyland's handing round to each a drop of claret, he having indeed but one bottle left, and, in an impertinent manner, excepting me alone, although I held the glass in my hand to receive it. Justly suspecting this insult to originate from my commander-in-chief, rather than appear to seek a quarrel, I endeavoured to make an apology, telling him, I had inadvertently erred in holding out my glass, not imagining I was to be distinguished from the other officers; assuring him it was not for the value of his wine, which I politely relinquished to my next neighbour. But this concession had no other effect than to increase the wrath of my fierce adversary who, apparently mistaking it for pusillanimity, became overbearing and scurrilous, in which he was seconded by all the other Swiss and Germans without exception. I said no more, and having tore away a wing of a boiled bird that stood before me (which bird had been shot by one of the rangers) I devoured it with little ceremony, and left the table with a determination to support my character or die. Thus resolved, I first went to the hut of a sick soldier, whose sabre I borrowed (my own being broken) on pretence of going out to cut a few sticks; after this I went in quest of Mr Meyland, and found him contentedly smoking his pipe by the waterside, looking at one of his friends who was angling. Having tapped him on the shoulder, I hastily told him, before the other, that now if he did not fight me that instant like a gentleman, I was determined to take revenge another way, with the flat of my sabre, where he stood. He at first declared that he had only meant a joke, and seemed for peace; but perceiving that I persisted, he with great *sang froid* knocked the tobacco ashes from his pipe against the heel of his shoe; then having brought *his* sabre, we walked together without seconds about half a mile into the wood. Here I stopped the captain short and, drawing my weapon, now desired him to stand on his defence. This he did, but at the same time observed that as the point of his sword was broken off, we were unequally armed; and so indeed we were, *his* being still near one foot longer than my own. Therefore calling to him that *sabres* were not made to thrust, but to cut with, I offered to make exchange; but he refusing, I dropped mine on the ground, and eagerly with both hands endeavoured to wrest his from him, till (as I had hold of it by the blade) I saw the blood trickle down all my fingers and was obliged to let go. I now grasped my own sabre, with which I struck at him many times, but without the least effect, as he parried every blow with the utmost facility; at last, with all his force, he made a cut at my head, which, being conscious I could not ward off by my skill, I bowed under it, and at the same instant striking sideways for his throat, had the good fortune to make a gash in the thick part of his right arm at least six inches long, the two lips of which appeared through his blue jacket, and in consequence of which his right-hand came down dangling by his side. I had, however, not escaped entirely unhurt, for his sabre, having passed through my hat without touching my skull, had glanced to my right shoulder, and cut it about one inch deep. At this time I insisted on his asking my pardon, or on firing both our pistols left-handed; but he chose the first, which ended the battle. I now reminded him that such Swiss jokes were always too serious to Englishmen, whereupon we shook hands and I conducted him, covered with blood, to the surgeon of his own corps, who having sewed up the wound, he went to his hammock and for the space of several weeks performed no duty. Thus was I reconciled to Captain Meyland, and what gave me the greatest satisfaction was his acknowledging the affront was offered as finding it would be agreeable to Fourgeoud to have me mortified. Ever after this acknowledgment we lived in the utmost intimacy. Peace, however, was not yet decreed to be my lot, for that very afternoon I found myself under the necessity of challenging two other officers who had espoused Meyland's quarrel against me at dinner; but in this I had the satisfaction of establishing my character without violence or bloodshed, both of the gentlemen acknowledged their error, and I became at once the favourite of the camp.

On the 9th of November both columns met, and encamped together on the north side of the Wana Creek, near its mouth, where it runs into the Cormoetibo, placing advanced guards at both creeks, at one mile distance from it; and this very evening I took the opportunity of acquainting Colonel Fourgeoud that I had nearly cut off the head of his beloved countryman in a duel (well knowing he must be informed of it by others); which trespass he was not only pleased graciously to pardon, but to tell me with a smile that I was a *brave garçon*, but in those smiles I put no more trust than I would in the tears of a crocodile.

My doubts of his friendship were soon confirmed, since my only true friend, Campbell, going down sick to Devil's Harwar, he would not so much as allow the boat or ponkee to wait till I had finished a letter, directed to Joanna, for some clean linen; however, a ranger (of which corps I by this time was become a remarkable favourite) found means to enable me to overtake this poor young man in a corialla or small canoe, composed of one single piece of timber. Shaking hands, we separated with tears, and I never saw him more, for he died in a few days after. Colonel Fourgeoud now being determined to scour the north banks of the Cormoetibo, we broke up in two columns, his own first, and that of Major Rughcop, to which last I still belonged, following; we left behind a strong guard with the provisions for the sick. Before we set out, I shall specify the substance of our orders to be observed on a march.

Article I. Quietness and sobriety was strongly recommended.

Article II. On pain of death none to fire without receiving orders.

Article III. Also death to whoever quits or loses his arms.

Article IV. The same punishment for those who dare to plunder while they are engaging the enemy.

Article V. An officer and sergeant to inspect the distribution of the victuals at all times.

Article VI. Each officer to be limited in the number of his black attendants.

The other orders were that in case our marines marched in two or three divisions or columns, they were to mark the trees with a sabre or bill-hook to give intelligence to each other where they had passed. Also when the troops marched over sandy deserts, heaths, or savannahs, they were occasionally to drop small twigs or reeds, tied together in the form of a cross: and in each camp, on the troops leaving it, were to be left a bottle and blank paper; if anything particular should happen, the same should be specified thereon. In case of the troops being attacked on a march, a small entrenchment was to be formed of the baggage-boxes, at the back of which the negro slaves were to lie flat on the ground; and this entrenchment to be defended by the rear-guard only, while the other troops had orders not to linger on the defensive, but vigorously, with bayonets fixed, to rush in upon the enemy's fire, nevertheless humanely giving quarter to all such as should be taken alive or surrender themselves to the troops.

These were the stated rules of our future military conduct; but for the present I beg leave to observe that everything was in the most unaccountable hurry and confusion. In this way, however, we proceeded, keeping our course towards the mouth of the Cormoetibo Creek, each officer provided with a pocket compass by which we were to steer, like sailors, through a dark wood where nothing is to be seen but the heavens, as at sea nothing appears but clouds and water. Thus those who were acquainted with navigation were the best qualified for marching and ran the least hazard of losing themselves in a black unbounded forest. But those wretches who most deservedly attracted my pity, were the miserable negro slaves who were bending under their loads; whose heads, on which they carry all burthens, bore the bald marks of their servitude. They were driven forward like oxen, and condemned to subsist on half allowance while they performed double drudgery. In short, to increase our misfortune, though in the dry season, the rains began to pour down from the heavens like a torrent, continuing all night: during this deluge (according to Colonel Fourgeoud's order) we were all ordered to encamp without huts or other covering of any kind, slinging our hammocks between two trees, under which, upon two small forked sticks, were placed our fire-arms, as the only method of keeping the priming powder dry in the pan; above this piece of architecture did I hang, like Mahomet betwixt the two loadstones, with my sabre and pistols in my bosom, and, in spite of wind and weather, fell most profoundly asleep.

On the 14th, at five o'clock in the morning, I was awaked by the sound of Up! up! up! when the rain still continuing, the half of the officers and men were sick, and I rose from my hammock soaked as in a wash-tub; having secured the lock of my firelock, in imitation of the rangers, with a piece of the bark of a palm-tree, and swallowing a dram with a piece of dry rusk biscuit for my breakfast, we again marched on. But I ought not to forget mentioning the negroes, who had the whole night slept in the water on the ground, and yet were in better health than any of the Europeans. Had we now been attacked by the enemy, we must inevitably have been all cut to pieces, being disabled from resisting with our firearms, in which not only the priming but even many of the cartridges were completely wet; this might have been prevented by having cased and waxed down our arms, as is practised by the buccaneers of America; but these were trifles not to be thought of. One thing, however, now happened which threatened to be no trifle, and that was that the provisions were gone, and those we expected to meet us in the creek not arrived, having by some mistake been neglected. By this accident we were now reduced, officers and men without exception, to subsist on one rusk biscuit and water for our allowance for twenty-four hours, to keep us from starving. In the midst however of this distress, we were again presented by one of the rangers with a large bird, called here *boossy-calcoo*, being a species of wild turkey; of this fortunate acquisition it was resolved in the evening to make broth, each throwing a piece of his rusk biscuit into the kettle, and (standing round the fire) beginning to ladle away as soon as the broth began to boil. Notwithstanding its being put over at six o'clock in the evening, at midnight the kettle was just as full as the first moment we had begun supper, though the broth was rather weaker, the heavy rain having dashed into it without intermission. During this severe storm we were as destitute of huts as the night before, but I availed myself once more of my English petticoat trousers which, loosening from my middle, I hung about my shoulders, and continuing to turn round before the fire (like a fowl roasting on a string) passed the hours with rather more comfort than my miserable coughing companions.

On the succeeding morning we marched again through very heavy rains, which by this time had swelled the water so high in the woods that it reached above our knees, and prevented us from crossing a small creek in our way without the help of a temporary bridge.

I prevailed therefore on the rangers, with the help of a few slaves, to erect one, which they did in the space of forty minutes, by cutting down a straight tree, which fell directly across the creek. To this they also made a kind of railing, but still our commander Rughcop, whose temper was soured by misery and whose constitution was already broken by hardships, was not pleased. He paid the rangers for their pains with oaths and reproaches, who, with a smile of contempt, left him swearing and crossed the creek, some by swimming, and others by climbing up a tree whose branches hung over it and dropping down on the opposite shore. In this I followed their example, and here we stopped till the arrival of the poor trembling and debilitated Major Rughcop, with two-thirds of his troops as sick as himself.

I still continued in perfect health, but I was much stung by different insects, and torn by a thousand thorns or *maccaws*, particularly one species, which are strong black prickles of several inches long that break short in the wound. Another inconvenience to be met with throughout all the low and marshy places in the forest, is a kind of roots called *matakee*, which rise above ground like nebees, three or four feet high, continuing thus to an almost endless length, and so thick that, like our brambles, no dog can get through them. Over these *matakees* it is extremely difficult to walk, as they every moment catch hold of the feet, and frequently trip up the body, unless at every footstep care is taken to step clear over them, which for short-limbed men is an absolute impossibility.

We marched again, with better weather, and arrived before noon at Jerusalem, near the mouth of Cormoetibo Creek, where I had formerly halted during my cruise. Here Colonel Fourgeoud, with his drooping soldiers, was arrived just before us, and here we made our appearance in such a shocking situation as will scarcely admit of description. It is sufficient to say, that the whole little army was exhausted by famine and fatigue, a very small number excepted; while several, unable to walk at all, had been carried upon poles by negro slaves in their hammocks. And during all this time we had discovered nothing. One thing is to be considered, that while the old gentleman himself went through all the above-mentioned hardships (to which he seemed as invulnerable as a machine of iron or brass) we had the less reason to complain of bad usage. In short, having as usual plunged in the river to wash off the mire and blood occasioned by the scratches, and having taken a refreshing swim, I looked round for my negroes to erect a comfortable hut; but in this I was disappointed as they were employed by Mr Rughcop to build his kitchen, although he had as yet nothing to dress in it. This piece of unpoliteness I for once overlooked, and the rangers having made me a nice bed of manicole-branches on the ground (there being no trees in the place to sling a hammock) and having lighted a blazing fire by the side of it, I lay quietly down next to them on my green mattress where, in a clear moonshine night and no rain, I fell sound asleep. But about two hours before daybreak I awaked, when the fire was out, the moon was down, and I almost dead with the cold dew and the damp that exhaled from the earth, being so stiff and benumbed that I had scarcely strength to crawl on hands and feet and awake one of my sable companions. He, however, having kindled a new fire, I recruited so as at six o'clock to be able to rise, but with such excruciating pain in one of my sides that I could not avoid groaning aloud; but to prevent Fourgeoud and the others from hearing, I hid myself in the skirts of the wood. The pain however still augmenting, I soon was prevented from breathing without the greatest difficulty, and at last fell down behind the rotten trunk of an old cabbage-tree. In this situation I was discovered by one of the negro slaves who was going to cut rafters, and who, supposing me dead, ran instantly back and alarmed the whole camp. I was taken up and carried in a hammock, by the care of a Captain Medler, under proper cover, and one of the Society surgeons instantly sent for to attend me. By this time I was surrounded by spectators, and the pain in my side became so acute that, like one in the hydrophobia, I tore my shirt with my teeth and bit whatever chanced to come near me; till being rubbed by a warm hand on my side with a kind of ointment, the complaint suddenly vanished like a dream, and I felt myself completely recovered.

To prevent a relapse, however, the first use that I made of my strength was to cut a cudgel, with which I swore to murder the Berbice ruffian, Geusary, who had the management of the slaves, if he did not instantaneously employ them to build for me a comfortable hut, let who would order the contrary, my life being the dearest thing I had to regard. Following him close at his heels, with my cudgel clubbed upon my shoulder, I had the satisfaction to be well housed in the space of two hours. I must not omit that Colonel Fourgeoud, during the crisis of my illness, had made me an offer of being transported to Devil's Harwar; but this I refused.

On the 18th the news arrived that poor Campbell died on the preceding day; and now Major Rughcop himself was sent down extremely ill, being the eleventh sick officer during this short campaign. Being now almost starving for want of provisions, we were most opportunely supplied by a quantity of fish, particularly the *jackee* and the *warappa*. These fish were so plentiful in the marshes, where they were left by the retreating waters, that our negroes caught many with their hands, but mostly by striking at hazard in the mud with their bill-hooks and sabres; after which, grasping with their fingers, they brought up pieces and half fishes in great abundance.

On the 20th we detached a captain, with twenty privates and twenty ranges, to reconnoitre the demolished village of Boucou. On the following day Major Rughcop died, and now Colonel Fourgeoud resolved to march himself to Boucou, leaving me the command of four hundred men, white and black, two hundred of whom were sick in their hammocks. But of that number I transported thirty to die at Devil's Harwar, while I sent sixty rangers with leave down to

Paramaribo. These latter went away declaring that Fourgeoud's operations were only calculated to murder his own troops instead of the enemy's. Such is the nature of the negroes that where they know nothing is likely to be done they will not march; it is indeed extremely difficult to maintain proper discipline among them, and when they expect to see the enemy, nothing can possibly keep them back. It is amazing to observe with what skill one negro discovers the haunts of another: while a European discerns not the smallest vestige of a man's foot in the forest, the roving eye of the negro-ranger catches the broken sprig, and faded leaf trod flat, without ever missing it. But when he finds the marks of the enemy being near, he can then no longer be restrained. This undoubtedly is inconsistent with modern tactics, but indicates that spirit of liberty which in ancient times alone completed the valiant soldier; and such was at this time the native and natural spirit of a people who had but yesterday been slaves.

On the evening of the 21st, I availed myself once more of being commandant, by sending two barges for provisions, the one to La Rochelle and the other to Devil's Harwar, which last brought back a box with Boston biscuit, sent me from Paramaribo.

On this day two slaves were put in confinement accused of having taken pork from the magazine, and I was addressed by the troops to inflict an exemplary punishment, the common soldiers despising the negro slaves as in their imagination greatly below themselves, and stupidly considering them as the causes of their distress. Having found a large piece of pork in their custody, yet having no proof that was sufficient to establish the theft, I found myself greatly at a loss to distribute justice with satisfaction to both parties; the Europeans unmercifully accusing, and the poor slaves vindicating their starved companions in such a clamorous style that the whole camp was in an uproar. The first persisted that the latter had stolen it, and the others that they had saved it from their allowance, to take to their families. Affecting, therefore, the style of a despotic prince, I ordered first a ring to be formed of the plaintiffs, and next the prisoners to be let within it. I then, with a stern and loud voice, commanded a block and a hatchet to be brought. It was with heart-felt satisfaction that I found this solemn apparatus, and the apprehension that we might commit a rash and criminal action, soon dispelled every feeling of resentment in the soldiers, and I was implored by the very accusers to show mercy. Obdurately stopping my ear, however, to all intreaty from either side, I made a strong negro slave take up the hatchet, and instantly chop the *pork* into three equal pieces; when, giving one share to the prosecutors, another to the malefactors, and the third to the executioner for having so well done his duty, the farce was ended to general satisfaction, and I heard no more of robberies or complaints.

On the 26th Colonel Fourgeoud, with his party, returned from his trip to Boucou, having surrounded three straggling rebel negroes unarmed as they were cutting a cabbage-tree for their subsistence. While one of them, called Passup, had escaped, another was taken alive, and a third, with his thigh shot to shivers by a slug cartridge, was first lashed hands and feet, and thus carried by two negroes on a pole, in the manner of a hog or a beer-barrel, bearing all the weight of his body upon his shattered limbs, which were dropping with blood, without a plaister or a bandage to cover the wounds, and with his head hanging downwards all the time. In this manner the unhappy youth—for he had not the appearance of being twenty—had been brought through thick and thin for above six miles distance from the camp, while he might just as well have been carried in one of the spare hammocks of the soldiers. I was shocked and surprised at this act of barbarity in Fourgeoud, whom I never had observed to be cruel in his cooler moments to an individual; indeed I must do him the justice to say quite the reverse. But on this occasion he was so flattered with this trophy of victory that every spark of feeling and humanity was extinct. The body being laid on a table, I implored one of the surgeons, called Pino, to dress his wounds; on which, that he might seem to do something, he put just as many round patches as the slugs had made holes, declaring he could never recover. Poor negro! what must have been his feelings! The fever increasing, he begged for some water, which I gave him myself clean out of my hat, when he said, 'Thank you, *Masera*,' sighed, and, to my inexpressible satisfaction, instantly expired. His companion, called September, was more fortunate, for Fourgeoud, in hopes of making some discoveries, regaled and treated him with more distinction than he did any of his officers. While September, looking as wild as a fox newly caught, was put in the stocks during the night, his companion was interred by the negro slaves with those marks of commiseration which his unhappy fate demanded from every human being. According to their custom, they spread his grave with the green boughs of the palm-trees, and offered a part of their scanty allowance by way of libation.

The following day Mr Stoelman, the militia captain, being arrived to stay one day only in the camp, I took the opportunity to remind Colonel Fourgeoud of what he had told me concerning his unbecoming insinuations, which I begged him now to repeat in that gentleman's hearing, as I was determined to have this matter cleared up and to obtain that satisfaction to which I thought myself entitled. But the gallant Colonel was not easily brought to proof. He now imputed all the blame to Major Rughcop, who was dead, and requested of me to say nothing more about it. I left him with contempt, shook hands with my supposed adversary, and then, to his inexpressible surprise, told him all that had happened. The consequence was that, in less than two hours, the captain quitted Fourgeoud and Jerusalem in disgust, and was followed by the remaining rangers.

On the 29th, Captain de Borgnes was made major in Rughcop's place, but no new subalterns were created, Fourgeoud declaring he had no more materials to fabricate them with. This might be true among the sergeants, but two brave youths, both gentlemen's sons, who had entered as volunteers and gone through every danger and fatigue, remained unnoticed in the ranks, the one named Sheffer, the other Meyer. Such ever was, and ever will be, *too frequently*, the consequence of wanting friends and fortune.

10

ON the 30th of November, 1773, the whole of the troops broke up together and, leaving Jerusalem, we once more marched back to the Wana Creek, but did not keep exactly the track that had brought us thither. Colonel Fourgeoud, however, revoking his former orders, now allowed his remaining party to sling their hammocks under cover, of which indeed he, at this crisis, condescended to set them the example; thus were we at least more comfortably lodged, but, I am sorry to add, not more comfortably victualled, while the old gentleman himself wanted for nothing that was good.

We continued our march for three days successively, with good weather; but I was every night awaked out of my sound sleep by a sentinel, who was sent by the colonel's orders to disturb me, with a charge of having whistled or spoke.

On the 3rd we arrived once more at the Wana Creek. Here, after a fatiguing march, I flattered myself with the hope of recruiting my exhausted strength and spirits by a quiet night's rest, but was once more awoken. So sound was my sleep, that the sentinel was obliged to shake me three or four times by the shoulder. I then started up, denying the charge, but Fourgeoud himself, sitting upright in his hammock, now swore, in a tremendous voice that he was determined to hang and quarter whoever should dare to disobey his orders, the dark and gloomy woods resounding with his bellowing threats. A deadly silence succeeded this storm throughout the camp, till I happened to break it by bursting out into an immoderate fit of laughter, in which I was instantly accompanied by so many others that he began to roar like thunder, without being able to distinguish one person's voice from another. In this music he was seconded by a large toad, called here the *pipa*, to which monster he actually gave shelter in his hut, and which kept croaking every night with such a voice as could only be exceeded by Fourgeoud himself. Morpheus I now invoked to befriend me again, but to no purpose, such was the impression which these several roarings had left on my mind.

The croaking of this pipa, the hammering of another which produces a loud and constant sound of *tuck*, *tuck*, *tuck*, from sun-set to sun-rise, the howling of the baboons, the hissing of the snakes, tigers, etc.—to which add the growling of Fourgeoud, and sometimes heavy rains into the bargain—made the night very uncomfortable and gloomy indeed. The rising sun, however, dispelled my resentment, and having taken a sound nap during the day, I was as well after it, and as well pleased as the forest of Guiana could make me.

On the morning of the 4th, I discovered a couple of fine *powesas* or peacock-pheasants on the branches of a high tree near the camp, and requested liberty from the chief to shoot one of them, which however was bluntly refused me, on pretence that the enemy might hear the report of my musket, though by the way, if it be not a solecism so to express myself, they knew better where we were than we did ourselves. A little after, however, a large snake appearing on the top of another tree, it was ordered to be shot immediately, whether from fear or antipathy I know not. On the discharge of the musket the animal fell to the ground, quite alive, and glided instantly into a thicket near the magazine. Upon this occasion I had an opportunity of remarking the uncommon intrepidity of a soldier who, creeping in after the reptile, brought it out from among the brambles, superstitiously pretending that he was invulnerable to its bite. However this may be, the snake, which was above six feet long, erected its head and half its body successively to attack him, and he as often knocked it down with his fist, and at last with his sabre severed it in two pieces, which ended the battle. For doing this he was regaled by Fourgeoud with a dram of rum.

On the 6th I received six gallons of rum from Paramaribo, four of which I gave as a present to Fourgeoud.

About six in the evening two of our slaves, who had been out to cut manicoles, brought intelligence that a gang of rebels had passed not above a mile from the camp, headed by a Captain Arico, with whom they had spoken on the banks of the Cormoetibo Creek, but could not tell which way they steered their course, so much had they been terrified. On this information we received orders to pursue them by break of day. The next morning, at five o'clock, all was ready, and we again broke up, leaving a detachment with the stores, and repaired to the spot whence the intelligence proceeded. Here we saw a large palm or *mawrisee* tree,* floating in the river, and moored to the opposite shore by a nebee, which plainly indicated that Arico, with his men, had crossed the creek, which they do by riding astride on the floating trunk, the one behind the other, in which manner they are ferried over (sometimes with women and children) by those who are the best swimmers.

Notwithstanding this plain evidence, the faith of our colonel, Fourgeoud, now began to waver, and he averred that it was no more than a stratagem of the rebels who, he said, had come from the place

* The largest of all the palm species.

to which we supposed them gone, and who had only tied the tree across the river to deceive us.

To this opinion neither myself nor the other officers could subscribe, but no arguments would prevail with him, and we marched directly away from them, instead of crossing and pursuing them as the rangers would certainly have done. Thus we kept on till it was near dark—though the bread was forgotten and the whole day not a drop of water to be obtained—marching through high sandy heaths or savannahs. After inclining a little to the right, we were just upon the point of making a camp when a negro called out that we were come to the Wana Creek. This in my ears was a welcome sound, and giving him a calabash and the best part of a bottle of my rum, I desired him to run to the creek and make me some grog. This he did, but the poor fellow, never having made grog before, poured in all the spirits and but very little water, doubtless thinking that the stronger it was the better. This beverage I swallowed to the bottom, without taking time to taste it, and I became instantly so much intoxicated that I could hardly keep my feet.

On the 9th we found ourselves returned to our old camp, from a fruitless cruise, when Colonel Fourgeoud set the captive negro September at liberty. But our commander-in-chief was indefatigable, and not only crossed and reconnoitred the west side of the creek himself, but filling our knapsacks, we the next morning set out in the same track we had kept on the eighth, he still persisting that he should overtake the enemy. Having thus marched till towards dark, we altered our course and passed the night in an old camp of the rebel negroes, having again passed the whole day without water.

The following day we still proceeded, but neither enemies nor water were to be found. The men and officers now began to be extremely faint, and some were already carried in their hammocks. It was by this time indeed insufferably hot, being in the very heart of the dry season. In this dilemma we dug a hole six feet deep, in the bottom of which a ball cartridge being fired, a little moisture began to trickle forth, but so slow and so black, that it proved not to be of the least use.

We still marched on, and encamped in an old weedy field where the rebels some time before had cultivated plantations. During the night it was truly affecting to hear the poor soldiers lament for want of drink; but to no purpose for, in spite of all this misery, Fourgeoud still persisted in going forward even the third day, building his hopes on meeting with some creek or rivulet to alleviate this general distress. In this he was however mistaken for, having again, on the 12th, marched over burning sands till about noon, he dropped down himself among a number of others. It was happy that in this situation we were not attacked by the negroes, as it must have been impossible to make any resistance, the ground being strewed with distressed objects that appeared to be all of them in raging fevers. Despair now seemed to be impressed even upon Fourgeoud's countenance as he lay prostrate on the earth, with his lips and tongue parched black; and in this condition, though so little deserving of it, he again attracted my pity.

During all this, some of the soldiers still devoured salt pork, while others crept on all fours and licked the scanty drops of dew from the fallen leaves that lay scattered on the ground. I now experienced the kindness of which a negro is capable when he is well treated by his master, being presented by one attending me with a large calabash of as good water as ever I drank in my life. This he had met with, after unspeakable difficulty, in the leaves of a few wild pineapple plants.

As Providence had graciously sent me this supply, I could not for my soul resist the impulse of sharing my relief with poor Fourgeoud, whose age and natural infirmities pleaded greatly in his favour. Being now refreshed, he at last saw himself obliged to return, without any further hope of overtaking the enemy. But so exhausted was the party that many were carried on long poles in their hammocks by the slaves.

As his last resource, our commander now detached the Berbicean negro, Gausarie, by himself, to try if he could bring him any intelligence while we continued our retreat. As we returned by our former footsteps and approached the pit we had dug yesterday, I was convinced that by this time it must contain clear water. I therefore dispatched my boy Quaco to the front, to fill one of my gallon bottles before it should be changed to a puddle. This he did, but was met on his return by Colonel Fourgeoud who, with the butt end of his gun, relentlessly knocked the bottle to pieces and, doubling his pace, placed two sentinels at the pit, with orders to preserve the water all for himself and his favourites. But at this moment, subordination being extinguished, the two protectors were forced headlong into the pit, followed by several others, who all fought to come at the water, which being now changed to a perfect mire, was good for nothing. Having slung our hammocks in an old rebel camp, a dram of *kill-devil* was distributed to each without distinction; but, as I never used this fluid, I offered my share to my faithful negro who had given me the water. This being observed by old Fourgeoud, he ordered it to be snatched out of the poor man's hand, and returned into the earthen jar, telling me, 'I must either drink it myself, or have none.' I was exceedingly exasperated at this mark of ingratitude, and finding means to procure that very evening a whole bottle, I gave it to the slave.

Near midnight, accidentally, good water was discovered. Good

God, what joyful news! How sweet the taste, surpassing any wine. Now all drank heartily, and Fourgeoud ordered a warm supper to be boiled for himself, but not so much as a fire to be lighted for any other person, forbidding even the cutting of a stick; thus were we forced to eat our salt beef and pork *raw*. However, having tied my small allowance to a string, I hung it quietly over the side of *his* kettle, to have it dressed; but his black cook chancing to drop a log of wood upon another in his eagerness to assist me, alarmed the hero, so that I was obliged to drop my luncheon into the kettle and take to my heels.

The old gentleman now insisting that some person had cut sticks against his orders, I quietly stepped up to his hammock in the dark, to undeceive him, and softly assured him that the whole camp was fast asleep. Whereupon he, on pretence of not knowing me, suddenly gave a loud roar, and with both his hands caught hold of me by the hair of the head. I escaped, and got fairly under cover, while he called, 'Fire at him! Fire at him!' to the infinite amusement of the whole camp, who lay in their hammocks convulsed with laughter. Having found out Quaco, I instantly sent him back to bring my luncheon; and such was his diligence, that he actually brought me back a piece of beef at least ten times as large as what I had left, and with it I had once more the satisfaction to regale the poor slaves.

The 13th we once more returned to the Wana Creek, fatigued beyond the power of description with these fruitless sufferings. Here the old gentleman regaled his friends with my rum in my presence, and without offering me a single drop. Here also I found a letter from the island of Ceylon in the East Indies, where my friend and relation, Mr Arnoldus de Ly, being governor of Point-de-Gale and Matury, I was invited to come and find my fortune ready made, but which for the present my evil stars prevented my accepting, as it would have been dishonourable to leave the service at this juncture.

The following day the negro Gausarie returned from his expedition, reporting that he had discovered nothing.

Captain Fredericy, who had marched on the 20th ult. with forty men, white and black, from Jerusalem, not having been heard of since, it was apprehended he had met with some dreadful accident and, in consequence, on the 15th, two captains, two subalterns, and fifty men, were dispatched to the river Marawina for some intelligence.

The post at the Marawina, which is called Vredenburgh, consists of houses surrounded with palisades, in a kind of square, all built of the manicole-tree with which the woods of Guiana so much abound. On the outer side are a guard and four sentinels, and the fort itself is defended by several cannon. It is situated in an opening, on the banks of the river, where is placed a large flag, and where the garrison communicates with the French post on the opposite shore, both being situated at but little distance from the mouth of the Marawina.

The barges etc. were ordered on the same day to bring up provisions and take down the sick; but at this very time the whole camp was attacked by that dreadful distemper the bloody flux, which is both infectious and epidemical, and daily carried numbers to their grave. An emetic, or some other medicine, administered at random, were the only relief in our power, as there was not a proper surgeon on the spot, all of them being engaged at the hospitals in Comewina and in Paramaribo.

The poor slaves were peculiarly unhappy, for, as I have stated, they had but half allowance and lived for months on the produce of the cabbage-tree, seeds, roots, wild berries, etc. and to this circumstance may be attributed the first introduction of this dangerous disease into the camp. So starved indeed were these wretched negroes, that they tied ropes or nebees about their naked bodies; this is a practice of the Indians when their abdomens are shrunk with hunger, as they find by experience, or at least fancy, that the pain occasioned by want of food is relieved by the compression. I, however, with a few others, escaped the infection, but I was laid up with a miserable bad cold and swelled foot—a disease called the *consaca*, and not unlike our chilblains in Europe, as it occasions a very great itching, particularly between the toes, whence issues a watery fluid.

The negroes are very subject to this complaint, which they cure by applying the skin of a lemon or lime, made as hot as they can bear it.

I have frequently had occasion to mention our provisions of salt beef, pork, rusk, biscuit and water, which were dealt out regularly every five or six days. The two former had perhaps made the tour of the world after leaving Ireland, and were so green, so slimy, so stinking, and sometimes so full of worms, that at other times they would not have remained upon my stomach. But I have not described our furniture. This, however, will not occupy much time, as it consisted only of a square box or chest for each officer, to carry his linen, and his fresh provisions and spirits, when he had either. These boxes served not only as cupboards, but as chairs and tables in the camp; on a march they were carried on the head of a negro. I must observe, moreover, that we had no light after six o'clock in the evening, that of the moon excepted, when all was solemn and melancholy beyond description.

I had not so much as a trencher, basin, spoon, or fork: for the first and second I made a negro's calabash serve me; a fork I wanted not, and a spoon but seldom; instead of that article, therefore, I used a folded leaf, agreeably to the practice of the slaves; and as for a knife, each person carried one in his pocket. I at last contrived to make a lamp by breaking a bottle; in which some melted pork produced a quantity of oil, and a slip of my shirt served for a wick. Necessity is proverbially ingenious, and in such a situation every nicety is forgotten. Indeed, could I now have had what formerly I left upon my plate, I should have ardently thanked God for it.

The whole camp was destitute of stockings, shoes, and hats. Colonel Fourgeoud walked a whole day barefooted himself to furnish an example of patience and perseverance, and to keep the few remaining troops from murmuring. In this respect I had fairly the advantage of all the company, my skin being (the swelled foot and a few scratches excepted) perfectly whole from my habit of walking thus, while not a sound limb was to be found among the rest, whose legs in general were broken out in dreadful ulcers, with a discharge of pus. I have already in part accounted for this inconvenience, and shall still further account for it by observing that, while the stockings and shoes of these unhappy people remained, they were never off the feet of many wearers who, after marching through water, mud, and mire, in this filthy condition, rested during the night in their hammocks, where, in fair weather, before morning this filth was dried upon their limbs, and in consequence caused an itching and redness on the skin, which by scratching broke out in many places. These wounds soon became scrofulous, and ended in open sores and ulcers which, from the want of care and proper application, often changed to mortification and intolerable swellings, by which some lost their limbs, and others even their lives when they were not saved by amputation. Such were the causes, and such the effects of the evils we had to struggle with; but they were far from the whole of our wretchedness, and might be called only the precursors of what we had still to undergo.

At this time a compliment of a fine ham and a dozen of port-wine being sent me by Captain Van Coeverden, I gave all in a present to poor Fourgeoud, who was emaciated with fatigue, except four bottles which I drank with the other officers; and next day, the 29th, I had the honour to be ordered *once more* on a patrol with Colonel des Borgnes and forty privates, to try if we could not take the negroes who had crossed the creek *three weeks* before.

Having dropped down the river with a barge, in which we lay all night, we landed the following morning, and marched north-east. Being without a compass, we soon lost our way, and having crossed a large sand savannah, slung our hammocks in the skirts of a thick and obscure wood. On the 31st we again set out the same course, in hopes of meeting with the marks of some former path cut upon the trees by some of our troops. But we were mistaken, for having got into a marsh where we waded till noon up to our chins at the hazard of being drowned, we saw ourselves under the necessity of returning the same way we came, perfectly soaked and in rags. After a forced march we encamped once more on the banks of Cormoetibo Creek, in a heavy shower of rain which caused so much confusion and hurry—each striving to build his shed and get under cover first—that I got a broken head, but persevering was one of the first in slinging my hammock under some spreading green boughs. Having lighted a comfortable fire, I fell most profoundly asleep in the middle of the smoke, which saved me from the stings of the mosquitoes.

While speaking of insects, I ought not to forget that this evening one of the negro slaves who had been looking for dry wood, presented me, to my great surprise, with a beetle no less than three or four inches in length, and above two in breadth, called in Surinam the *rhinoceros* on account of its proboscis or horn, which is hooked, forked, and thick as a goose-quill; on the head it has many hard polished knobs, the limbs are six, the wings are large, and the whole animal is perfectly black, being the largest of all the beetle kind in America.

Having slept most soundly for six or seven hours, in spite of the rains, the smoke, the mosquitoes, and my broken head, I turned out perfectly refreshed at five, and at six we commenced the year 1774 by marching up along the banks of the Cormoetibo till midday, when we arrived once more at the *grand* encampment at the mouth of the Wana Creek, after, as usual, a fruitless cruise.

On the 3rd, to our joy, Captain Fredericy also returned with his party, bringing in a captive negro in chains, called Cupido, and relating that a poor soldier of the Society troops, on receiving his pardon when on his knees to be shot, was gone out of his senses.

Colonel Fourgeoud being finally determined to break up this campaign, sent out a party of sixty men to cruise on the way to Patamaca before him.

I now washed my shirt, the last I had, in the Wana Creek (but was obliged to keep swimming till it was dried by the sun), my letter, sent for linen, having never reached Paramaribo, and what I had brought with me being torn to rags.

On the 4th of January, at six o'clock in the morning, all were ready to decamp. Thus having sent down the barges with the sick to Devil's Harwar, we at last crossed Cormoetibo Creek and marched first directly south for Patamaca, over steep mountains covered with stones and impregnated with minerals. In the evening we encamped at the foot of a high hill, where we found a small rivulet of good water and a number of manicole-trees, the two chief requisites. It is curious, and indeed beautiful, to behold, in the space of an hour, a green town spring up as it were from nothing, and a little after all the fires lighted on which the men are boiling their hard fare, while others are employed in drying their clothes.

This night, however, the whole camp was disturbed by a diuretic complaint occasioned by drinking the water we found here, which indeed was very pure, but was so impregnated with minerals, that it tasted almost like that of Bath or the German Spa. This is a circumstance which I think indicates that these mountains contain metals, if the Dutch would go to the expense of searching in their bowels.

On the 5th we marched the same course again over mountains and dales, some of which were so excessively steep that one or two of the slaves, not being able to ascend them loaded, threw down their burdens, and deserted, not to the enemy, but found their way to their masters' estates, where they were pardoned; others tumbled down, burthen and all, from top to bottom.

This evening we found our quarters ready-made, and lodged in the *wigwams* or huts that were left standing when the Rice Country was destroyed and Bonny with his men put to flight; in that where I lay I found a very curious piece of candle, which the rebels had left behind, composed of bees-wax and the heart of a bulrush.

Bonny's own house, where Fourgeoud lodged, was a perfect curiosity, having four pretty little rooms and a shed or piazza enclosed with neat manicole palisades.

The whole corps appearing on the 6th excessively fatigued, Fourgeoud ordered a general day of rest, only detaching Captain Fredericy with six men, as he knew the country best, to reconnoitre the banks of the Claas Creek, a water that issued from near this place in the upper parts of Rio Cottica. They had hardly marched off when the eye of our chief by chance falling on me, he ordered me instantly to follow *alone*, and return with a report of what I could discover on the *other* side the creek. I overtook the party soon, and after a short march we were in water up to our very armpits. Fredericy now ordered a retreat, but desiring him to wait for me, I took off all my clothes, and with only my sabre in my teeth, swam by myself across the Creek, where having ranged the opposite shore and finding nothing, I again swam back, after which we all returned to the camp.

At noon, making my report to Colonel Fourgeoud, he was astonished indeed at this desperate action, which in fact he had not expected; but I was not less amazed when he took me by the hand, entertaining me with a bottle of wine and ordering Monsieur Laurant to set some bacon-ham before me, to find, however incredible it may appear, that the one was actually sour, and the other creeping with live worms. My own provisions, *now his*, which were fresh, were withheld me. This meanness so much exasperated me, that, starting up, I left Fourgeoud, his valet, his wine, and his reptiles, with that contempt which they deserved, alleviating my hunger with a piece of dry rusk biscuit and a barbecued fish, called *warappa*, which I got from a negro.

On the 7th of January we marched again and this evening we encamped near the Patamaca Creek, where a poor negro woman cried bitterly and scattered some victuals and water at the root of a tree by way of libation, as being the spot where her husband was interred, having been shot in some former skirmish by the Europeans.

Here Captain Fredericy and myself, walking outside the skirts of the camp in a sandy savannah, discovered the fresh footsteps of a large tiger with her young, at which time they are extremely ferocious: we thought it prudent therefore to make a sudden retreat. I measured the diameter of the dam's claws printed in the sand, which were nearly of the dimensions of an ordinary pewter-plate.

Having marched a few hours longer the succeeding morning, we at last arrived at the Society post La Rochelle in Patamaca, such a display of meagre, starved, black, burnt, and ragged tatterdemallions, and mostly without shoes or hats, as I think were never before beheld in any country. Here we found a set of poor wretches ready to enter the woods which we had just left, and destined to undergo in the same manner the severest misery that ever was inflicted on sublunary beings. I have already mentioned the prickly heat, ring-worm, dry gripes, putrid fevers, biles, consaca, and bloody flux, to which human nature is exposed in this climate; also the mosquitoes, Patat and Scrapat lice, chigoes, cockroaches, ants, horse-flies, wild-bees, and bats, besides the thorns and briars, and the alligators and peree in the rivers; to which if we add the howling of the tigers, the hissing of serpents, and the growling of Fourgeoud, the dry sandy savannahs, unfordable marshes, burning hot days, cold and damp nights, heavy rains, and short allowance, the reader may be astonished how any person was able to survive the trial. Notwithstanding this black catalogue, I solemnly declare I have omitted many other calamities that we suffered, as I wish to avoid prolixity, though perhaps I have been already too often guilty of it.

The reader may form some conception of the famished state in which we came hither, when I inform him that, the moment of our arrival, observing a negro woman supping on plantain broth from a calabash, I gave her half-a-crown, and snatching the basin from her hands, I devoured the contents with a greater relish than I have ever tasted any delicacy before or since during my whole existence. I now observed to Colonel Fourgeoud how pitiable it was not to regale his remaining soldiers with vegetables and fresh beef or mutton, besides providing them with hats, stockings, shoes, etc. But he replied that Hannibal had lost his army at Capua by too much indulgence. In short, he quoted not only Hannibal but Horace for his example and appeared fully convinced, that no persons will behave so desperately in action as those who are tired of their lives.

On the 11th, the other party which had left Wana the day before ourselves, arrived, having, according to custom, neither taken nor seen anything.

On the 12th, one of the rebels with his wife came to La Rochelle, and surrendered himself voluntarily to the commander in chief. This day Fourgeoud acquainted me that I was at liberty to go and refit at Paramaribo when I thought proper. This proposal I gladly accepted, and that moment prepared for my departure with some other officers, leaving behind us himself and a band of such scarecrows as would have disgraced the garden or field of any farmer in England. Among these was a Society captain, named Larcher, who declared to me he never combed, washed, shaved, or shifted, or even put off his boots, till all was rotted from his body. At last arrived the happy hour, when, taking leave of my tattered companions, I and five more, with a tent-boat and six oars, rowed straight down for Paramaribo, still in good health and in a flow of spirits, and at the very summit of contentment.

At Devil's Harwar I met a cargo of tea, coffee, biscuit, butter, sugar, lemons, rum, and twenty bottles of claret, sent me by my friends, directed to La Rochelle. Again, notwithstanding the barbarous usage that I had so lately met with, I gave all in a present to poor Fourgeoud, twelve bottles of wine excepted, which we drank in the barge to the healths of our wives and mistresses. Nor could I help pitying Colonel Fourgeoud, whose age (he being about sixty) and indefatigable exertions claimed the attention of the most indifferent; for during this trip, though but few rebels were taken, he had certainly scoured the forest from the river Comewina to the mouth of the Wana Creek, dispersed the enemy, and demolished their habitations, fields, and gardens, and thus cut them off from all prospect of support.

On the evening of the 13th, we supped at the estate Mondesire, and thence kept rowing down all night and day, shouting and singing till the 15th at noon, when, the tide serving, we went on shore at the fortress Amsterdam. Then, crossing the river, we arrived before Mr de Lamar's door at Paramaribo and I stepped ashore among a crowd of friends, who all flocked round to see and to welcome me to town.

I next sent for my inestimable Joanna, who burst into tears the moment she beheld me, not only for joy at my still existing (for it had been reported that I was no more) but also from seeing my very distressed situation.

11

BEING once more arrived at Paramaribo, it will not be improper to introduce in this place some account of that beautiful town. Before I commence the description however, I must observe that, being long accustomed to walk bare-footed, I could not bear the confinement of shoes and stockings for some time; they heated and even swelled my feet so much that, dining on the 16th of January with my friend Kennedy, I was actually obliged to throw them off at his house, whence he was so kind as to send me home in his whisky. I have already mentioned that Paramaribo is situated on the right side of the beautiful river Surinam, at about sixteen or eighteen miles distance from its mouth. It is built upon a kind of gravelly rock, which is level with the rest of the country, in the form of an oblong square, its length about a mile and a half, and its breadth about half as much. All the streets, which are perfectly straight, are lined with orange, shaddock, tamarind, and lemon-trees, which appear in ever-lasting bloom, while at the same time their branches are weighed down with the richest clusters of odoriferous fruit. Neither stone nor brick is made use of here for pavement, the whole being one continued gravel, not inferior to the finest garden walks in England, and strewed on the surface with sea-shells. The houses, which are mostly of two, and some of three stories high, are all built of fine timber, a very few excepted; most of the foundations are of brick and they are roofed with thin split boards, called shingles, instead of slates or tiles. Windows are very seldom seen in this country, glass being inconvenient on account of the heat, instead of which they use gauze frames; some have only the shutters, which are kept open from six o'clock in the morning until six at night. As for chimneys I never saw one in the colony, no fires being lighted except in the kitchens, which are always built at some distance from the dwelling-house, where the victuals are dressed upon the floor, and the smoke let out by a hole made in the roof: these timber houses are however very dear in Surinam, as may be evinced by that lately built by Governor Nepveu, which he declared had cost him above £15,000 sterling. There is no spring water to be met with in Paramaribo; most houses have wells dug in the rock, which afford but a brackish kind of beverage, only used for the negroes, cattle, etc. and the Europeans have reservoirs or cisterns, in which they preserve rain-water for their own consumption; those of nicer taste let it first drop through a filtering-stone into

Name of
introducer.................................M/ship No. ....
MR MRS MISS

Address ....

....

Free books for introductions

Fill in below the names of any of your friends who you believe would enjoy membership of the Folio Society. For each new enrolment which results from your introduction you may choose—free of charge—any volume which is still available from the list of 'Earlier Publications' in our current prospectus.

PLEASE SEND DETAILS OF THE SOCIETY TO:

1...MR MRS MISS

....

....

2...MR MRS MISS

....

....

IN THE EVENT OF THE ABOVE JOINING THE SOCIETY PLEASE SEND ME A FREE COPY OF

....

....

....

(*Please give an alternative choice for each introduction*)

PLEASE USE BLOCK LETTERS

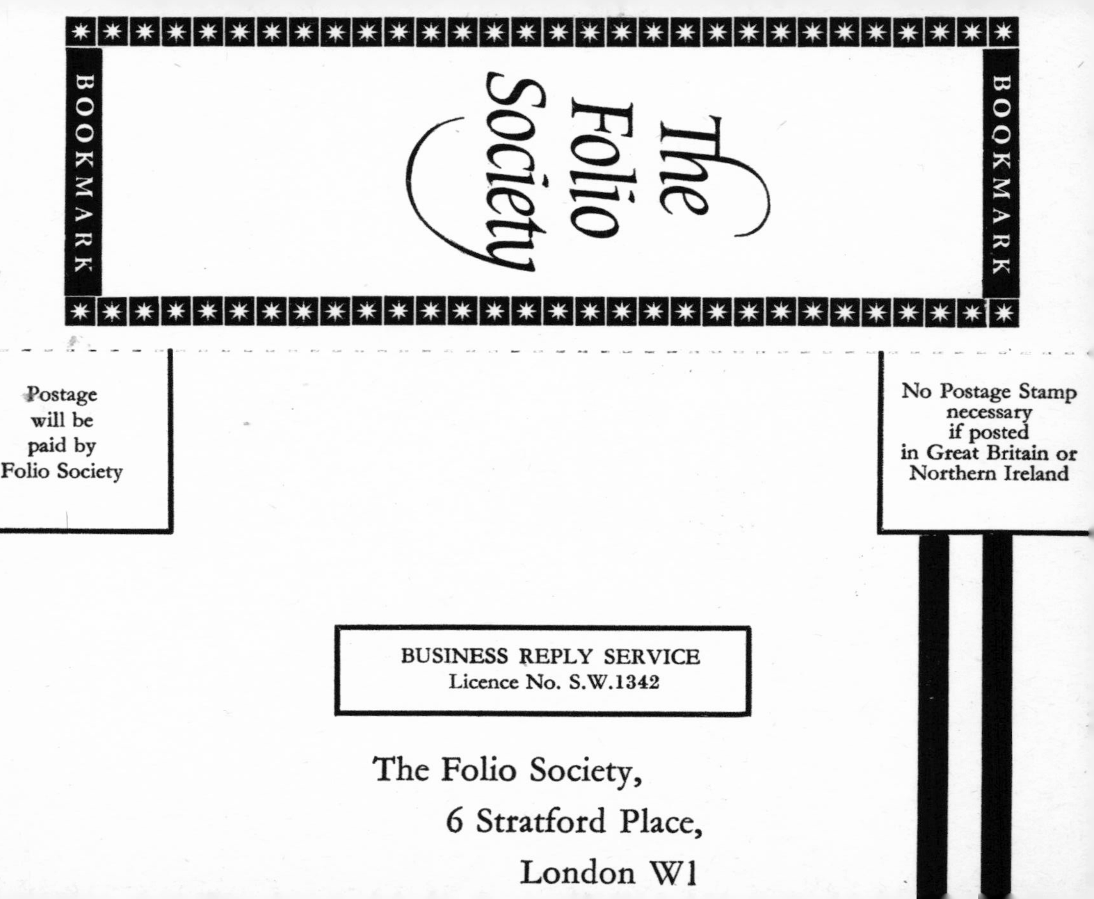
BOOKMARK
The Folio Society
BOOKMARK
Postage will be paid by Folio Society
No Postage Stamp necessary if posted in Great Britain or Northern Ireland
BUSINESS REPLY SERVICE
Licence No. S.W.1342
The Folio Society,
6 Stratford Place,
London W1

large jars or earthen pots, made by the native Indians on purpose, which they barter at Paramaribo for other commodities. The inhabitants of this country, of every denomination, sleep in hammocks, the negro slaves excepted, who mostly lie on the ground; the hammocks used by those in superior stations are made of cotton, ornamented with rich fringe; these are also made by the Indians, and sometimes worth above twenty guineas; neither bedding nor covering is necessary, except an awning to keep off the mosquitoes. Some people indeed lie on bedsteads; in that case they are surrounded, instead of curtains, with gauze pavilions, which admit the air freely, and at the same time keep off the smallest insect. The houses in general at Paramaribo are elegantly furnished with paintings, gilding, crystal chandeliers, china jars, etc.; the rooms are never papered or plastered, but beautifully wainscoted with cedar, Brazil, and mahogany wood.

The number of buildings in Paramaribo is computed at about one thousand four hundred, of which the principal is the governor's palace. This house, and that of the commandant, which has lately been burnt, were the only brick buildings in the colony. The townhall is an elegant new building, and covered with tiles; here the different courts are held, and underneath are the prisons for European delinquents, the military excepted, who are confined in the citadel of Fort Zelandia. The Protestant church, where divine worship is performed both in French and Low Dutch, has a small spire with a clock; besides which there is a Lutheran chapel, and two elegant Jewish synagogues, one German, the other Portuguese. Here is also a large hospital for the garrison, and this mansion is never empty. The military stores are kept in the fortress, where the Society soldiers are also lodged in barracks, with proper apartments for some officers. The town of Paramaribo has a noble road for shipping, the river before the town being above a mile in breadth, and containing sometimes above one hundred vessels of burthen, moored within a pistol shot of the shore; there are indeed seldom fewer there than fourscore ships loading coffee, sugar, cacao, cotton, and indigo, for Holland, including also the Guinea-men that bring slaves from Africa, and the North American and Leeward Island vessels, which bring flour, beef, pork, spirits, herrings, and mackerel salted, spermaceti-candles, horses, and lumber, for which they receive chiefly molasses to be distilled into rum. This town is not fortified, but is bounded by the river on the south-east, by a large savannah on the west, by an impenetrable wood on the north-east, and is protected by Fort Zelandia on the east. This citadel is only separated from the town by a large esplanade, where the troops parade occasionally. The fort is a regular pentagon, with one gate fronting Paramaribo, and two bastions which command the river; it is very small but strong, being made of rock or hewn stone, surrounded by a broad fosse well supplied with water, besides some out-works. On the east side fronting the river, is a battery of twenty-one pieces of cannon. On one of the bastions is a clock, which is struck with a hammer by the sentinel, who is directed by an hour-glass. On the other is planted a large ensign-staff, upon which a flag is hoisted upon the approach of ships of war, or on public rejoicing days. The walls are six feet thick, with embrasures but no parapet.

Paramaribo is a very lively place, the streets being generally crowded with planters, sailors, soldiers, Jews, Indians, and Negroes, while the river is covered with canoes and barges constantly passing and repassing, like the wherries on the Thames, often accompanied with bands of music; the shipping also in the road adorned with their different flags, guns firing, not to mention the many groups of boys and girls playing in the water, altogether form a pleasing appearance; and such gaiety and variety of objects serve, in some measure, to compensate for the many inconveniences of the climate. Their carriages and dress are truly magnificent; silk embroidery, Genoa velvets, diamonds, gold and silver lace, being daily worn, and even the masters of trading ships appear with buttons and buckles of solid gold. They are equally expensive at their tables, where everything that can be called delicate is produced at any price, and served up in plate and china of the newest fashion and most exquisite workmanship. But nothing displays the luxury of the inhabitants of Surinam more than the number of slaves by whom they are attended, often twenty or thirty in one family. White servants are seldom to be met with in this colony.

The current money is stamped cards of different value, from five shillings to fifty pounds. English and Portuguese coin are sometimes met with, but mostly used as ornaments by the Mulatto, Samboe, Quadroon, and Negro girls. The Negro slaves never receive any paper money, for as they cannot read they do not understand its value; besides in their hands it would be liable to many accidents, from fire or children, and particularly from the rats, when it becomes a little greasy.

This town is well supplied with provisions such as butcher's meat, fowls, fish, and venison. Vegetables in particular the country abounds with; besides the luxuries peculiar to this climate, they import whatever Europe, Africa, and Asia can afford. Provisions, however, are excessively dear in general, especially those imported, which are mostly sold by the Jews and masters of ships. The first enjoy extraordinary privileges in this colony; the latter erect temporary warehouses for the purpose of trade, during the time their ships are loading with the productions of the climate. Wheat flour is sold from fourpence to one shilling per pound; butter two shillings; butcher's meat never under one shilling, and often at one shilling and sixpence; ducks and fowls from three to four shillings a couple. A single turkey has cost me one guinea and a half; eggs are sold at the rate of five, and European potatoes twelve for sixpence. Wine three shillings a bottle. Jamaica rum a crown a gallon. Fish and vegetables are cheap, and fruit almost for nothing. My black boy, Quaco, has often brought me forty oranges for sixpence, and half a dozen pineapples for the same price, while limes and tamarinds may be had for gathering. House-rent is excessively high. A small room unfurnished costs three or four guineas a month; and a house with two apartments on a floor, lets for one hundred guineas yearly. Shoes sell for half-a-guinea a pair; and a suit of clothes, with silver binding, has cost me twenty guineas.

The whites or Europeans in this colony, who reside principally in town, are computed at five thousand, including the garrison; the negro slaves at about seventy-five thousand. The military mount guard every morning at eight o'clock in the fortress; but the safety of the town is entrusted to the burghers or militia, who keep watch during the night. At six o'clock in the morning, and the same hour in the evening, the morning and evening guns are fired by the commanding ship in the harbour; at the evening signal, all the flags are instantly lowered on board the different vessels; their bells are set a ringing, whilst the drums and fifes beat the *tattoo* through the town. The watch is then set, and no negro of either sex is allowed to appear in the streets or on the river without a proper pass signed by his owner; without this he is taken up, and infallibly flogged the next morning. At ten at night, a band of black drums beat the burgher, or militia retreat, through the streets of Paramaribo.

At this time the ladies begin to make their appearance, who are particularly fond of a *tête-à-tête* by moonlight, when they entertain with sherbet, *sangaree*,* and wine and water. Besides the most unreserved and unequivocal conversation concerning themselves, as well as the peculiar qualifications of their husbands, they also talk of the situation of their female slaves, whom they propose the acceptance of to the gentlemen they converse with at so much per week, according to their own estimation. Sometimes placing half a dozen of them in a row, the lady says, 'Sir, this is a *callebasee*, that is a maid, and this is not'—thus are they not only unreserved in their conversation, but also profuse in their encomiums upon such gentlemen as have the honour of their instructive company, and whose person or figure meets with their approbation.

They are also rigid disciplinarians, as the backs of their poor slaves, male and female, sufficiently testify. Thus every country has its customs, and from these customs exceptions are to be made; for I

* Water, Madeira wine, nutmeg, and sugar.

have known ladies in Surinam whose delicacy and polite conversation would have graced the first circles in Europe. Besides the amusements of feasting, dancing, riding, and cards, they have a small theatre, where the inhabitants of fashion act plays for their own amusement and that of their friends. As they are elegant in their dress, so they keep their houses extremely clean. They use the finest linen, exquisitely well washed with Castile soap; its whiteness can only be compared to mountain snow, and would make the best bleached linen in Europe appear like canvas. Their parlour floors are always scoured with sour oranges cut through the middle, which gives the house an agreeable fragrance.

But to return to my narrative. Being once more reconciled to shoes, I visited Colonel Westerloo on board a West-India ship bound for Holland. This gentleman, who had relieved me at Devil's Harwar when I was ill, was now himself in a most miserable condition, having lost the use of his limbs. In this debilitated state, it was doubtful whether anything but the air of his native country would recover him. Several officers were now under the necessity of selling their effects to procure a subsistence, not being able either to procure their pay or allowance from Fourgeoud. I felt this hard usage the less, from the kindness I experienced from my numerous friends.

On the 28th of January, as I was walking in the morning by the river side, I saw a fish brought ashore that deserves to be mentioned for its size and goodness, being sometimes near two hundred pounds weight. It is here called *grow-muneck*, or grey friar, and is said to be of the cod genus, to which it bears some resemblance in shape and colour, the back being a dark olive brown and the belly white; it was soon cut up into large slices, several of which I purchased and sent as presents to my friends, as it was, in my opinion, even superior to turbot. It is an inhabitant of the sea, but is sometimes to be met with in the rivers. The negroes here are the only fishermen, and are regularly trained up to this profession by their masters, who make them pay a certain sum weekly. If they are expert and industrious, they soon acquire money for themselves, and some even become rich; but, on the contrary, if they are indolent and do not fulfil their weekly engagements, they are certain to be punished very severely.

This custom is also common to many other trades, and by perseverance and sobriety they are actually enabled to live happily. Thus I have known slaves in Surinam, who have bought slaves for their own use. Some purchase their freedom from their masters, whilst others keep their money, preferring to be the slave of an indulgent master, being, so long as they continue slaves, free from all duties and taxes which, in case of manumission, they become liable to. A particular instance of this kind was a negro blacksmith, named Joseph, who being offered his liberty upon account of his long and faithful services, positively refused it, choosing rather to be the slave of a worthy master. This man had several slaves of his own, kept a decent house, with handsome furniture and some plate, and when visited by his humane master or mistress, entertained them with sangaree, port or claret. I must, however, acknowledge this to be a very singular instance, and observe that although a few live comfortably at Paramaribo, the greatest number are wretched, particularly those governed by a lady, who have many weals to show, but not the smallest indulgence to boast of.

Among the slaves, those of the class called Quadroons are in general much respected for their affinity to Europeans; a Quadroon being the offspring of a white and a mulatto, and they are very numerous in this colony.

Here one not only meets with the white, the black, and olive, but with

> 'The Samboe dark, and the Mulatto brown,
> The Mæsti fair,* the well-limb'd Quadroon.'

These boys are generally placed out to some good trade, such as cabinet-makers, silversmiths, or jewellers; whilst the girls are employed as waiting-women, and taught the arts of sewing, knitting, and embroidery to perfection: they are generally handsome, and take much pride in the neatness and elegance of their dress.

But to change the subject, the tyranny of our commander, Colonel Fourgeoud, seemed daily to increase. Lieutenant Count Runtwick, who, being sick, was to proceed for Holland with Colonel Westerloo, was ordered to remain in Surinam for having only said that he had been ill treated by him. As a specimen of his justice, I will only observe that all the officers had now subsisted a whole year upon a private soldier's allowance of salt provisions, a few weeks at Paramaribo only excepted. This accommodation cost me thirty pounds, but I have already mentioned he kept back our money, and why should he not our allowance also, it not being the part of a good soldier to enquire after trifles?

On the 2nd of February I received intelligence that Lieutenant Colonel Becquer, scorning any longer to partake of Fourgeoud's bounty, had suddenly given up the ghost, by which in rotation I became possessed of his vacant company. This was some compensation for so much trouble and fatigue. But to counterbalance this good fortune, a certain lady, whose husband had shewn me extraordinary civilities, now made me an offer which I could not with honour

* The offspring of a European and of a Quadroon.

accept. But persisting in my refusal of her favours and golden presents, I at last felt the effects of a woman's hatred and revenge. Her husband, who had lately been so much my friend, and whose honour I, in this instance, so much respected, was suddenly perverted into a bitter enemy. I bore their frowns with resignation, conscious of my own rectitude in not committing a trespass of which too many others would have made a boast. Shortly after, however, this gentleman again became my friend, even more than before this affair happened, having been perfectly undeceived.

On the 6th, a poor drummer of the Society brought me a present of some *alligato*, or more properly *avocado* pears and oranges, for having supported him, he said, in Holland against my servant, who had knocked him down. This trait of gratitude afforded me more pleasure than the coolness of my late friend had given me pain. The avocado pear grows on a tree above forty feet high, and not unlike a walnut-tree: the fruit, about the size and colour of a large pear, a pale green, is the most exquisite, in my opinion, of any in the colony, or even in the world; the inside is yellow and the kernel is enclosed in a soft rind like a chestnut. The pulp is so salubrious and nutritious that it is often called the vegetable marrow, and is frequently eaten with pepper and salt; nor can I compare it to anything so well as a peach, melting in the mouth in the same manner, not so sweet indeed, but incomparably more delicious.

On the 16th, the news arrived that Colonel Fourgeoud, with the remaining troops, having marched from La Rochelle, had been attacked by the rebels, and that, among others, Captain Fredericy, marching in the front, had been shot through both thighs. This brave officer, clapping both his hands on the wounds, and sitting in water up to his breast to conceal the bleeding and prevent his misfortune from discouraging the troops, remained in this situation until the surgeon had dressed them, when he was carried in his hammock by two negroes.

Nothing, indeed, could exceed the zeal which both this officer and Fourgeoud's adjutant, Captain Vangewrike, shewed during the whole expedition. But honour was the only advantage they derived from a five years assiduous and extraordinary attendance. In my opinion, Colonel Fourgeoud never recompensed them according to their merit, while he treated the subalterns, and even some field officers, worse than ever I did my corporals.

I now made another offer to join him in the woods; but instead of permission, he sent me orders to hasten to L'Esperance, in English the Hope estate, as I shall henceforth call it, situated in the upper part of the Comewina, there to take the command of the whole river during his absence. Being new to me, I repaired to this post with the greater satisfaction.

Having provided myself with a complete camp-equipage and purchased provisions, I was soon ready to depart for my new station. But before I leave Paramaribo, I must remark, that during my stay there no less than nine negroes each had a leg cut off, for running away from their masters. This punishment is a part of the Surinam administration of justice, performed at the desire of the proprietor, and executed by a Mr Greuber, the surgeon of the hospital. During this inhuman operation, the poor sufferers very deliberately smoked their pipe of tobacco. For this service the surgeon received about six pounds a limb but, notwithstanding his great abilities, four of them died immediately after the operation. A fifth destroyed himself by plucking away the bandages and bleeding to death during the night. These amputated negroes are common in this colony, and are employed in rowing the boats and barges of their masters. Others are seen deprived of an arm, the forfeit for daring to raise it against a European.

I embarked on the 17th of February for the Hope on board a decent tent-boat rowed by six negroes, having once more bid adieu to my beloved Joanna. In the evening I passed the Sporkesgift estate in the Matapaca Creek; the next day I arrived at Arentrust in Comewina, having passed the Orelana Creek and the fortress Somelsdyk, which is about sixteen miles above Fort Amsterdam, and forms the separation between that and the river Cottica, commanding the two opposite shores by the fire of its cannon.

On the 19th, about noon, I reached the Hope. This estate, where I now took the command, is a valuable sugar plantation, situated on the left side of the Comewina, at the mouth of a rivulet called Bottle Creek, and almost opposite to another creek called Cassivinica: the Bottle Creek communicating with the Comewina and Perica, as the Wana Creek does with the Cottica and Marawina.

Here the troops were lodged in temporary houses built with the manicole-tree, but the situation was so low and marshy as at spring-tides to be entirely under water. The officers were all crowded in one apartment of the same construction, while the planter's fine house, which might have been serviceable for the pleasure and health of these gentlemen, was made use of by nobody but the overseer of the estate.

About a cannon-shot higher up the river is the estate Clarenbeek, where I went, on the 22nd to examine the state of the hospital, and where I found the troops more disagreeably quartered than at the Hope, owing chiefly to the amazing number of rats with which this place was infested, destroying the men's clothes and provisions, and running over their faces by dozens as they lay in their hammocks. The only mode of remedying this horrid inconvenience, was to break holes in the bottoms of quart bottles, and then string them like beads upon the lashings of each hammock, both at head and foot: when this was properly done, their polish rendered it impossible for the rats to reach the canvas.

Here the crowded hospital afforded a melancholy spectacle, and humanity suffers so much from such scenes, that I felt myself happy upon my return to the Hope. My orders here were much the same as they had been at Cottica: to protect the estates from the enemy. The parole or watchword was regularly sent me by Colonel Fourgeoud.

I became daily more charmed with my situation; I was at liberty to breathe freely, and my prospects of future contentment promised amply to compensate for my past hardships and mortifications. Respected as the prince of the river, caressed by the neighbouring planters, who plentifully supplied me with presents of game, fish fruit, and vegetables, I was scarcely the same man, and had very few wishes unsatisfied.

One day (the 5th of March) during my residence here, I was surprised by the waving of a white handkerchief from a tent-boat that was rowing up the river. To augment my happiness, it unexpectedly proved to be my Mulatto, accompanied by her aunt, who now preferred Fauconberg estate, four miles above the Hope, to residing in the town; and to this plantation I immediately accompanied them.

Here Joanna introduced me to a venerable old slave, her grandfather, who made me a present of half a dozen fowls. He was grey-headed and blind, but had been comfortably supported for many years through the kind attention of his numerous offspring. He told me he was born in Africa, where he had once been more respected than any of his Surinam masters ever were in their country.

It will no doubt appear surprising to many of my readers to find me mention this female slave so often, and with so much respect; but I cannot speak with indifference of an object so deserving of attention, and whose affectionate attachment alone counter-balanced all my other misfortunes. Her virtue, youth, and beauty gained more and more my esteem; while the lowness of her birth and condition, instead of diminishing, served to increase my affection.

On the 6th of March I returned to the Hope, loaded with fowls, aubergines, brocoli, agoma, and a few Surinam cherries. The aubergines are a species of fruit which grows in the shape of a cucumber; they are of a purple colour without, and white within; they are cut in slices and eaten like salad, sometimes stewed: they are very good and wholesome. The leaves of the tree which bears this fruit are large and green, covered with a purple-coloured down. The agoma is a bitterish vegetable: the brocoli as in Europe, but scarce. The cherries are ribbed, very sour, and unless very ripe fit only for preserving.

On the Prince of Orange's anniversary, the 8th of March, I invited some company to drink his health, while Colonel Fourgeoud kept scouring the bushes; but the sum of his operations amounted only to having some of his men shot by the negroes, some lost in the woods, while the rebel Cupido escaped with all his chains. Of two men he sent me for the hospital at Clarenbeek, one was terribly cut by the rebels.

I received a present of a haunch of venison on the 17th, and one of my slaves presented me with a lizard called *sapagala*, which is less in size and less agreeable food than the iguana. Of this last dainty I did not partake, but gave it to the overseer, while with the venison I entertained all my officers.

On the 21st, having visited Mr and Mrs Lolkens at Fauconberg, we, after dinner, walked to a brick manufactory, called Appe-cappe, which lies in the neighbourhood and belongs to Governor Nepveu, and where they make as good brick, and as expeditiously, as in Europe. It is also a profitable business, not being common in Surinam. This I only relate as a proof of the abundant advantages of this country where, moreover, the wood for burning the bricks may be had for cutting, if the inhabitants choose to be industrious. We were here, however, so pestered with clouds of insects, called *monpeira*, that I was glad to take my leave and return to the Hope. The monpeira are the smallest kind of gnats, but equally troublesome with the larger species called mosquitoes. They fly so thick and close together that they appear like a cloud of black smoke: they are so small that numbers of them stick in the eyes, whence they cannot be extracted without pain and even danger.

I always visited by water, having at the Hope an elegant tent-boat, with half a dozen negroes at my command, who also shot and fished for me. Upon the whole, I was here so happy and so much respected, that I could almost have engaged never more to change my situation.

12

I HAVE already said that I was happy at the Hope; but how was my felicity augmented, when Mr and Mrs Lolkens came to visit me one evening, and not only gave me the address of Messrs Passalage and Son at Amsterdam, the new proprietors of my Mulatto, but even desired me to take her to the Hope, where she would be more agreeably situated than either at Fauconberg or Paramaribo. This desire was unquestionably most readily complied with by me; and I immediately set my slaves to work, to build a house of manicole-trees for her reception.

In the meantime I wrote the following letter to Messrs Passalage and Son.

GENTLEMEN,

Being informed by Mr Lolkens, the administrator of the estate Fauconberg, that you are the present proprietors, and being under great obligations to one of your Mulatto slaves named Joanna, who is the daughter of the late Mr Kruythoff, particularly for having attended me during sickness, I in gratitude request of you, who are her masters, to let me purchase her liberty without delay; which favour shall be ever thankfully acknowledged, and the money for her ransom immediately paid, by

Gentlemen,

Your most obedient servant,

JOHN GABRIEL STEDMAN,

Captain in Colonel Fourgeoud's
Corps of Marines

This letter was accompanied by another from my friend Lolkens, who much cheered my prospects by the assurance of success.

Having dispatched these letters to Holland, I had now the opportunity of observing the whole process of a sugar plantation, of which I shall endeavour to give an accurate description.

The buildings usually consist of an elegant dwelling-house for the planter, outhouses for the overseer and book-keeper, besides a carpenter's lodge, kitchens, storehouses, and stables, if the sugar-mills be wrought by horses or mules. But on the Hope these are not requisite, as the wheels move by water stored in canals during the spring-tide by means of sluices, which being opened at low water pour out like a deluge and set the machinery in motion. A sugar-mill is built at the expense of four thousand, nay sometimes seven or eight thousand pounds.

Adjoining the mill-house is a large apartment, also built of brick, in which are fixed the coppers or large cauldrons to boil the liquid sugar. These are usually five in number; opposite to these are the coolers, which are large square flat-bottomed wooden vessels, into which the sugar is put from the cauldrons to cool before it is put into hogsheads, which are placed near the coolers upon strong channelled rafters that receive the molasses as it drops from the sugar, and convey it into a square cistern placed underneath to receive it. The distillery joins this apartment, where the dross or scum of the boiling sugar is converted into a kind of rum, mentioned before, and known by the name of *kill-devil*. Every estate in Surinam keeps a tent-boat and several other craft for the conveyance of their produce; they have also a covered dock, to keep them dry and repair them.

The sugar estates in this colony contain five or six hundred acres; the parts for cultivation being divided into squares where pieces of cane, about one foot long, are stuck into the ground in an oblique position, in rows straight and parallel. They usually plant them in the rainy season, when the earth is well soaked and rich. The shoots that spring from these joints are about twelve or sixteen months in arriving at maturity, when they become yellow and are from six to ten feet in height, with pale green leaves like those of a leek, but longer and denticulated, which hang down as the crop becomes ready for cutting. The principal business of the slaves during the growth of the canes is pulling up the weeds, which would otherwise impoverish them.

Some sugar estates have above four hundred slaves. The expense of purchasing these, and erecting the buildings, frequently amounts to twenty or twenty-five thousand pounds sterling, exclusive of the value of the ground.

We shall now examine the progress of the sugar-cane through the mill: here it is bruised between the three cylinders or rollers through which it passes twice, once it enters, and once it returns, when it is changed to trash, and its pithy substance into liquid, which is conducted as extracted through a grooved beam from the mill to the boiling-house, where it is received into a kind of wooden cistern.

So very dangerous is the work of these negroes who attend the rollers, that should one of their fingers be caught between them, which frequently happens through inadvertency, the whole arm is instantly shattered to pieces, if not part of the body. A hatchet is generally kept ready to chop off the limb before the working of the mill can be stopped. Another danger is that should a poor slave dare to taste that sugar which he produces by the sweat of his brow, he runs the risk of receiving some hundred lashes, or having all his teeth knocked out by the overseer. Such are the hardships and dangers to which the sugar-making negroes are exposed.

From the above wooden cistern the liquor is let into the first copper cauldron, filtering through a grating to keep back the trash that may have escaped from the mill; here, having boiled some time and been scummed, it is put into the next cauldron, and so on till in the fifth or last it is brought to a proper thickness or consistency to be admitted into the coolers: a few pounds of lime and alum are thrown into the cauldrons to make it granulate; thus it is boiled gradually stronger and stronger, until it reaches the last cauldron. When it is put into the wooden coolers the sugar is well stirred, and scattered equally throughout the vessels; when cold it has a frozen appearance, being candied, of a brown glazed consistency, not unlike pieces of highly polished walnut-tree. From the coolers it is put into the hogsheads which, upon an average, will hold one thousand pounds weight of sugar; there it settles, and through the crevices and small holes made in the bottoms it is purged of all its liquid contents, which are called molasses and, as I have said, are received in an underground cistern. This is the last operation, after which the sugar is fit for exportation to Europe, where it is refined and cast into loaves. I shall only further observe that the larger the grain the better the sugar, and that no soil can be more proper for its cultivation than Guiana, the richness of which is inexhaustible, and produces upon an average three or four hogsheads per acre. In 1771, no less than twenty-four thousand hogsheads were exported to Amsterdam and Rotterdam only, which, valued at six pounds per hogshead, though it has sometimes sold for double, returned a sum of near one hundred and fifty thousand pounds sterling, besides the vast quantity of molasses and *kill-devil*; the first computed at seven thousand hogsheads, and sold to the North Americans for twenty-five thousand pounds; the second, which is distilled in Surinam and used chiefly by the negroes, valued at as much more, which produces no less than two hundred thousand pounds per annum.*

The *kill-devil* is also drunk by some of the planters, but too much by the common soldiers and sailors and, when new, acts as a slow pernicious poison upon a European constitution. On the contrary, it never hurts the negroes, but is even necessary and wholesome, especially in the rainy seasons when they are sometimes indulged with a single dram per day by their masters, though this custom is far

* The first sugar was refined anno 1659.

from being general. There is no part of this salutary plant useless, the chaff refuse and leaves of the cane being used for manure and fuel. All the estates are closely surrounded by the uncultivated forest, whence the herds of wild deer often commit very great ravages; being surrounded by armed negroes, and dogs set in to disperse them, they are frequently shot. From what I have said upon this subject alone, the reader may form an idea of the riches with which this country abounds; which, nevertheless, did not seem to stimulate its enemies during the late war to attempt the possession of it. But I must say, I doubt whether Surinam, in the hands of any other nation than the Dutch, would not cease to be of its present consequence, the Hollanders being indisputably the most patient, persevering, industrious people that inhabit the globe.

Notwithstanding, however, the immense wealth that the West Indies in general afford, it will ever be my opinion that the Europeans might live as comfortably, if not more healthily, without them; the want of sugar, coffee, cotton, cacao, indigo, rum, and Brazil wood, might be amply supplied by honey, milk, wool, Geneva, ale, English herbs, British oak, etc.

On the 1st of April 1774, Joanna came down the river in the Fauconberg tent-boat, rowed by eight negroes, and arrived at the Hope. I communicated to her immediately the contents of my letter to Holland, which she received with that gratitude and modesty in her looks which spoke more forcibly than any reply. I introduced her to her new habitation, where the plantation slaves, in token of respect, immediately brought her presents of casada, yams, bananas, and plantains, and never two people were more completely happy. Free like the roes in the forest, and disencumbered of every care and ceremony, we breathed the purest ether in our walks, and refreshed our limbs in the limpid stream: health and good spirits were now again my portion, while my partner flourished in youth and beauty, the envy and admiration of all the colony.

Colonel Fourgeoud now intending to quit the woods and encamp at Magdenberg, a post near the source of the Comewina, I sent a large barge with provisions, escorted by an officer and twenty men, to that place; and upon reviewing my remaining marines, they did not amount to twenty men, besides a small detachment at Calis, near the mouth of Cassivinica Creek. Higher up the same creek, at an estate called Cupy, were also posted an officer and a few soldiers.

On the morning of the 4th, I was witness to a very wonderful battle between two snakes, the one about three feet long, the other no more than fourteen inches. After a severe contest of near half an hour, during which time the many wreathings and twistings were truly curious, the largest gradually shifting his grip, at length caught the smallest by the head, and absolutely swallowed him alive.

My negro boy about this time throwing out some red-hot embers, I was surprised to see the frogs eat them with avidity, without receiving any visible damage from the fire, which most probably they had mistaken for the firefly. I saw another frog in the sugar-mill, feasting upon a regiment of ants, which are here very numerous, licking them up with his tongue as they marched before him. Another of these animals slept every day upon one of the beams of my cottage, which it regularly left every night; this was called *yombo-yombo* by the negroes, from its great power in leaping. It is very small, almost flat, a fine yellow with black and scarlet specks, and is frequently found in the upper stories of houses, where it arrives by climbing up the walls. We thought it a pretty little animal, and would allow nobody to hurt it.

On the morning of the 8th, between six and seven o'clock, while we were interring one of my sergeants, we heard the report of several minute guns towards the river Perica, in consequence of which, I immediately detached an officer and twelve men to give assistance. They returned next day with an account that the rebels had attacked the estate of Kortenduur where, after they had pillaged some powder, the plantation slaves, armed by their master, had bravely beaten them back before my assistance could be of use.

A small detachment from Colonel Fourgeoud at Wana Creek arrived at the Hope on the 11th, with September, the negro prisoner, who related that the rebels had spoken to Fourgeoud, and even laughed at him, having overheard him giving his orders not to fire on them, but to take them alive. Among those lost in the woods was the unlucky Schmidt, who had lately been so unmercifully beaten and had never yet recovered.

About the 13th, the spring floods broke down the dams and laid our whole post under water, except the spot where I had pitched my cabin, which remained dry, but unfortunately by this accident the officers and men were up to the knees in water. My worthy friend Mr Heneman, the volunteer, arrived at this time from Colonel Fourgeoud's camp at Wana Creek, with a barge full of men and ammunition; he was now entered a lieutenant in my company. He informed us, that the remaining troops were marching for Magdenberg in Upper Comewina, there to go into quarters. This poor young man was much emaciated with misery and fatigue; I therefore introduced him at his first landing to the care of Joanna, who was a most incomparable nurse, and under her care he felt himself extremely happy.

On the 14th, Colonel Fourgeoud with his troops being arrived at Magdenberg, the officers and privates of the Society, and the rangers to the amount of near two hundred men, were sent down in barges to be stationed on different parts of the river Perica. Some landed at the Hope to refresh, and behaved so very disorderly as to oblige me and my officers to knock them down by half dozens, to keep the peace till they departed the same day. After which I dispatched a tent-boat and eight oars to row the commander in chief with some of his favourites to Paramaribo, from which place he at last permitted the much-injured Count Rantwick to sail for Holland.

Colonel Fourgeoud moved from Magdenberg on the 20th, with all his troops, in order to establish his headquarters nearer the infirmary. His army being in a very sickly condition, he fixed upon the estate called New Rosenback, situated between the Hope and the hospital, for his encampment. Thither I immediately repaired, to pay my respects to the chief; there I saw the remainder of his miserable army landed, and received a further detail of the campaign. I have already mentioned Captain Fredericy's being wounded, one man lost by neglect, another cut and disarmed, the captives running away—chains and all—and the hero scoffed at and ridiculed by his sable enemies. I shall now add that a sick marine was left to die or recover by himself, and that one of the slaves, by bad usage, had his arm broke. The captive negro woman was also gone—never more to return to her conqueror—considerably increased in size from her connection with the troops, and likely to present a new recruit to her dusky monarch. These were the particulars of the last campaign. But I must mention the humanity of a poor slave who, at every hazard, deserted Fourgeoud to attend the dying marine, and having performed the last sad office of friendship, returned to receive his punishment, but to his infinite surprise he was pardoned.

In justice to Colonel Fourgeoud I must say that upon such expeditions, and in such a climate, many of these accidents cannot be prevented; and that while he killed his troops by scores without making captures on the enemy, he nevertheless did the colony considerable service by disturbing, hunting, and harassing the rebels, and destroying their fields and provisions. For it is certain no negro will ever return to settle in those haunts from which he has been once expelled. Colonel Fourgeoud's partaking personally in every danger and fatigue at his age, must make some amends for the other faults that stained his character, and may even serve, in some measure, to establish his reputation as a man of patience and fortitude. It would give me infinitely more pleasure to write nothing but in his praise; but truth, and the general benefit of mankind, requires that while I display his good qualities I also point out his failings, as they may serve to correct others, and by these means even his vices may be rendered useful.

On the 21st, several officers came to visit me at the Hope, whom I entertained with a fish dinner. We were very happy, and my guests perfectly satisfied with their entertainment. But on the morning of the 22nd my poor Joanna, who had been our cook, was attacked with a violent fever and desired to be removed to Fauconberg, there to be attended by one of her female relations. This I complied with, but on the evening of the 25th she was so extremely ill that I determined to visit her myself. This I would do as privately as possible, since Fourgeoud was to visit me at the Hope the next day and his satirical jokes upon such an occasion I could very well dispense with. I also knew the most laudable motives were no protection against the ungovernable sallies of his temper.

I had to pass close to his post, but I, however difficult the undertaking, was, like another Leander determined to cross the Hellespont. Having informed my friend Heneman, I set out about eleven at night in my own barge, but coming opposite New Rosenback, I heard Fourgeoud's voice very distinctly, as he walked on the beach with some other officers. Immediately the boat was hailed by a sentinel, and ordered to come ashore. I now thought all was over, but, persisting to the last, I told the negroes to answer *Killestyn Nova*, the name of an adjoining plantation, and thus got leave to proceed unmolested. Soon afterwards I arrived safe at Fauconberg, and found my dearest friend much better.

But on the 26th, in the morning, mistaking the daylight for moonshine, I overslept myself and knew not how to return to the Hope, as my barge and negroes could now not pass without being well known to the Colonel. Delay was useless, so out I set, trusting entirely to the ingenuity of my slaves, who put me ashore just before we came in sight of the headquarters. One of them then escorted me through the woods, and I arrived safe at the Hope. But here my barge soon followed under a guard, and all my poor slaves prisoners, with an order from Fourgeoud for me to flog every one of them, as they had been apprehended without a pass, while their excuse was that they had been out fishing for their *Masera*.

Their fidelity to me upon this occasion was truly astonishing, as they all declared they would have preferred to be cut in pieces rather than betray the secrets of so good a master. However, the danger was soon over, as I confirmed what they had said, and added that the fish were intended to *regale the hero*; after which I made a donation of two gallons of rum among my sable privy-counsellors. This passage, however trifling, may serve as a sample not only of European weakness, but of African firmness and resolution.

Notwithstanding my preparation, still Colonel Fourgeoud did not visit me on the 27th, but the next morning Joanna arrived, accompanied by a stout black who was her uncle, and whose arm was decorated with a silver band on which were engraved these words: 'True to the Europeans.' This man, who was named Cojo, had voluntarily fought against the rebels, before his companions, by the inhuman treatment of Mr D. B. and his overseer, had been forced to join them. Holding a little girl, called Tamera, by the hand he related to us the following remarkable story. 'This child's father,' said he, 'is one whose name is Jolly Coeur, the first captain of Baron's men and, not without cause, one of the fiercest rebels in the forest, as he has lately shown on the neighbouring estate of New Rosenback, where your colonel now commands. On that estate one Schults, a Jew, was the manager at the time when the rebels suddenly appeared and took possession of the whole plantation. Having tied the hands of Schults and plundered the house, they next began feasting and dancing, before they thought proper to end his miserable existence. In this deplorable situation the victim lay, only waiting Baron's signal for death, when his eyes chanced to catch Jolly Coeur's and he addressed him nearly in the following words: "O Jolly Coeur, now remember Mr Schults, who was once your deputy-master; remember the dainties I gave you from my own table when you were only a child, and my favourite, my darling, among so many others: remember this, and now spare my life by your powerful intercession." The reply of Jolly Coeur was memorable—I remember it perfectly well. "But you, O tyrant, recollect how you ravished my poor mother and flogged my father for coming to her assistance. Recollect that the shameful act was perpetrated in my infant presence. Recollect this—then die by my hands, and next be damn'd." Saying this, he severed his head from his body with a hatchet at one blow, and having played at bowls with it upon the beach, he next cut the skin with a knife from his back and spread it over one of the cannon to keep the priming dry.' Thus ended the history of Mr Schults; Cojo, with young Tamera, departed, and left me to go, with an increased impatience, to receive the news that I was soon to expect from Amsterdam of when the deserving Joanna should be free from the villainy of such pests of human nature.

On the 28th, Colonel Fourgeoud arrived about ten o'clock with one of his officers, and with the very devil painted in his countenance, which much alarmed me. I, however, instantly introduced him to my cottage, where he no sooner saw my mate, than the clouds (like a vapour by the sun) were dispelled from his gloomy forehead, and I must confess, that I never saw him behave with more civility.

Having entertained him in the best manner we were able, and now related the story of the Hellespont, he laughed heartily at the stratagem, and giving us both a shake by the hand departed to New Rosenback, in good-humour and perfectly contented. From all the preceding circumstances, the above chapter may be stiled the golden age of my West India expedition.

13

HAVING delayed his departure to the 29th of April, Colonel Fourgeoud now finally rowed down for Paramaribo, accompanied by a few of his officers, to refresh themselves, while the remaining emaciated troops (which were melted down to a very small number, and unfit, till recruited in their constitutions, for any further military service) greatly required some rest. Just before the chief's departure, he sent me (who now commanded the river) the following very curious instructions which, as a proof of his generalship, I cannot help inserting. Among others, 'to ask the planters if the rebels were come to their estates, in which case to attack and drive them away, but not to follow them unless I was sure that I certainly should conquer them; for any miscarriage I should be called to an account.' In plain English: 'if I attacked the enemy without success, I must be punished, and if I did not attack them at all, I was to be called to account for neglect of duty.' However judicious the other articles I had received, I could not help thinking the above so very absurd that I immediately returned them back by an officer, and had the good fortune to get them changed into common sense.

How happy was I at this time in particular, who wanted for nothing, and who had such an agreeable partner constantly near me, whose sweet conversation was divine music to my ears, and whose presence banished every languor and hardship from my mind!

Thus I spent the most agreeable hours, constantly accompanied by my young mulatto, upon this Elysian plantation. But alas! all at once, in the midst of my hopes, my truly halcyon days were blasted, and I was almost plunged into despair by receiving the fatal news of the death of Mr Passalage at Amsterdam, to whom I had written to obtain my mulatto's manumission. What redoubled my distress was the situation in which she proved to be, promising fair to become a mother in the space of a few months. It was now that I saw a thousand horrors intrude all at once upon my dejected spirits; not only my friend but my offspring to be a slave, and a slave under such a government! Mr Passalage, on whom I relied, dead—the whole estate going to be sold to a new master—I could not bear it, and was totally distracted; nay, must have died of grief, had not the mildness of her temper supported me by suggesting the flattering hopes that Lolkens would still be our friend. In the midst of these reflections, on the evening of the 4th, we heard the report of several alarm-guns towards the north-east, on which, by daybreak next morning, I sent a detachment to the Perica, which returned about noon with the account of the rebels attacking the estate Merseille, in the river Cottica, but they had been beaten back by the plantation slaves, as they had before by those of Kortenduur. The other news was that they had ill treated a party of poor Indians, suspecting them to have assisted the estates in making their defence; also that, at Paramaribo, an insurrection was discovered among the negroes, who had determined to join the rebels, after first having massacred all the inhabitants; that, however, they were detected, and the ringleaders executed.

On the morning of the 6th, we again heard several musket-shot in the woods, which apprehending to be some European party that had lost their way, I made my sentinel answer the signals of distress by firing his piece alternately with theirs, shot for shot, to which I added two drums that kept beating for several hours without intermission as the report of their fire-arms gradually approached nearer and nearer. At length appeared a Society sergeant and six privates that belonged to Reedwyk in Perica, and had been lost in the forest for three days, nearly starved, without hammocks, meat, or drink, excepting water. Having refreshed them in the best manner I was able, they all recovered to my very great satisfaction, though one of them remained perfectly blind for several hours, with the sting of a kind of wasp, known in this country by the name of *marobonso*. The only thing that I can say of them is that they are extremely large, live in hollow trees, are the strongest of the bee kind, and sting so violently that the pain is excruciating, and always occasion a fever.

Having, on the 12th, swam twice across the river Cottica, which is above half a mile broad, I came home in a shiver, and next day had an intermitting fever. By abstaining, however, from animal food, and using plenty of acid with my drink, I had no doubt of getting well in a few days; the more so, as tamarinds grew here in profusion.

Indeed, on the 16th, I was almost perfectly recovered (weakness excepted) when about ten in the morning, as I was sitting with Joanna before my cottage, I had an unexpected visit from a Mr Steger, who happened to be one of our surgeons. After having felt my pulse, and examined my tongue, he declared without ceremony that I should be dead before the morrow, unless without further delay I made use of his prescription. I acknowledge the sentence staggered me so much that, though at other times I never used medicines at all, I instantly swallowed the dose which he had prepared for me in a tumbler, without hesitation, but almost as instantly I dropped down on the ground.

In this manner I lay till the 20th, being four days before I came to my senses, when I found myself stretched on a mattress in my little house, with poor Joanna sitting by me alone, and bathed in tears. She begged me at that time to ask no questions, for fear of hurting my spirits, but next day related to me the dismal transaction. The moment I fell, four strong negroes had taken me up, and by her direction placed me where I now was; the surgeon having put blisters on several parts of my body, had finally declared that I was dead and had suddenly left the plantation. A grave and coffin were ordered for my burial on the 17th, which she had prevented by dropping upon her knees to implore a delay. She had then dispatched a black to her aunt at Fauconberg for wine-vinegar and a bottle of old Rhenish, with the first of which she had constantly bathed my temples, wrists, and feet, by keeping without intermission five wet handkerchiefs tied about them, while with a teaspoon she had found means to make me swallow a few drops of the wine mulled. During all that time I had lain motionless, while she had day and night, by the help of Quaco and an old negro, attended me, still hoping for my recovery. To all this I could only answer by the tear of sympathy that started from my eyes, and a feeble squeeze of my hand.

I had, however, the good fortune to recover, but so slowly that, notwithstanding the great care that was taken of me by that excellent young woman (to whom alone I owed my life), it was the 15th of June before I could walk by myself, during all which time I was carried by two negroes on a species of chair supported on two poles like a sedan, and fed like an infant, being so lame and enervated that I was not able to bring my hand to my mouth. Poor Joanna (who had suffered too much on my account) was for several days following very ill herself.

Great was the change from what I had been but so shortly before—then the most healthy and most happy in body and mind, and now depressed to the lowest ebb, in my constitution and my spirits. My friend Heneman, who visited me every day, at this time told me that he had discovered the medicine which had so nearly killed me to be only tartar-emetick and ipecacuanha, but in too great a quantity—four grains of the first, mixed with forty grains of the latter—the surgeon having measured my constitution by my size, which is above six feet. I was so much incensed at this piece of stupidity that, on the 4th of June, having drunk his Britannic Majesty's health in a rummer of Madeira, and the fatal surgeon coming to make me a bow, he no sooner put his foot on the landing-place where I was sitting in my palanquin or chair, than, having previously clubbed one of the poles that carried me upon my shoulder, I let it fall upon his guilty pericranium, my strength being as yet too feeble to aim a blow. The poor fellow no sooner felt the weight of the pole, than forgetting the rest of his compliments, he skipped back into his boat with all expedition and to our no small entertainment, as fast as the negroes could row him.

About this time, while the troops were doing nothing, two of the bravest men in the colony, Captain Fredericy and the militia captain, Stoelman, with the rangers, entered the woods. They killed three or four of the rebels, and took a few more prisoners who had been starving for want of subsistence ever since Fourgeoud had ransacked the surrounding forest and destroyed their fields. In the creek Patamaca, two rebel negroes, attempting to plunder Mr Winey's plantation, were shot by his slaves, who sent their right hands barbecued to Paramaribo.

Being still so weak that I was unfit for any duty, even at the Hope, I now surrendered the command of that post to the next officer in rank. Expecting that a change of air would be beneficial to me, I went, with the previous knowledge of Colonel Fourgeoud, on a visit to a neighbouring estate, called Egmond, where the planter, Monsieur de Cachelieu, a French gentleman, had given me, with Joanna, my boy Quaco, and a white servant, a most hearty invitation. At this place I was extremely comfortable, and nothing could be better calculated for my speedy recovery than this Frenchman's hospitality and good-humour. How inconsistent with this was his injustice and severity to his slaves! For instance, two young negroes, who well deserved a flogging by breaking in and robbing their master's storehouse, came off with a few lashes; while two old ones, for a trifling dispute, were each condemned to receive no less than three hundred.

On my asking the cause of this partiality, I was answered by Monsieur de Cachelieu, that the young ones had still a very good skin and might do much work, whereas the old ones had long been disfigured, worn out, and almost unfit for any service; nay, that killing them altogether would be a benefit to the estate. At Arentrust, a few plantations lower down, some days before, a poor negro was sent with a letter from his proprietor to the manager there. This last, not liking the contents, gave the messenger four hundred lashes, telling the innocent man, at the same time, to carry that for the answer to his master.

But to return to my French host (who was, in this alone excepted, as polite, hospitable, and well-bred a man as ever I would wish to converse with) I must mention that nothing could be better than the oranges and china apples that I found on his estate.

Nor ought I to forget his excellent French wines, which were perfectly unadulterated and truly delicious, particularly his muscadel. But in spite of all these good things, I still continued a valetudinarian, being oppressed with weakness and indigestion. Thus, in hopes that exercise on horseback might do me good, I determined to take leave of my hospitable French friend, and ask leave of absence to go for some time to Paramaribo.

In consequence, on the 9th, Colonel Fourgeoud arriving in the river at the estate Cravassibo and expecting soon to renew his manoeuvres, I, on the 10th, wrote him a letter for the above purpose, and also for above six months' pay which was due to me. I was answered, on the 12th, not only with a negative to both my requests, which had been granted to other officers, but in so truly impertinent a style as I could not, even from himself, have expected—such as calling in question my zeal, though he knew I was sick, and refusing me my own money, or even the proper remedies and means of recovering. This incensed me so much that I wrote him a second letter, to let him know I was incapable of doing or asking anything unbecoming my character, but on the contrary (ill as I was) ready to give him such proofs of my honour as should leave him no further room to doubt of it, should he be pleased to put it to the proof. This epistle, weak and unfit as I was for service, I followed in person two days after, with my French friend Cachelieu for my companion and voucher, who gave me the use of his tilt-barge with eight oars for the purpose.

On our arrival I expected to see Fourgeoud raging with resentment, and that he would put me under an arrest and ask an explanation of our last correspondence. But I dreaded not the worst that he could do after the many trials to ruin me which he had already put in execution, and death itself was almost preferable to his cruelty.

Monsieur de Cachelieu and I, however, were both disappointed. He not only took us politely by the hand, but solicited us to dine with him as if nothing had happened. But this affectation I despised, and with contempt refused to accept of his invitation, in which I was followed by the French planter. When, in my turn, I enquired for the cause of his refusing my request, and sending me so strange a letter, this was the answer—that thirty or forty of the Ouca negroes, who were our allies by treaty, had deceived him in doing nothing while they had been in the woods and during the time he had been at Paramaribo; that he was in consequence determined to push on the war with double vigour, on which account he had not only forbidden me to go to town, but had since ordered even all the sick officers to come up and to follow the enemy, while they had strength or breath remaining, not so much as leaving one at Paramaribo to guard the colours and the regiment's chest, which had both been left to the care of a quartermaster. This, indeed, was literally the fact; but to this he might safely, and without hurting his conscience, have added the inveteracy of his disposition with which he had determined to persecute me and some others to annihilation. I ought to mention that it was not till about this time that he issued orders to be observed on a march, and that previous to this everything was performed in perfect hurry and confusion, which indeed even afterwards was too frequently the case.

Having now been near two months on the estate Egmond, where I could not recover, and not being permitted to go to Paramaribo, I preferred returning back again to take the command at the Hope.

At the Hope I found my friend Mr Heneman (who was now made a captain) very sick, with several others. All these, as well as myself, were left without a surgeon, medicines, or money, while, as I stated before, the many hogsheads of wine sent from Amsterdam, together with scores of kegs containing preserved vegetables and other fresh provisions, were for ever kept invisible from the poor, emaciated, and languishing troops, for whom they had certainly been intended by that city. I indeed here made one more attempt to recover our property, but to no purpose; money, medicines, wine, and refreshments, were all kept back. Thus did we continue to pine and lose strength, instead of gaining it. I mean the greatest part of us: as for myself, I had the least cause to complain, being well attended by Joanna and my servants (who the next day all arrived from Egmond) besides receiving presents, which were as usual sent me from all quarters. One additional inconvenience I felt however—my feet were infested with chigoes, which I partly impute to having, during my illness, worn stockings and shoes.

On the 21st I received a letter from the commander-in-chief, not an answer to my last, but orders to send him up to the estate Cravassibo (which was at present his headquarters) all the provisions, kettles, axes, etc. that could be spared from the Hope, as he was preparing to re-enter the woods. I accordingly dispatched them the next day; but the supply of victuals was not great, for a whole barge, with beef and pork, bound for the Hope, had been shipwrecked in the river.

On the 25th Mr Steger, the surgeon who had so nearly poisoned me that I could not yet get the better of the effects of his ignorance, was discharged from the regiment, as incapable of his profession. Still, notwithstanding my unsettled state of health, as several officers were going to join Fourgeoud about this time, and weak as I was, I entreated once more to be one of the party. But on the morning of the 26th, his adjutant, with another surgeon, visiting all the troops that were in Comewina, I was deemed totally incapable of supporting the

Manner of sleeping in the forest

Rural retreat—the cottage

fatigue: indeed so much so, that relapsing on the 29th, I was even glad to be superseded in the command of the river by the major, Mr Medlar, who arrived at the Hope this day for that purpose. Nevertheless I was condemned to linger at this place, while one month at Paramaribo might have perfectly recovered me.

On the 11th of September, Fourgeoud at last broke up from Cravassibo and, with all the able troops he could collect (which were now not much more than one hundred) he again marched into the forest after the enemy.

On the 19th of this month in the forenoon, a herd of wild swine, called *pingos* (more than two hundred in number), having lost their way in the forest, came to the Hope, galloping over the plantation, when above a score of them were killed by the negroes who knocked them down with their bill-hooks and axes. The *pingos* are about the size of our English small hogs; they are black, and have coarse bristles thinly scattered; they live in herds of sometimes above three hundred, in the thickest parts of the forest, and run always in a line, the one closely following the other. When the foremost or leader is shot, the line is instantly broken, and the whole herd is in confusion; for which reason the Indians take care (if possible) to knock their captain on the head before the rest; after this the others even often stand still, stupidly looking at one another, and allowing themselves to be killed one by one, of which I have been a witness. They do not attack the human species, nor make any resistance at all, like the European wildboar, when wounded.

On the morning of the 29th, we again heard the report of several guns towards the river Cottica, where it since appeared the rebels were a second time beaten back from the plantation Merseille by the fidelity and bravery of the slaves belonging to that estate.

On the 8th of the succeeding month, we received the news that Colonel Fourgeoud, having discovered and destroyed some fields belonging to the enemy (who had again kept up a distant conversation with him) and having found the mangled remains of poor Schmidt, who had been murdered by the rebels, was once more come with his troops to Magdenberg, where he encamped till the eleventh. He then re-entered the forest, previously sending to the Hope the sick, and with them a young officer under arrest, in order to be tried for not being able to undergo the fatigues as well as himself. In other words, having been ordered to watch two days and two nights, the youth had proved unequal to the task, and had dropped asleep under arms as he was sitting on the ground. The climate indeed was such that even without these trials nature was often overcome.

The preservation of Fourgeoud's vigour hitherto may, in a great measure, be attributed to his continually drinking a medicine he called *tisan*, in large full basins. This had a most nauseous taste, and was composed of the jesuits bark, cream of tartar, and stick-liquorice, boiled together, which he drank as hot as he could bear it. Having accustomed his constitution to it, he could not do without it. In this, however, he was followed by none of the rest, as they were apprehensive that when this should once cease to operate (which it must at last), all other medicines in time of real need would be ineffectual. As for my own part, I still continued to be so exceedingly weak, that I almost despaired of evermore recovering; while my depressed spirits, on account of Joanna's critical and almost hopeless situation, greatly contributed to prevent the restoration of my health. These alarms were not diminished on the 21st, when, being visited by Mr and Mrs Lolkens at the Hope, this gentleman told me that the whole estate Fauconberg was again transferred, with its dependants; that the new proprietor was a Mr Lude of Amsterdam, with whom he had not the smallest interest; and that there was in town a general report that we had both been poisoned. This sentence was, however, greatly alleviated by the kindness of his lady, who insisted that my Joanna should accompany her to Paramaribo immediately, where, at her own house, she should meet with every care and attention that her situation could require, till perfectly recovered. For this I thanked her in the best manner I was able, and poor Joanna wept with gratitude. Having therefore conducted them as far as their estate Killestyn-Nova, where we dined, I took my leave of them and Joanna, and bid them all an affectionate farewell for the present.

At my return to the Hope, my indignation was scarcely to be restrained within the bounds of prudence, when I found myself upbraided by my mess-mates for taking care of my own offspring: 'Do as we do, Stedman,' said they, 'and never fear. If our children are slaves, they are provided for; and if they die, what care we, should they be d—n'd in the bargain? Therefore keep your sighs in your own belly, and your money in your pocket, my boy, that's all.' I repeat this in their own language, to show how much my feelings must have been hurt and disgusted with similar consolation.

The following morning, awaking by daybreak in my hammock, the first thing that I saw, when looking up, was a snake about two yards long, hanging with its head downwards like a rope, and straight above my face, from which he was not one foot distance, while his tail was twisted round the rafters under the thatch. Observing his eyes bright as stars, and his forked tongue in agitation, I was so distressed that I scarcely had power to avoid him, which however I did by running out. After this, I heard a rustling in the dry thatch, where the negroes attempted to kill him, but in vain, he having escaped, and thus I cannot say what species he belonged to. Being now by myself, and rather startled by this unwelcome guest, I shut up my house and lodged and messed with my friends the major, Heneman, and Macdonald.

On visiting my boxes, I now found that great depredations had been committed by the ants, which are throughout all Guiana so very numerous, and of so many different species, that once I had a pair of new cotton stockings perfectly destroyed by them in one night only. Those which frequent the estates are generally small, but very troublesome. The only way possible to keep them from the refined sugar, is by hanging the loaf to the ceiling on a nail, and making a ring of dry chalk around it, very thick, which crumbles down the moment the ants attempt to pass it.

My friend Captain Van Coeverden, at this time marching in the woods, suffered a much worse depredation at Paramaribo, where not the ants, but the negro-slaves, had broken open his boxes and robbed him of all his best effects and near twenty guineas in money.

On the 6th, a marine drowned himself, in one of those frenzy fevers which are so common in Guiana. About the same time another Society soldier was shot by order of a court-martial. Thus perished those men who were spared by the climate or the enemy.

Having written to a Mr Seifke to enquire whether it was not in the power of the Governor and Council to relieve a gentleman's child from bondage, provided there was paid to its master such a ransom as their wisdom should judge adequate, I received for answer, that no money or interest could purchase its freedom without the proprietor's consent, since, according to law, it was just as much a slave as if it had been born in Africa and imported from the coast of Guinea. This information now perfectly completed my misery, and I at last had recourse to drinking, which temporary relief, however, only caused my spirits to flow higher, in order to make them sink lower after its evaporation. During this conflict it happened that I was invited with the Major to dine at an estate called Knoppemonbo, in the Casavinica Creek, where a Mr de Graav, the proprietor, did everything in his power to amuse me, but to no purpose. At last, seeing me seated by myself on a small bridge that led to a grove of orange-trees, with a settled gloom on my countenance, he accosted me, and taking me by the hand, to my astonishment, pronounced the following words:

'Sir, I am acquainted by Mr Lolkens with the cause of your just distress. Heaven never left a good intention unrewarded. I have now the pleasure to acquaint you that Mr Lude has chosen *me* for his administrator, and that from this day I shall pride myself in making it my business to render you any service with that gentleman, as well as the virtuous Joanna, whose deserving character has attracted the attention of so many people, while your laudable conduct redounds to your lasting honour throughout the colony.'

No angel descending from above could have brought me a more welcome message, and no criminal under sentence of death could have received a reprieve with greater joy. The weight of a mill-stone was removed from my labouring breast, and having made Mr de Graav repeat his promise, I felt I should yet be happy. Soon after this I was surrounded by several gentlemen and ladies, to whom my friend had communicated his generous intentions. They congratulated me on my sensibility, and on having met with so valuable an acquaintance. All seemed to partake in the pleasure that I now felt; and the day being spent in mirth and conviviality, I returned to the Hope much better pleased than when I left it. Next day the whole company was entertained by Major Medlar, nor did we separate, or cease feasting up and down the river, till the 13th, when we once more spent the day at Knoppemonbo.

Here Mr de Graav, having bought some new slaves, gave a holiday to all the negroes on his estate, and here I had the opportunity of seeing the diversions peculiar to that people. But of these I must reserve the particular account to another occasion, and for the present only give a short description of the Loango dancing, as performed by the Loango negroes, male and female, and not by any others; it consists from first to last in such a scene of wanton and lascivious gestures, as nothing but a heated imagination and a constant practice could enable them to perform. These dances, which are performed to the sound of a drum to which they strike time by clapping of hands, may properly be considered as a kind of play or pantomime divided into so many acts, which lasts for some hours. But the most remarkable is, that during this representation, the actors, instead of being fatigued, become more and more enlivened and animated, till they are bathed in sweat like post-horses, and their passions wound up to such a degree, that nature being overcome, they are ready to drop into convulsions.

However indelicate the above exhibitions may be, fashion has rendered them no more disgusting than any other diversions to the European and Creole ladies who, in company with the gentlemen, crowd about them without the least reserve, to enjoy what they call a hearty laugh; while such scenes would change an English woman's face from white to scarlet.

On the 14th I returned to the Hope, where I saw my cottage unroofed by a storm. But now, expecting no more to inhabit it, I permitted it to go to ruin. Be that as it may, I had passed in it the happiest days of my whole lifetime.

On the 26th Colonel Fourgeoud marched once more to the Wana

Creek, but having taken the troops from the Jew Savannah, the rebels availed themselves of their absence, and not only pillaged a plantation in the river Surinam, but burnt several dwellings in the Creek Casavinica. From the above river they were bravely pursued by a feeble Society detachment, which chanced to be there, but without success; two soldiers were killed, and Mr Negle their leader, with several others, wounded. The major now broke up the new post formed at Oranjebo, which he also dispatched after the enemy; but having ranged a whole week in the forest, they also returned without any manner of success. These frequent miscarriages evince how difficult it is for European troops to carry on a war in the forests of South America.

The 30th of this month being the anniversary of St Andrew, and now finding myself in excellent spirits, I roasted a whole sheep, with which I entertained all the officers on the Hope, as well as with a couple of gallons of good Jamaica rum in punch, which we drunk to the healths of all our friends on the old continent. This festivity I repeated on December the 4th, on receiving the tidings that my Joanna was delivered of a strong and beautiful boy. That very morning I dispatched another letter to Mr Lude at Amsterdam, to obtain her manumission, couched much in the same terms as that which I had written to his predecessor Mr Passalage, only praying for dispatch, as I was now uncertain how much longer the expedition was to last. In this request I was again seconded by my new friend Mr de Graav, as I had been before by Mr Lolkens. Afterwards I entertained the sick with a dozen of old Rhenish received from the former gentleman, which had been in his cellar since 1726.

Walking round the plantation the morning of the 10th with my gun, I found the whole of the slaves on the estate in a mutiny, on account of the cruel usage inflicted by the managers: happily for all parties the interference of the military soon ended this matter to mutual satisfaction. These frequent disturbances, which I have at different times mentioned, plainly indicate the inclination of the negroes to break out in an open rebellion, and this would certainly have been more often attempted had they not been awed by the troops.

On the 11th the estate Rectwyk in Perica was attacked, but the enemy was beaten back by the military.

Colonel Fourgeoud being now again arrived at Magdenberg, and I at last, being perfectly recovered after seven months' illness, I ventured to propose, by another letter to the commander, that I might accompany him on his future excursions in the woods, or go for some time to Paramaribo; but neither the one or the other request was yet granted. In this situation I wrote a letter to town, to inform my poor friend that I was well, with which I went to the riverside to look out for a boat, and towards noon hailed the tent-barge belonging to Fauconberg, which was rowing with the overseer to Paramaribo. This was, unfortunately, a new superintendent and, not knowing me, he refused to come ashore for the message. However, seeing the negroes rest upon their oars, I took the letter in my teeth and leaped instantly into the river. Having swum with the stream, in my shirt and trousers, till I came within two oars' length of the boat, I held up the letter in my hand, and called out, 'Who the devil are you, that refuse to take on board a piece of paper?' Being answered in French, 'Je suis Jean Bearnee, paysan de Guascogne, à votre service,' I had the mortification to see them pull away without a possibility of overtaking them, or of returning. In this distress I had now nothing left but to perish, it being impossible to swim against the stream, especially as I was incumbered with my clothes. I struggled, however, but sank twice to the bottom in the attempt, and must inevitably have been drowned had I not caught hold of a projecting paling that was erected in the river for the purpose of catching fish. To this I remained sticking fast, while a Dutch carpenter, who observed me from the top of the sugar-mill, called out that the English captain was trying to kill himself.

On this news a dozen stout negroes immediately leapt into the river and, having dragged me safe ashore (under the direction of my good friend Medlar, who was inclined to believe the report), lifted me upon their shoulders to carry me home. The disappointment, the danger, the anger, vexation, and shame (for there was no contradicting them) had by this time wound up my passions to such a height, and made such an impression on my spirits, that I became perfectly mad, and had almost perpetrated the act of which I was accused. On crossing over a small bridge, I gave a sudden twist and, from their shoulders, threw myself with a jerk headlong over the balustrades once more into the water. Here a second time I was picked up by the negroes, and now the suspicion being confirmed that I intended suicide, I was put to my hammock, with two sentinels appointed to guard me during the night, while several of my friends were shedding tears around me. Having, however, drank some mulled wine, I enjoyed a sound nap till morning. Then, appearing calm and perfectly composed, my words, to my great joy, began to gain credit, and the apprehensions of my companions were dispelled. Such was the danger to which I was exposed by the unkind and inhospitable behaviour of this Frenchman, who nearly obliterated the memory of this transaction by his many succeeding instances of unprecedented brutality. The following day, however, by one of my negroes and a small canoe, I sent my letter to Paramaribo.

On the 16th another officer arrived from our hero under an arrest for the crime of contending with the free negro Geusary for a bunch of plantains. This young man was afterwards sent to Europe by Fourgeoud, in expectation that he would be broken by a court-martial; but, after a very short confinement, he was honourably acquitted, to the joy of the whole corps and the mortification of this hectoring Swiss. Such was the inveteracy of this old gentleman, who had not the smallest consideration for the foibles of youth, and who constantly saw the mote in the eye of his neighbour, overlooking the beam that appeared so conspicuously in his own.

Obtaining my friend Medlar's concurrence, I now took a trip on the 18th to Paramaribo, where I found my boy bathing in Madeira wine and water,* while his mother was happy and perfectly recovered. Having seen them well and presented Joanna with a gold medal that my father had given my mother on the day of my birth, also thanked Mrs Lolkens for her very great kindness, I immediately returned to the Hope, where I arrived on the 22nd.

The poor negro whom I had sent before me with a letter had been less fortunate than I was, having his canoe overset in the middle of the river Surinam, by the roughness of the water. With great address, however, he kept himself in an erect posture (for this man could not swim), and by the buoyancy and resistance of the boat against his feet, he was enabled just to keep his head above the water, while the weight of his body kept the sunk canoe from moving. In this precarious attitude, he was picked up by a man-of-war's boat, who, taking away the canoe for their trouble, put him on shore at Paramaribo. He kept the letter, however surprising, still in his mouth, and being eager to deliver it, he accidentally ran into a wrong house, where, being taken for a thief (for refusing to let them read it), he was tied up to receive four hundred lashes; fortunately he was reprieved by the intercession of an English merchant of the name of Gordon, who was my particular friend, and knew the negro. Thus did the poor fellow escape drowning and being flogged, either of which he would have undergone sooner than disclose what he called the secrets of his *masera*.

But I must once more return to the operations of our commander in chief, who having rested a few days at Magdenberg, again marched, on Christmas Day, with the remaining handful of his men, to the Jew Savannah, whence he returned (having seen nothing) back to Magdenberg, with the new title of being himself the wandering Jew. This did not prevent me and Major Medlar from renewing our solicitations to accompany him in his expeditions; but we were still

* This, however uncommon it may appear to a European, is often practised in Surinam by such as can afford it, among which class was the hospitable Mrs Lolkens, who generously presented Joanna with the wine.

prevented by his going to town, where about this time a fresh supply of troops was hourly expected to arrive from Europe. At last, however, he gave me leave to follow him, with some other officers who were actually in want, at a time when fifteen hogsheads of fine claret, and fifteen thousand florins in specie, were waiting his commands at Paramaribo.

14

On the 18th of January 1774, I at last bid farewell to the Hope, slept at the estate Arentrust, and next day dined at the beautiful plantation Catwyk. In the evening I rowed to Paramaribo with the ebb tide, which gave me an opportunity of seeing the mangroves that line the banks of the river Surinam full of oysters, stuck in the branches like fruit, from the water's edge up to high-water mark. These oysters attaching themselves to trees as they do to rocks, has given rise to the vulgar error that they grow or vegetate like fruit. At some distance they look like mushrooms and are indeed very small and trifling; for one hundred are not comparable to one dozen that come from Colchester. In Surinam are also a kind of mussels, but these are so small and insipid that they are scarcely worthy of mention.

On the 25th a great number of Indians, or natives, arrived at Paramaribo, which afforded me an opportunity of seeing and describing this people, who are the aborigines of the country. All these tribes of Indians are in general of a copper-colour; while the negroes of Africa, that live under the same degree of latitude, are perfectly black. This, however inconceivable it may appear, is easily accounted for, when one considers that the American Indians in Guiana are constantly refreshed by the cooling sea breeze, or easterly wind, that blows between the tropics, and that those who dwell in Terra-Firma and Peru, on the West coast, enjoy that same easterly breeze, still kept cool by the great chain of inland mountains over which it passes, and which have their summits perpetually covered with snow. The inhabitants of Africa, south of the river Senegal, get the same east wind rather heated than cooled, because of the prodigious quantity of inland, hot, sandy deserts over which it passes.

This is the most probable reason why the Americans are of a copper-colour or red, and the inhabitants of Africa, called Negroes, are black, not because they are two distinct races of people: no person who examines and reflects, can avoid seeing that there is but one race of people on the earth, who differ from each other only according to the soil and the climate in which they live. I am further of opinion, that these aborigines, or Indian natives, will appear to have still less title to be called a distinct people from those of the old continent, when we consider the proximity of Russia to North America, whence apparently they have emigrated, and hitherto but thinly peopled the

New World, the Mexicans, and a few others excepted, till they were butchered by Spanish avarice and superstition. A happy people I call them still, whose peace and genuine morals have not been contaminated with European vices; and whose errors are only the errors of ignorance, and not the rooted depravity of a pretended civilization, and a spurious and mock Christianity.

All the Guiana Indians believe in God as the supreme author of every good, and never inclined to do them an injury; but, to prevent his afflicting them with evil, they worship the devil, whom they call *Yawahoo*, and to whom they ascribe pain, disease, wounds, and death. Where an Indian dies, the whole family, in order to avert future fatality, soon after leave the spot as a place of residence.

The Guiana Indians are a perfectly free people, having no division of land, and being without any government, excepting that in most families the oldest acts as captain, priest and physician, to whom they pay a reverential obedience: these men are called *Peïi* or *Pagayers*, and, as in some civilized nations, live better than all others.

Polygamy is admitted among them, and every Indian is allowed to take as many wives as he can provide for, though he generally takes but one, of whom he is extremely jealous, and whom he knocks on the head the moment he receives a decided proof of her incontinency. These Indians never beat their children on any account whatever, nor give them any education, except in hunting, fishing, running and swimming; yet they never use abusive language to each other, nor steal, and a lie is totally unknown among them. To which I may add, that no people can be more grateful when treated with civility, but I must not forget that, on the other hand, they are extremely revengeful, especially when, as they suppose, they are injured without just provocation.

The only vices with which to my knowledge they are acquainted, if such among them they may be called, are excessive drinking when opportunity offers, and an unaccountable indolence—an Indian's only occupation, when he is not hunting or fishing, being to lounge in his hammock, picking his teeth, plucking the hairs from his beard, and examining his face in a bit of broken looking-glass.

The Indians in general are a very cleanly people, bathing twice or thrice every day in the river or the sea. They have all thick hair, which never turns grey, and the head never becomes bald; both sexes pluck out every vestige of hair on their bodies, that on the head only excepted: it is of a shining black, which the men wear short, but the women very long, hanging over the back and shoulders to their middle as if they had studied the scriptures where it is said that long hair is an ornament to a woman but a disgrace to a man.

The Guiana Indians are neither tall, strong, nor muscular; but they are straight, active, and generally in a good state of health. Their faces have no expression whatever, that of a placid good-nature and content excepted; and their features are beautifully regular, with small black eyes, thin lips, and very white teeth. However, all the Guiana Indians disfigure themselves or less by the use of arnotta or rocow, by them called *cosowee*, and by the Dutch *orlean*. The seeds of the arnotta being macerated in the juice of lemon, and mixed with water and gum that exudes from the *mawna* tree, or with the oil of castor, composes a scarlet paint with which all the Indians anoint their bodies, and even the men their hair, which gives their skin the appearance of a boiled lobster; they also rub their naked bodies with *caraba* or crab-oil. This, it must be allowed, is extremely useful in scorching climate, where the inhabitants of both sexes go almost naked. One day, laughing at a young man who came from the neighbourhood of Cayenne, he answered me in French, saying, 'My skin, sir, is kept soft, too great perspiration is prevented, and the mosquitoes do not sting me as they do you: besides its beauty, this is the use of my painting red. Now what is the reason of your painting white?' (meaning powder in the hair) 'You are, without any reason, wasting your flour, dirtying your coat, and making yourself look grey before your time.'

These Indians also make use of a deep purple blue, which they call *tapowripa*; but this is purely for ornament, and is absolutely indelible for about nine days. It is the juice of a fruit in size like a small apple that grows on the *lawna* tree, and which is bruised and macerated in water. With this these people make figures on their faces and all over their bodies, resembling hieroglyphics. So very permanently does this paint adhere to the skin, that one of our officers, who could not believe the fact, having by way of a frolic made a pair of enormous whiskers with it on his face, was obliged, to our great amusement, to parade Paramaribo with them for above a week, and wait till they gradually disappeared.

The only dress worn by these Indians consists of a slip of black or blue cotton worn by the men to cover their nakedness. Being wound round their loins, it passes through between their thighs, and the ends of it, which are very long, they either throw over their shoulders, or negligently let them trail on the ground. For the same purpose, the women wear an apron of cotton, with parti-coloured glass beads strung upon it. This covering is of no great size, being only about one foot in breadth by eight inches in length, ornamented with fringes, and fastened round the waist with cotton strings; but being heavy, though of no larger dimensions, it answers all the purposes for which it was intended. Many also wear a girdle made of human hair round their waist, through which, before and behind, they fasten a square broad piece of black cotton.

In the inland parts, many Indians of both sexes go quite naked, without any covering whatever. The Indian women also, by way of ornament, often cut small holes in their ears and their lips, in the first of which they wear corks or small pieces of light wood, and through their lips they stick thorns, and sometimes all the pins they can lay hold of, with the heads inside against the gums, and the points like a beard dangling down upon their chins. Some wear feathers through their cheeks and through their noses, though this is but seldom. But the most unaccountable ornament in my opinion is, that the girls at ten or twelve years old work a kind of cotton garter round their ankles, and the same below the knee; which being very tight, and remaining for ever, occasions their calves to swell to an enormous size by the time they are grown women, and gives their limbs a very odd and unnatural appearance. They also wear girdles, bands, and bracelets, of various coloured beads, shells and fish-teeth, about their necks, across their shoulders, or round their arms, but generally above the elbow. Upon the whole, the Indian women, naturally disagreeable in their shapes, with their toes turned inwards, are still less attractive by their ornaments.

The ornaments of the men consist of crowns of various coloured feathers, or a sash of boar's or tiger's teeth across one shoulder, as a token of their valour and activity. The chiefs of families sometimes wear the skin of a tiger; they also frequently have small oval bits of silver in the cartilaginous separation of their noses, and sometimes a green or yellow coloured stone.

All these nations live in the forest, near rivers, and along the sea-coast, where they are scattered in small villages or hamlets. Their houses or wigwams are built as those of the negroes, but instead of being covered with the leaves of the manicole-tree, they are covered with the leaves of rattans or jointed canes. Their furniture is very simple, but sufficient for their wants, consisting of a few black earthen pots of their own making, a few calabashes or gourds, a few baskets, a stone to grind, and another to bake their cassava bread, a fan to blow the fire, a wooden stool, a sieve, a press to squeeze the wet cassava, and a cotton hammock or net for them to sleep in.

Besides these, since their intercourse with the Europeans, many of them are furnished with a hatchet and a knife, which last, like a dagger, the Indians always wear by their side. But I must not forget that every Indian family is provided with a large boat or canoe to carry all that they possess when they travel by water, which is not unfrequent.

The only vegetables cultivated by these people are yams, plantains, and bananas, and particularly *cassava*. The sweet cassava, roasted in hot ashes, and eaten with butter, is an agreeable and healthy food, tasting much like the chestnut. But the bitter cassava, which when raw is the most fatal poison both to man and beast, is (however strange it may seem) when prepared by fire, not only a very safe food, but the most natural bread of the Indians in this country, as well as of several Europeans and negroes.

The other food of the Indian consists of sea and land turtle, and crabs, called *seereeca*, which last are seen in great quantities in the mud all along the coast of Guiana at low water. Of these they are extremely fond, as also of the river lobsters called *sarasara*, which are here in great abundance; but nothing pleases them so much as the *iguana* or *wayamacca* lizards. Everything they eat is so highly seasoned with Cayenne pepper, that the mere tasting of their food excoriates the mouth of a European. They use little or no salt, but barbecue their game and fish in the smoke, which equally preserves it from putrefaction; and if an Indian has neglected to provide food by hunting or fishing, his hunger is assuaged by eating the seeds of the *green-heart* or the *eta* tree, or of similar productions of the forest.

Their drink consists of various fluids, such as the juice of the *coumoo* fruit. The *coumoo* tree is one of the smallest of the palm kind. Its seed grows in bunches of purple blue berries, resembling grapes, the pulp of which thinly adheres to a round hard stone, about the size of a pistol bullet. These berries are dissolved and maçerated in boiling water, making a beverage which, when mixed with sugar and cinnamon, is frequently used by the fair inhabitants: it tastes very much like chocolate. A drink they call *piworree* is a composition of the cassava bread, chewed by the females and fermented with water, which has something of the taste of ale and will intoxicate. It appears at first very extraordinary, that what has been within the teeth, mixed with the saliva and spit from the mouths of others, should be drank without loathing by the people of any country; but those who have read Cook's Voyages will find that this practice was so common in the islands he discovered, that had he not complied with it, his refusal might have fatally offended the inhabitants.

In pronunciation the language of the Indians in general much resembles the Italian, their words being sonorous and harmonious, mostly terminating with a vowel. They have no calculation of time, a string with some knots being the only calendar they are acquainted with. Their musical instruments consist of a kind of flute called *too-too* and made of a single piece of thick reed, on which they make a sound no better than the lowing of an ox, without either measure or variety. Another instrument is also used by them to blow upon, called *quarta*, and consists of reeds of different lengths, that are joined together like the pipes of an organ, but even at the top, which they hold with both hands to the lips, and which, by shifting from side to side, produces a warbling of clear but discordant sounds, agreeable to none but themselves. Never have I seen a better representation of the god Pan playing on his chaunter, than a naked Indian among the verdant foliage playing upon one of those reedy pipes. They also make flutes of the bones of their enemies, of which I have one now in my possession. Their dancing, if such it may be called, consists in stamping on the ground, balancing on one foot, and staggering round in different attitudes for many hours, as if intoxicated.

The Indians are a very sociable people among themselves, and frequently meet together in a large wigwam that is in every hamlet for the purpose, where, if they do not play or dance, they amuse each other with fictitious stories, generally concerning ghosts, witches, or dreams, during which they frequently burst out into immoderate fits of laughter. They greatly delight in bathing, which they do twice at least every day, men, women, boys, and girls, promiscuously together. They are all excellent swimmers without exception. Among these parties not the smallest indecency is committed, in either words or actions.

The employments of the men are, as I have stated, but very few, and, indeed, may be comprised in two words, hunting and fishing: at both of these exercises they are indisputably more expert than any nation whatever. For the first they are provided with bows and arrows of their own manufacturing, the arrows being of different kinds for different purposes. Some are pointed like a lance, others are doubly and trebly barbed, and so contrived as to stick in the wound. These are used mostly for game and fish. Some arrows have blunted heads instead of points, about the size of a large chestnut; with these they do not kill, but stun the macaws, parrots, and small monkeys, so that they can take them with their hands. Soon afterwards they recover, and are sent alive to Paramaribo. Some of the arrows for killing fish have the appearance of a trident, with three and sometimes five barbed sticks instead of one, which enables them to shoot fish even at random. A few of the above arrows are frequently dipped in the *woorara* poison,* which is instantaneously fatal: but when intent on certain destruction, this people make use of another kind of arrow that is not above ten or twelve inches long, extremely thin, and made of the hard splinters of the palm-tree bark. Instead of feathers, one end

* The bark of a tree so called, mixed with others.

is wound round with a tuft of raw cotton, so as to fill up a hollow tube made of reed near six feet in length, through which they blow them with their breath. These little implements of death will carry to the distance of forty paces, and with so much certainty that the intended victims never escape.

I must not forget that every Indian carries a club, which they call *apootoo*, for their defence. These clubs are made of the heaviest wood in the forest; they are about eighteen inches long, flat at both ends, and square, but heavier at the one end than the other. One blow with this club, in which is frequently fixed a sharp stone, scatters the brains. They are used by the Guiana Indians like the tomahawk by the Cherokees, and on these, besides other hieroglyphical figures, they often carve the number of persons they have slain in battle. The manner of fixing the stone in the club is by sticking it in the tree while it is yet growing, where it soon becomes so fast that it cannot be forced out; the wood is then cut and shaped according to fancy.

The women are occupied in planting cassava, plantains, and other roots, in dressing the victuals, and in making earthen pots, bracelets, baskets or cotton hammocks.

The Indian girls arrive at the time of puberty before twelve years old, indeed commonly much sooner, at which time they are married. The ceremony consists simply in the young man's offering a quantity of game and fish of his own catching, which, if she accepts, he next proposes the question, 'Will you be my wife?' If she answers in the affirmative, the matter is settled, and the nuptials celebrated in a drunken feast, when a house and furniture is provided for the young couple. Their women are delivered without any assistance, and with so little inconvenience or suffering that they seem exempt from the curse of Eve. They go about the menial services for their husbands the day after their delivery; then, however ridiculous and incredible it may appear, it is an absolute fact that every one of these gentlemen lie in their hammocks for above a month, groaning and grunting as if they had been themselves in labour, during which time all the women must attend them with extraordinary care and the best food. This the Indian calls enjoying himself, and resting from his labour. Most of these people esteeming a flat forehead a mark of beauty, they compress the heads of their children, it is said, immediately after their birth, like the Chactaws of North America.

No Indian wife eats with her husband, but serves him as a slave: for this reason they can take but very little care of their infants, which, nevertheless, are always healthy and undeformed. When they travel, they carry them in small hammocks slung over one shoulder, in which sits the child having one leg before and the other behind the mother. For an emetic they use the juice of tobacco, which they seldom smoke.

When the Indians are dying, either from sickness or old age, the latter of which is most frequently the cause, the devil or *Yawahoo* is at midnight exorcised by the *peii* or priest, by means of rattling a calabash filled with small stones, peas and beads, accompanied by a long speech. This office is hereditary, and by these pretended divines no animal food is publicly tasted, and yet on the whole they live better than all the others. When an Indian is dead, being first washed and anointed, he is buried naked, in a new cotton bag, in a sitting attitude, his head resting on the palms of his hands, his elbows on his knees, and all his implements of war and hunting by his side. During this time his relations and neighbours rend the air by their dismal lamentations, but soon after, by a general drunken riot, they drown their sorrows till the following year. At the expiration of the year, the body, being rotten, is dug up, and the bones distributed to all the friends and acquaintances, during which ceremony the former rites are repeated for the last time, and the whole neighbourhood look out for another settlement. Some tribes of Indians, having put their deceased friends in the above posture, place them naked for a few days under water, where the bones being picked clean by the *piree* and other fish, the skeleton is dried in the sun, and hung up to the ceiling of their houses or wigwams; and this is done as the strongest instance of their great regard for their departed friend.

When these Indians travel by land, their canoe, which is made of a large tree hollowed by means of fire, is always carried along with them to transport their luggage across swamps, creeks and rivers; it is, like themselves, all over besmeared with arnotta.

Notwithstanding the Guiana Indians are upon the whole a peaceable people, they sometimes go to war among themselves, purely for the sake of capturing prisoners; to this they are too much encouraged by the Christians, who receive them in exchange for other commodities, and make them slaves. But these kind of slaves are only for show and parade, as they absolutely refuse to work, and if at all ill-treated, or especially if beaten, they pine and languish like caged turtles, even refusing food, till by affliction and want they are exhausted and finally expire.

The Indians always fight their battles by midnight: indeed their contests resemble more a siege than a battle, as these broils consist only in surrounding the hamlets of their enemies while they are asleep, making prisoners of the women, boys and girls, while they shoot the men with poisoned arrows, or with their clubs or apootoos divide their skulls when they come to close quarters; they also scalp their male prisoners, bring home their hair, and even their bones, as tro-

A Surinam planter in his morning dress

phies of war and presents to their wives, unless they intend to sell them to the Europeans at Paramaribo. In their open encounters, which happen very seldom, the bows and barbed arrows are their principal weapons of offence; with these they often kill at the distance of sixty paces, and the swiftest bird in its flight, provided it has the magnitude of a crow, seldom escapes them.

15

I NOW once more return to the principal object of my Journal, Fourgeoud's military operations. I have before mentioned, that a supply of fresh troops was expected to reinforce our decayed little army, and, on the 30th of January, 1775, the news came to Paramaribo that the transport ship *Maastroom*, Captain Eeg, was arrived in the river Surinam and come to an anchor before the fortress Amsterdam, with Colonel Seyburgh and two divisions, consisting together of one hundred and twenty men, under his command, two more divisions being expected.

The following day I went down with a row-boat to welcome them; and having dined on board together, the ship weighed anchor, and I sailed up with them till before the fortress Zelandia, where they moored and were saluted by a few guns. Till this date I had been the oldest officer in the corps, excepting only Colonel Fourgeoud.

On the arrival of the troops, our commander invited them to a dinner which consisted of salt beef, pork, barley, and hard pease, of which I had the honour to partake, to my no small amusement, when I observed the significant looks which were directed by these new-comers on their commander and his entertainment. In the evening we conducted them to the play-house, where the death of Caesar, and Crispin Doctor, were performed, the one exactly as laughable as the other. I must however confess that I was better entertained the next day, when the governor gave to all a superb dinner and supper, where the strangers seemed to be as much surprised with the magnificence of the feast as they had been the day before amazed with Colonel Fourgeoud's frugality.

On the 5th of February, the troops that were so lately landed were sent to the upper parts of the river Comewina to be encamped. I speak of the privates, for most of the officers remained to partake of a feast at the house of a Mr Mercellus, by whose command (to crown the banquet) half a dozen negroes continued blowing the trumpet and French horn in the room where we dined, till the company were absolutely deafened by discordancy and noise.

On the 6th, the whole corps, without exception, received orders to leave Paramaribo and to encamp at Magdenberg, a mountain near the Tempaty Creek, in the upper parts of the river Comewina, to which, as I have just mentioned, the reinforcement was already dispatched. Having, therefore, prepared myself to set out on my fourth campaign, and taken leave of my little family and friends, I repaired to the waterside, to set out in the same barge with Colonel Seyburgh. He erroneously supposing that the troops which came with him from Holland were a distinct corps from those arrived with Fourgeoud in 1773, made the negroes shove off the boat in my presence, when I was not a stone's cast from it, and left me on the beach, to my utter surprise and mortification. I knew Fourgeoud had swore that he should 'dance just as much to his pipes as the youngest ensign in the regiment' and in that he was perfectly right: I therefore strenuously supported the chief against his antagonist, and setting off immediately with another boat, soon overtook him (to his astonishment) when we all went ashore at the plantation Vossenburgh, in the river Comewina. The next day we came to the estate Arentrust, having passed the heavy barges that departed from Paramaribo on the 5th; and on the 10th we made the Hope.

On the 11th, we arrived at the plantation Cravassibo, where we passed the night. Here the overseer, a Mr De Bruyn, was so very impertinent that, as I already had no abundance of affection for the fraternity of overseers, I gave him such a sound beating that, with a bloody face, he suddenly decamped from the estate in a small canoe with one negro, and in this trim, at twelve o'clock at night, like Banquo the ghost, appeared before the amazed Fourgeoud, who thought proper to give him no other consolation than to dismiss him with a heavy curse.

On the 12th we arrived safe at Magdenberg—Fourgeoud, the officers, and the barges with the privates. After the Hope, the estates began to appear thinner; and after passing Goet-Accord, about ten or twelve miles farther upwards, not a cultivated spot was to be seen, the plantations having been all laid in ashes by the rebels in 1757, as I have already mentioned. The river above Goet-Accord becomes very narrow, being lined on each side with impenetrable brush-wood, like the river Cottica between Devil's Harwar and Patamaca; and the Tempaty Creek, which may be considered as the source of the whole river Comewina, becomes also much narrower. Magdenberg, which is about a hundred miles from Paramaribo, was formerly an estate, but has now not a vestige of cultivation left, a poor old orange-tree excepted, and is at present neither more or less than a barren desolate mountain.

On the 17th the news reached us that the transport ship, the *Maria Helena*, with the remaining two divisions of one hundred and twenty men, commanded by Captain Hamel, had also arrived in the river Surinam on the 14th instant. Thus the reinforcements together consisted of two hundred and forty men, and, on the 5th day of March they all arrived in heavy barges at Magdenberg, where I may now say that Colonel Fourgeoud's whole forces were assembled. The same day one hundred negro slaves also arrived, to carry the loads when we should march. One of the new negroes being missed from on board a military barge and marks of blood discovered in it, the commanding officer, a Mr Chatteauview, and a sentinel were both put under an arrest to be tried for murder. On the same eventful day also, two of our captains fought a duel, in which one of them received a wound in his forehead.

On the 13th, a barge with provisions, coming from Paramaribo (shocking to relate!) found the negro that was missed on the 5th at the water's edge, lying in the brush-wood, with his throat cut from ear to ear, but still alive, the knife having missed the wind-pipe. This miserable apparition of skin and bone they took on board and brought to Magdenberg, where, by a skilful surgeon, the wound was sewed up and the man surprisingly recovered, having lain nine days in that dreadful condition without any subsistence or covering whatever, and weltering in his own blood, even without a bandage. The week after I had nearly lost my own life by an accident. Two negroes of the estate Goet-Accord being employed in hunting and fishing for Fourgeoud, one of them, named Philander, proposed to me to accompany them in the wood, where we might chance to meet with some *pingoes* or *powesa*; but a heavy shower of rain coming on when we had only walked two miles, we determined to relinquish the project and repair to the small spot called the Jacob for shelter, to gain which we were obliged to pass through a deep marsh. Having waded till up to our arm-pits, Philander, who was the finest man without exception that I ever saw, began to swim with one hand as did his companion, holding their fowling pieces above the water with the other, and desired me to follow them. This I tried, having nothing on but my shirt and trousers, but after swimming two or three strokes, I sunk to the bottom like a stone, with the weight of my musket; relinquishing it, I immediately rose to the surface, and begged that Philander would dive for it, and he brought it up without difficulty. At this moment a thundering voice called out through the thicket: 'Who *somma datty?* and another *sooto sooto da Bonny kiry da dago?* Who is that? Who is there? Fire! shoot! it is Bonny, kill the dog!' Looking up, we saw the muzzles of six muskets presented upon us at a very little distance indeed. I instantly dived, but Philander answering that we belonged to Magdenberg, we were permitted to come on shore one by one at the Jacob, and found that these trusty negro slaves, having heard a flouncing in the water, and seeing three armed men in the marsh, took it for granted that the rebels were coming, headed by Bonny himself, for whom they had mistaken me as I was almost naked and so much sunburnt; besides my hair, which was short and curly, I entirely resembled a mulatto. Being refreshed with some rum, and having dried ourselves by a good fire, we now returned back to Magdenberg, where I congratulated myself on my escape.

On the 21st, Fourgeoud reviewed with pleasure his recruited little army, where I was sorry the rangers did not appear. He now dispatched one hundred men as a patrol to reconnoitre the skirts of his new encampment, of which number I had the honour to be one. During this time nothing remarkable happened, though, on my return to Magdenberg, I narrowly escaped being crushed to death by an enormous tree, which dropped by age just at my feet. These accidents frequently happen in the forest, but this only slightly wounded two or three of our marines. During this trip we had much rain, and were obliged to cross over a small creek. We cut down one of the palm-trees on the water's edge, which falling across the river formed a temporary bridge.

I now paid a visit to the miserable negro who had been found with his throat cut, and who was so well as to be able to converse. He declared to me that he committed this violent action with his own hand, and the suspected officer and sentinel were, therefore, instantly acquitted.

I now to my sorrow received a letter from Mr Kennedy, who was preparing to visit Holland, requesting that my boy Quaco might be returned to his estate. I accordingly sent him down with a letter, offering to buy him off his master as soon as it should be in my power to pay him.

On the 2nd of April, Colonel Fourgeoud ordered all the sick remaining in the colony to Magdenberg, where he had erected an hospital and a large victualling magazine. Thus all the invalids from Clarenbeek arrived here, with surgeons, apothecaries and attendants. At this period the old gentleman was particularly ill-natured, and abused both friend and foe without distinction, swearing that not a soul should be exempt from duty provided they could but stand on their legs.

It was now, in the midst of the rainy season, that Fourgeoud declared his intention of scouring the woods and, in consequence, gave orders for two strong columns to march the next day. The reason for choosing this season was that if he could now dislodge the rebels they must starve for want, which would not be the case in the dry months, for then the forest abounds with fruits and roots of many kinds. This was, however, in my opinion, a false piece of generalship, if we consider the dreadful havoc which the wet weather must produce among his troops, of which he killed, I suppose, twenty to each rebel negro.

On the morning of the 3rd of April, at six o'clock, the two columns set out upon their march, the one commanded by Colonel Seyburgh, the other by Fourgeoud. Our poor men were now loaded like asses. They were ordered to put their fire-locks in their knapsacks, the muzzles of course excepted: this was to keep them from the rain, which absolutely poured in torrents. Our course was south by east, up among the banks of the Tempaty Creek, where we soon came to swamps, and were marching in the water above our knees.

On the 4th of April we marched again, our course south by east, till two o'clock, when we changed our course to south-south-west. The word of command being again given on the 5th, we unslung our hammocks, then marched south-south-east, and south by east, through deep and dangerous marshes up to our breasts in water, and in very heavy rains; in which helpless situation we were suddenly alarmed, not by a party of rebels, but by a company of large monkeys, which we discovered in the tops of the trees, knocking a kind of nuts against the branches to break them for their contents. One of these nuts, falling from a considerable height, broke the head of one of our marines, and it was this sound that we had mistaken for the rebel negroes cutting wood with an axe.

In the evening we encamped near the Tempaty Creek, where we made large fires and built comfortable huts, so that this night we slept protected from the wet.

On the 6th we marched again, keeping due west till twelve o'clock, through very heavy rain and deep water, when we changed our course to the north, and passed over very high mountains, by many supposed to be pregnant with treasure.

We still continued marching north, on the 7th, over mountains from which, at intervals, we had undoubtedly the most enchanting prospects, as well from the wildness of the country as the beautiful variegated verdure displayed in so many different shades through this amazing forest. Here I saw a bird which is called a woodcock, which appears to have much of the colour of those in Europe, but which flew very heavily: I was, however, informed that it can run with incredible swiftness.

Having crossed an arm of the Mapany Creek in the evening, we once more returned to our camp at Magdenberg. Mr Noot, one of our officers, and several others, were so ill that they were carried in their hammocks upon poles by the negro slaves, and a great number were so very weak that they could scarcely support the weight of their emaciated bodies; but to complain of sickness was to mutiny, till they dropped down almost ready to expire. During this expedition, in which we still perceived nothing of the enemy, I was remarkably fortunate, having neither suffered by fatigue, nor been persecuted by extraordinary bad usage. The succeeding day Colonel Seyburgh's column arrived, having, like us, seen no appearance of the rebels.

On the 9th, my boy Quaco returned from Paramaribo, his master, Mr Walter Kennedy, having, to my great joy, sold him to me for the sum of five hundred Dutch florins, amounting with the expenses to near fifty pounds, for which Colonel Fourgeoud very civilly gave me a bill on his agent. The payment of this faithful servant's ransom of course revived my impatience for the long-wished moment of emancipation of my poor Joanna and her boy, from whose new master I had not yet received any answer.

Colonel Fourgeoud now treated me with the greatest politeness, and he now gave me leave, for fourteen days, to go to town to wish Mr Kennedy a prosperous voyage to Europe. Availing myself therefore of his good humour, I left Magdenberg within one hour, and made such dispatch that I came to Paramaribo on the 22nd, where I found my friends and little family all well.

The first visit I now made was to Mr Kennedy, to bid him farewell; I then paid five hundred florins for the black boy, for which he gave me a receipt, and Quaco was mine. About this time I fell ill with a fever which, however, lasted but a few days. On the 2nd of May, being again perfectly recovered, I took leave of Joanna and her Johnny—for thus he was named after myself though the ceremony of baptism could not yet be performed—while I set out once more for Magdenberg in a tent-boat with six oars.

On the 3rd, I called at Egmond, on my French friend Monsieur Cachelieu, and next day stopped at Oranjebo or Ornamibo, where I was heartily entertained by my old adversary Captain Meyland, with whom I had fought at the Wana Creek. But now this gentleman declared that he loved me better than any man in the colony.

On the 5th, I arrived at Magdenberg. Here Colonel Seyburgh, and what he called his officers, seemed to form a distinct corps from those of Fourgeoud. They appeared totally destitute of politeness, and treated each other with the greatest rudeness, while their colonel was most cordially hated by the commander-in-chief. This state of things contributed to render our situation still more disagreeable. I, however, had at this time little reason to complain, being for the present, at least, in the good graces of Fourgeoud.

On the 9th, an accident had nearly befallen me which must have caused me much poignant and lasting sorrow. My black boy, washing my cotton hammock in the Tempaty Creek, was suddenly carried to the bottom by the rapidity of the stream, and entangled in the hammock's lashings, so that both the one and the other disappeared; the boy, however, luckily extricated himself, though with great difficulty, and to my great joy, though more than half drowned, appeared once more on terra firma.

The following day, as Captain Hamel was angling, his tackle got fast at the bottom of the creek and, in diving to clear it, I struck my ankle with such violence against a rock that it was several months before it was perfectly recovered.

Accidents like this appeared greatly to entertain Colonel Seyburgh, while in return I could not help feeling a degree of indignation at what I considered as unhandsome behaviour; but the most extraordinary circumstance was, that this disgust between Seyburgh and myself seemed to gain me the favour of old Fourgeoud, almost as much as if I had destroyed half the rebel negroes in the colony.

Whatever may be thought of Fourgeoud's manoeuvres in not being able to bring the rebels to a pitched battle, it is very certain that he exerted himself and his troops to the utmost, and that by his constantly traversing the upper parts of the rivers and scouring the skirts of the colony, he prevented many depredations on the estates—undoubtedly a very essential service to the inhabitants, though at a dreadful expense of blood and money.

By the 2nd of June, the Hope in Comewina was become so very unwholesome for want of cleanliness (as it was much neglected by the newly-arrived troops which were now stationed there), that the commanding officer and most of his men were rendered unfit for duty by sickness, and many of them already buried. To this place Colonel Fourgeoud ordered down Captain Brant to take the command, with a fresh supply of men, and orders to send, not to town but to Magdenberg, all the invalids he should relieve. These orders he gave to the above officer in such a brutal manner, and dispatched him so suddenly that he had not even time to pack up his clothes, while Colonel Seyburgh deprived him of his only servant, whom he took for himself. This usage so much affected Captain Brant that he burst into tears and declared he did not wish longer to survive such galling treatment: he then departed to the Hope, truly with a broken heart.

Upon his arrival he was informed that Captain Brough, the late commanding officer, was dead. This poor man had been on hard service in the woods and, being very corpulent, could no longer support the fatigues and excessive heat; he melted down very fast, and a putrid fever at last occasioned his dissolution. Captain Brant was soon followed by Colonel Seyburgh to the Hope, with orders to inspect the sick.

On the 7th, the sick officers and soldiers arrived from the Hope in barges; some of the latter, being too ill to bear removing, died on the passage without medicines and without assistance. One of our surgeons died also this day in camp, and a number of the privates died daily. This was the consequence of having marched so much in the wet season, which was judged however by our chief to be the only season in which he was likely to root the rebels from the forest of Guiana.

16

As I now seemed to be on a friendly intercourse with Colonel Fourgeoud, I one day presented the old gentleman with a plan and bird's-eye view of all the encampment of Magdenberg, which pleased him so much that he sent it to the Prince of Orange and the Duke of Brunswick, as a specimen of his military manoeuvres. This present had the desired effect, for I not only became one of his favourites but, declaring his highest esteem for the Scots and English, he even promised to recommend me in particular at court. I was so satisfied with this change in his behaviour, that I now took the blame of all former animosity on myself. His attention, however, was suddenly attracted by affairs of more consequence, since, on the 14th of June, the news arrived that some rebel huts were discovered near the sea-side; that Captain Meyland had marched in quest of the enemy with one hundred and forty men of the Society troops, and had actually discovered them; but in wading through a deep marsh, had been first attacked by the negroes, who had killed several of his people, wounded more, and beaten back the whole detachment after they had already passed the marsh and were mounting fast on the opposite beach to storm the village. From this news it was evident that our sable foes were not to be trifled with, and since they were thus discovered, orders were immediately issued for all the troops that were able to march to keep in readiness. These included Fourgeoud's marines, the Society regiment and my favourite rangers, who wanted no spur and now could hardly be restrained till the others were prepared. In consequence of these orders all was activity and vigour in the camp, in hopes that this decisive stroke would end the war and their misery together; and this, therefore, was the time to lead them on to a spirited attack. But, for reasons best known to himself, our commander delayed his movement till the 20th of August, which was above two months.

In the meantime the disagreeable news arrived that Captain Brant was almost dead with a violent illness at the Hope, and for the command at this place (as being one of his favourites) Fourgeoud now singled me out, declaring that I might thank my sound constitution for bestowing on me this honour. From this conduct, I plainly discovered that all his friendship was entirely interested, and I felt my resentment involuntarily rekindled against him for thus sending me to an inglorious death when he had so fair an opportunity of employing me honourably on actual service.

On my arrival at the Hope, my orders were to send poor Captain Brant not down to Paramaribo, but to Magdenberg. This young man, however, frustrated the tyrannical command; justly suspecting it, he had, a few hours before I came, set out with a tent-barge to town, where he was no sooner carried to his lodgings than he expired from the effects of a burning fever and a broken heart. No man could be more regretted than Captain Brant; nor did Fourgeoud ever lose a better officer, or I a sincerer friend.

On the 20th of June, a few days after my arrival, I had the honour to receive a visit from the governor, Mr Nepveu, on his return from his estate Appecappe to Paramaribo, with whom I condoled on the loss of his lady, who had died very lately. I also received daily visits from several planters, who complimented me with refreshments from their plantations.

A planter in Surinam, when he lives on his estate (which is but seldom, as they mostly prefer the society of Paramaribo) gets out of his hammock with the rising sun, about six o'clock in the morning, and makes his appearance under the piazza of his house, where his coffee is ready waiting for him. This he generally takes with his pipe instead of toast and butter, and there he is attended by half a dozen of the finest young slaves, both male and female, to serve him. At this *sanctum-sanctorum* he is next accosted by his overseer, who regularly every morning attends at his levee, and having made his bows at several yards distance, with the most profound respect informs his greatness what work was done the day before, what negroes deserted, died, fell sick, recovered, were bought or born, and, above all things, which of them neglected their work, affected sickness, or had been drunk or absent. The prisoners are generally present, being secured by the negro-drivers, and are instantly tied up to the beams of the piazza or a tree without so much as being heard in their own defence, and the flogging begins, with men, women, or children, without exception. The instruments of torture on these occasions are long hempen whips, that cut round at every lash and crack like pistol-shot, during which they alternately repeat, '*Dankee, masera*' (Thank you, master). In the meantime he stalks up and down with his overseer, affecting not so much as to hear their cries, till they are sufficiently mangled, when they are untied and ordered to return to their work without so much as a dressing.

This ceremony being over, the dressy negro (a black surgeon) comes to make his report. After he has been dismissed with a hearty curse for *allowing* any slaves to be sick, a superannuated matron next makes her appearance with all the young negro children of the estate, over whom she is governess. These, being clean washed in the river, clap their hands and cheer in chorus, when they are sent away to breakfast on a large platter of rice and plantains, and the levee ends with a low bow from the overseer, as it begun.

His worship now saunters out in his morning dress, which consists of a pair of the finest Holland trousers, white silk stockings, and red or yellow Morocco slippers, the neck of his shirt open and nothing over it, a loose flowing nightgown of the finest India chintz excepted. On his head is a cotton nightcap, as thin as a cobweb, and over that an enormous beaver hat that protects his meagre visage from the sun. This is already the colour of mahogany, while his whole carcase seldom weighs above eight or ten stone, being generally exhausted by the climate and dissipation.

Having loitered about his estate, or sometimes ridden on horseback to his fields to view his increasing stores, he returns about eight o'clock when, if he goes abroad, he dresses, but if not, remains just as he is. Should the first take place, having only exchanged his trousers for a pair of thin linen or silk breeches, he sits down and holding out one foot after the other, like a horse going to be shod, a negro boy puts on his stockings and shoes, which he also buckles, while another dresses his hair, his wig, or shaves his chin, and a third is fanning him to keep off the mosquitoes. Having now shifted, he puts on a thin coat and waistcoat, all white; then, under an umbrella, carried by a black boy, he is conducted to his barge, which is in waiting for him with six or eight oars, well provided with fruit, wine, water and tobacco by his overseer, who no sooner has seen him depart, than he resumes the command with all the usual insolence of office. But should this prince not mean to stir from his estate, he goes to breakfast about ten o'clock, for which a table is spread in the large hall, provided with a bacon ham, hung-beef, fowls, or pigeons broiled; plantains and sweet cassavas roasted; bread, butter, cheese, etc. with which he drinks strong beer, and a glass of Madeira, Rhenish, or Moselle wine, while the cringing overseer sits at the farther end, keeping his proper distance, both being served by the most beautiful slaves that can be selected.

After this he takes a book, plays at chess or billiards, entertains himself with music, etc. till the heat of the day forces him to return into his cotton hammock to enjoy his meridian nap, which he could no more dispense with than a Spaniard with his *siesta*, and in which he rocks to and fro, like a performer on the slack-rope, till he falls asleep without either bed or covering. During this time he is fanned by a couple of his black attendants, to keep him cool.

About three o'clock he awakes by natural instinct when, having washed and perfumed himself, he sits down to dinner, attended as at breakfast by his deputy governor and sable pages. Here nothing is wanting that the world can afford in a western climate, of meat, fowls, venison, fish, vegetables and fruits, and the most exquisite wines are often squandered in profusion; after this a cup of strong coffee and a liqueur finish the repast. At six o'clock he is again waited on by his overseer, attended as in the morning by negro-drivers and prisoners, when the flogging once more having continued for some time, and the necessary orders being given for the next day's work, the assembly is dismissed, and the evening spent with weak punch, sangaree, cards and tobacco. His worship generally begins to yawn about ten or eleven o'clock, when he withdraws and is undressed by his sooty pages. He then retires to rest, where he passes the night in the arms of one or other of his sable sultanas (for he always keeps a seraglio) till about six in the morning, when he again repairs to his piazza walk, where his pipe and coffee are waiting for him, and where, with the rising sun, he begins his round of dissipation, like a petty monarch, as capricious as he is despotic and despisable.

Such absolute power indeed, cannot fail to be peculiarly delightful to a man who, in all probability, was in his own country, Europe, a—nothing. Exceptions, however, take place in every circumstance of life; and I have known many planters in Surinam as good men as I ever would desire to be acquainted with, which I have already mentioned.

As for the ladies, they indulge themselves just as much, by giving way to their unbounded passions and especially to the most relentless barbarity. But while I can bear witness to the exalted virtues of a few women whose characters shine with treble lustre, I shall draw a veil over all the imperfections too common to their sex in this climate. Before I drop this subject, however, I must attest that hospitality is in no country practised with greater cordiality or with less ceremony, a stranger being everywhere at home, and finding his table and his bed at whatever estate necessity or choice may occasion him to visit. This is the more to be regarded as no inns are to be met with in the neighbourhood of any of the Surinam rivers.

The Hope was now truly a most shocking place of residence where not a man was to be seen without an ague or fever, or some other wasting complaint. The dysentery also began to make its appearance and, to add to our distress, we had neither surgeon, medicines, nor so much as a light, and very little bread left. I was moved with the situation of the troops, and again distributed all my biscuits, lemons, oranges, sugar, wine, ducks and fowls, among the unhappy sufferers, with a few spermaceti candles.

On the 23rd I sent up to the hospital at Magdenberg two sick officers, with all the privates that could bear to be transported, and, at the same time, I repeated my humble entreaties to be soon relieved from so very disagreeable a situation (for the confinement to which there was not the least necessity), and requested to be one of the party to march against the rebels.

An order at last came for my relief, and I immediately set out for Goet-Accord, where the planter received me with great hospitality. This sugar estate being the farthest that is cultivated on the Comewina, and consequently exposed to the neighbourhood of the rebel negroes, makes the slaves liable to their seductions; they are therefore treated with peculiar kindness and indulgence, to prevent their concurring in any insurrection, or being persuaded to leave their present situation.

Here we saw a great novelty indeed, the young negro women waiting at the table all stark naked as they came into the world. I was at first startled at the unusual appearance, and asking the cause, was modestly answered by the lady of the house that it was ordered so by their mothers and matrons to prevent (by such means of detection, said they) their too early intercourse with the males, and child-bearing, which would spoil their shapes, weaken their strength, and cramp their growth. Indeed finer made figures I never beheld than were both the men and the women on this plantation.

Next day we departed for Magdenberg an hour before sun-set, in a small barge covered only with a loose awning. We had not rowed above two miles when not only night came on, but we were overtaken by such a shower of rain as had nearly sunk us, the boat's gunwale not being more than two inches above the water. However, by the help of our hats and calabashes, we kept her afloat, while a negro sat upon the bow, holding out a boat-hook straight before him to prevent us from being overset by inadvertently running, in pitch darkness, against the roots of mangroves which thickly lined both the banks of the river all the way upwards.

In this state of wet and obscurity, at ten o'clock at night, we came to the Jacob, being just afloat and no more. I had no sooner leaped on the beach, than the boat sank with all that was in her, the slaves luckily swimming ashore. Alas! among the wreck, was my poor box, with my journal and all my paintings, which had cost me above two long years so much labour, care, and attention. I was truly distressed at this loss, when a skilful negro dived several times to the bottom and at last brought up my little treasure, which, though thoroughly soaked, I was very happy to have again in my hands. Having drank some warm grog and slung our hammocks, we all fell asleep round a good fire, by which I made shift to dry myself, and, what was of more consequence, my papers.

The following morning we again set out, and rowed for Magdenberg, but about half-way our voyage was once more obstructed by an enormous tree which had accidentally fallen across the creek, so that we could neither drag the boat over nor under it. Thus we were again obliged to return to the Jacob, whence we now proceeded to Magdenberg on foot, through thorns, roots, brambles and briars, and finally arrived wet and bloody—my ankle, which had been nearly well, fresh wounded to the bone, the skin and flesh being quite torn away by the numberless obstructions to our steps.

17

THE rainy season again approaching, Colonel Fourgeoud, having selected all the remaining healthy people—who now amounted to but one hundred and eighty in number—proceeded on the 3rd of July, 1775, on his march for Barbacoeba, in the river Cottica. This spot he appointed for the general rendezvous, previous to the grand attack on the rebels. Of this party I had the honour to be one, but on the surgeon's declaring that I should run the hazard of losing my foot if I marched in the woods, I was ordered to remain at Magdenberg, with liberty, if I soon recovered, to join Fourgeoud and make the best of my way to Barbacoeba. My limb, indeed, was now so swelled, and my wound so black with the mortification, that an amputation was dreaded by Mr Knollaert, Fourgeoud's surgeon, and I could not even stand without excruciating pain.

I have said that all the officers and most of the privates who had lately been stationed at the Hope, had died or been sent up dangerously ill, while I had escaped the contagion. But, alas! now it became my turn, having only had a reprieve and no more: on the 9th I was seized with the same burning fever that had carried off the rest, and even my black boy Quaco was very ill.

On the 14th, necessity forced me to give up the command to another officer, and depart from this inhospitable spot for Paramaribo. I could however reach no farther than Goet-Accord, and there, on the 15th, all expected my death until an old negro woman found means to make me partake of some buttermilk boiled with some barley and molasses, which was the first food I had tasted since I was taken ill. This certainly did me infinite service, and the day following I was again able to be transported. My black boy also was much better.

The evening of the 15th I reached Fauconberg, where I was met by a packet of six or eight letters from different friends, accompanied with presents of hung-beef, bullocks' tongues, madeira, porter, rum, and a fine bacon ham and a beautiful pointer. But two letters gave me greater pleasure than all the things I received put together. One from Mr Lude at Amsterdam, and the other from Mr de Graav, his administrator at Paramaribo, acquainted me finally, and to my heartfelt satisfaction, that the amiable Joanna and the little boy were at my disposal, but at no less a price than two thousand florins, amounting, with other expenses, to near two hundred pounds sterling, a sum which I was totally unable to raise. I already owed the sum of fifty pounds that I had borrowed for the black boy Quaco's redemption, but Joanna was to me invaluable, and no price could be too dear for a young woman, possessing so much excellence, provided I could pay it.

I now found myself, though exceedingly weak, so much better, that on the next day I went down so far as the estate Bergshove, whence the administrator humanely caused me to be transported to Paramaribo in a decent tent-barge with six oars; but relapsing, I arrived just alive on the evening of the 19th, having passed the preceding night on the estate called the Jalosee, apparently dead.

Being now in a comfortable lodging at Mr de la Mare's, and attended by so good a creature as Joanna, I recovered apace, and on the 25th was so well, that I was able to walk out for the first time, when I dined with Mrs Godefroy, Mr de Graav not being in town to concert matters relative to the emancipation of Joanna, who had now once more literally saved my life. At this table there was never wanting all the wholesome and refreshing nourishment that I stood in need of, with the best of fruits and wines.

About this period several American families arrived at Paramaribo, on account of the war which broke out between the mother country and her colonies. For many of these I felt very much, and must ever declare that no people could have a better heart or greater friendship for a British individual than they had for me, which they showed on many different occasions.

On the 3rd of August, Mr de Graav being arrived in town, I now thought proper to take the first opportunity of settling matters with him, by proposing him to give me credit till I should have it in my power to pay the money for which Joanna and my Johnny had been sold to me. This I was determined to save out of my pay, if I should exist on bread, salt and water, though even then this debt could not be discharged in less time than two or three years. Providence however interfered, and at this moment sent that excellent woman, Mrs Godefroy, to my assistance. No sooner was she acquainted with my difficult and anxious situation, than she sent for me to dine with her and addressed me in the following terms:

'I know, good Stedman, the present feelings of your heart, and the incapacity of an officer, from his income only, to accomplish such a purpose as the completion of your wishes. But know, that even in Surinam virtue will meet with friends. Your manly sensibility for that deserving young woman and her child must claim the esteem of all rational persons, in spite of malice and folly, and so much has this action recommended you to my attention in particular, that I should think myself culpable in not patronizing your laudable intentions.

Permit me then to participate in your happiness, and in the future prospect of the virtuous Joanna and her little boy, by requesting your acceptance of the sum of two thousand florins, or any sum you stand in need of. With this money go immediately, Stedman, go and redeem innocence, good sense, and beauty from the jaws of tyranny, oppression, and insult.'

Seeing me thunder-struck, and gazing upon her in a state of stupefaction, without the power of speaking, she continued, with a divine benignity:

'Let not your delicacy, my friend, take the alarm, and interfere in this business: soldiers and sailors ought ever to be the men of fewest compliments, and all I expect from you is, that you say not one word more on the subject.'

I was no sooner returned home, than I acquainted Joanna with all that had happened. She, bursting into tears, called out, '*Gado sa bresse da woma*!'—'God will bless this woman!' and insisted that she herself should be mortgaged to Mrs Godefroy till every farthing should be paid; she indeed was very anxious to see the emancipation of her boy, but till that was done, she absolutely refused to accept of her own freedom. I shall not here endeavour to paint the contest which I sustained between affection and duty, but bluntly say that I yielded to the wish of this so charming creature, whose sentiments endeared her to me still more. Thus I instantly drew up a paper, declaring my Joanna, according to her desire, from this day to be the property of Mrs Godefroy, till the last farthing of the money she lent me should be repaid. On the following day, with the consent of her relations,* I conducted her to Mrs Godefroy's house, where, throwing herself at the feet of that incomparable woman, Joanna herself put the paper into her hands. But this lady having raised her up, no sooner had read the contents, than she exclaimed: 'Must it be so? Then come here, my Joanna, I have a spirit to accept of you not as my slave, but more as my companion: you shall have a house built in my orange-garden, with my own slaves to attend you, till Providence shall call me away, when you shall be perfectly free, as indeed you now are the moment you wish to possess your manumission; and this you claim both by your extraction and your conduct.' On these terms, and on no other, I accepted of the money on the 5th, and carrying it in my hat to Mr de Graav's, I laid it on his table, demanding a receipt in full.

Mr de Graav, on counting the money, addressed me in the following terms: 'Stedman, two hundred florins of this sum belong to me as administrator. Permit me also to have a small share in this happy

* Without the consent of parents, brothers, and sisters, no respectable slaves are individually sold in Surinam.

event, by not accepting this dividend, as I shall find myself amply paid by the pleasure of having been instrumental in bringing about what seems so much to contribute to the enjoyment of two deserving people.'

Having thanked my disinterested friend with an affectionate shake by the hand, I immediately returned the two hundred florins to Mrs Godefroy, and all were happy.

On the 7th of August, matters being thus far settled, I wrote a letter to Mr Lude, at Amsterdam, to give him intelligence, and to thank him for having parted with the *most valuable* property of his estate. My ankle being now pretty well recovered, I also wrote to Colonel Fourgeoud, that I should have the honour to join him in a few days. This letter I directed to Barbacoeba, for there he still continued, while the intrepid and active militia captain, Stoeleman, was beating up the woods with a few rangers at another quarter, and who this day sent in four captive rebel negroes to Paramaribo.*

On the 10th, finding myself sufficiently recovered, and ready once more to enter the forest, I bade farewell to my sweet family and friends—leaving the first still at Mr de la Mare's, at their request—and cheerfully set off with a tent-boat on my fifth campaign, in the hopes of accompanying Fourgeoud. He, having assembled all his remaining forces, and made the necessary arrangements to attack the enemy, was now determined to march in a very few days.

On the 14th I arrived with a boat at Barbacoeba, in the upper part of the river Cottica, and found the old gentleman (who civilly welcomed me) ready to start the following day. I never saw the troops in such fine spirits, or so eager for service—some in the hopes of plunder, some of revenge on the rebels, and some from a wish to see the war at an end. Others, I believe, were tired of existence by continual illness and hard service, and heartily wished for a glorious end of all their miseries.

On the 15th of August 1775, the rebels, flushed with their late victory over Captain Meyland and his party, whether with a design to brave Fourgeoud or to intimidate his troops—being well apprised by their spies that he was at Barbacoeba—had the assurance to set fire to all the huts in two different camps which had been left standing by his patrols, while they continued shouting and hallooing the whole night within our hearing. But this only proved an incentive to action, and enraged our veteran commander so much that he now declared he would have ample revenge at all hazards. During

* It is a maxim with the rangers to chop off the right hand of every rebel negro they kill, for which they receive twenty-five florins; and for every one they send in alive fifty florins; also for finding a town or village one thousand florins.

this night a large tiger also alarmed the camp, but did no damage of any kind.

An hour before day-break next morning, Colonel Fourgeoud, with his troops, was ready to march, and immediately entered the woods. They now amounted exactly to two hundred Europeans fit for service, the rest being ill and unfit for service; but no rangers were as yet arrived, though they had been expected. The fact was, they were so much disgusted with Fourgeoud's command that they did not appear at all, which afforded this gentleman for once an opportunity of stigmatizing them as a band of pusillanimous rascals; and I confess I was myself extremely astonished at this wilful absence of my black favourites, who were at other times so eager to rush upon the enemy, and had declared their satisfaction at the hopes of a decisive engagement with their sable countrymen.

This whole day our course was due east, and after proceeding about eight miles (which is a great distance in this country where the pioneers with bill-hooks must constantly open a path), we erected huts, and encamped.

On the 16th we continued our march due east upon a ridge or elevated ground. These ridges, if I mistake not, run generally in this country east and west as do also most of the marshes and swamps. Having advanced rather a less distance than we did the day before, we were ordered early to sling our hammocks and to sleep without any covering to prevent the enemy from hearing the sound of cutting the trees; nor were any fires allowed to be lighted nor a word to be spoken, while a strict watch was kept round the camp. These, in fact, were all very necessary precautions; but if we were not discovered by the enemy, we were almost devoured by the clouds of gnats or mosquitoes which arose from a neighbouring marsh. For my own part I suffered more here than I had even done on board the fatal barges in the upper Cottica, as we could make no smoke to drive them away. In this situation I saw the poor men dig holes with their bayonets in the earth, into which they thrust their heads, stopping the entry and covering their necks with their hammocks, while they lay with their bellies on the ground. To sleep in any other position was absolutely impossible.

By the advice of a negro slave, I however enjoyed my rest. 'Climb,' said he, '*masera*, with your hammock to the top of the highest tree that is in the camp, and there go sleep; not a single mosquito will disturb you, the swarm will be sufficiently attracted by the smell of the sweating multitude below.' This I immediately tried, and slept exalted near one hundred feet above my companions, whom I could not see for the myriads of mosquitoes below me, nor even hear them, from the incessant buzzing of these troublesome insects.

This was the principal distress of the night, while during the day, we had frequently been attacked by whole armies of small emmets, called here *fire-ants*, from their painful biting. These insects are black, and very diminutive, but live in such amazing multitudes together, that their hillocks have sometimes obstructed our passage by their size, over which, if one chances to pass, the feet and legs are instantly covered with innumerable of these creatures, which seize the skin with such violence in their pincers, that they will sooner suffer the head to be parted from their body, than let go their hold. I can aver that I have seen them make a whole company hop about, as if they had been scalded with boiling water.

On the 17th we continued our march still due east till nine o'clock, when we altered our course to the north and had to scramble through great quantities of mataky roots, or trumpeters, which proved that we were descending into the low grounds, and indeed the soil soon became very marshy; fortunately, however, though it was now the wet season, we had as yet very little rain.

This evening we encamped about four o'clock, Colonel Fourgeoud being seized with a cold fit of the ague.

As I was slinging my hammock between two large branches, but not so high as the preceding night, my eye chanced to fall upon what I conceived to be the leaf of a tree, but which appeared to move and crawl up the trunk. I called several officers to see it, when a gentleman of the Society exclaimed, '*C'est la feuille ambulante.*' That is the walking leaf. Upon closer examination it proved to be an insect, whose wings so perfectly represent a leaf that by many it has been mistaken for a vegetable production.

I now returned to my hammock where I fell into a profound sleep, which I enjoyed till near midnight, when we were all awaked in pitch darkness and a heavy shower of rain, by the hallooing and shouting of the rebel negroes, who discharged several muskets. But as the shot did not reach our camp, we were extremely astonished, the darkness rendering it impossible to form any just idea of their meaning. This disturbance continuing till near day-break made us expect every moment to be surrounded, and we kept a very sharp look-out.

In the morning early we unlashed our hammocks, and marched due north towards the place whence we conjectured the hallooing noise to have proceeded, being all much fatigued for want of rest, especially Colonel Fourgeoud, who could hardly support himself so much was he weakened by the ague. We had not marched above two miles, I having the vanguard, when a rebel negro sprang up at my feet from under a shrub, where he had been asleep; but as we had orders not to fire upon stragglers, he escaped, running with almost the swiftness of a stag among the brambles. I no sooner made report to the old hero, than, swearing he was a spy—which I believe was true—he shook off his illness and quickened his pace with redoubled vigour. But our pursuit was to no purpose, at least this day, for about one o'clock we got into a bog from which we could hardly extricate ourselves, and were forced to return to our last night's encampment, missing two privates of the Society troops, whom we supposed to have perished in the marsh.

In the evening a slave presented me with a bush-spider of such magnitude that, putting him into a case-bottle above eight inches high, he actually reached the surface with some of his hideous claws, while the others were resting upon the bottom. No creature can be more dreadfully ugly than this enormous spider, which the people of Surinam erroneously call the *tarantula*. It is such a hideous creature, that the very sight of it is sufficient to occasion a tremor of abhorrence, even in persons most accustomed to inspect the deformities of nature.

Such were the pests that we had to struggle with in this baneful climate, while our poor men were dying in multitudes, without proper assistance, unpitied, and frequently without a friend to close their eye-lids, neither coffin nor shell to receive their bones, but thrown promiscuously into one pit like heaps of loathsome carrion.

On the 19th, we again left our encampment, and after keeping a little south marched east till ten o'clock, when, to my great satisfaction, we were overtaken and joined by a party of one hundred rangers. At this period we mustered three hundred men, and however little Colonel Fourgeoud affected at other times to value these black soldiers, he was now not at all displeased with their company upon our near approach to an enemy with whom the rangers were well acquainted, and whom they knew how to engage much better than the marines. It will ever be my opinion that one of these negroes is preferable to half a dozen white men in the forest of Guiana; it indeed seems their natural element, while it is the bane of the Europeans.

Colonel Fourgeoud now issued orders for our little army to march in three lines or columns, his own regiment in the centre, the Society troops on the right, the rangers or black soldiers on the left, all within hearing of each other, with a few flankers or riflemen outside the whole: thus formed we advanced till about noon, when we changed our course from east to north-east and continued our march over a *biree-biree* swamp, or quagmire. These are very common and dangerous in this country, being a deep soft miry bog covered over with a thin crust of verdure, sufficient in most places to bear the weight of a man, and quaking when walked over; but should this crust give way, whoever breaks it is swallowed up in the chasm, where he must inevitably perish if not immediately extricated.

Quicksands are quite different, as they overwhelm by a gradual suction, whereas the effects of a quagmire are instantaneous. To avoid accidents, we opened our files as much as possible, but even with this precaution several men sunk through it as if the ice had broken under their feet, but were fortunately, though with much difficulty, extricated.

In the afternoon we passed through two old cassava fields, which indicated our near approach to the rebel settlement. The evening being too far advanced to attack the enemy, we once more encamped a few miles from the swamp in which Captain Meyland and his party had been defeated.

Having had a long march and the men being much fatigued, Colonel Fourgeoud allowed, during this night, both huts and fires. This surprised me greatly, being so near the rebels, as he had forbidden these comforts when we were at a very considerable distance from them. I however availed myself of his bounty, and having got some pigeon-peas from my sergeant—which he had picked up in the old cassava grounds—and laid hold of one of the kettles, I invited him and a captain of the black corps called Hannibal, to a share. Having thrown their salt-beef and rusk-biscuit into the mess with mine, and stirred it round with a bayonet, we made a very excellent supper, though in a sad dreary night and heavy rain.

On the 20th in the morning, no one could awake to a more beautiful day and in better spirits than I did, until they were damped by observing that at so critical a time, and even in the moment before the conflict, instead of that kind treatment which it would have been prudent to have shown to those from whose exertions we were to expect a happy period to our sufferings, there was even then such discouragement of the subaltern officers and private men as involuntarily drew from me the reflection that (if possible to avoid it) princes and ministers should never invest any one individual with unlimited authority, especially in a foreign country, without being perfectly well acquainted with the rectitude of their moral principles and disposition.

At six o'clock we advanced north-east by north towards the marsh, my melancholy evaporating with the rising sun. About eight o'clock we entered this formidable swamp, and soon found ourselves above our middle in water, well prepared nevertheless for the warm reception we expected from the opposite shore, as the former party had so fatally experienced. After wading above half a mile, our grenadiers rapidly mounted the beach with cocked firelocks and bayonets fixed;

the main body instantly followed and also mounted the beach, all without the smallest opposition. We now beheld a spectacle sufficient to shock the most intrepid, as the ground was strewn with skulls, bones, and ribs still covered with human flesh and besmeared with the blood of those unfortunate men who were killed with Captain Meyland. That officer had indeed found means to bury them, but the rebels had dug them up for the sake of their clothes, and to mangle the bodies which, like ferocious animals, they had torn limb from limb.

This being the second or third heap of human bones we had met with in our march, I frankly acknowledge did not operate upon me as a stimulative to engage with negroes; yet these awful relics spurred on the common soldiers to take revenge for the loss of their massacred companions.

We now followed a kind of foot-path made by the enemy, which after a little turning led us in a westerly direction. At ten o'clock we met a small party of the rebels, each with a green hamper upon his back; they fired at us, dropped their bundles, and taking to their heels ran back towards their village. A little after this we perceived an empty shed, where a picquet had been stationed to give notice of any danger, but they had precipitately deserted their post. We now vigorously redoubled our pace till about noon, when two more musket shots were fired at us by another advanced guard of the enemy, as a signal to the chief, Bonny, of our approach. Major Medlar and myself, with a few of the vanguard and a small party of the rangers, rushing forward, soon came to a fine field of rice and Indian corn. We here made a halt for the other troops, particularly to give time for our rear to close up, some of whom were at least two miles behind us. During this period we might have been cut to pieces, as we were afterwards informed that the enemy, unknown to us, had surrounded the field in which we were.

In about half an hour the whole body joined us, when we instantly proceeded by cutting through a small defile of the wood, into which we had no sooner entered than a heavy fire commenced from every side, the rebels retiring, and we advancing until we arrived in the most beautiful field of ripe rice in the form of an oblong square. From here the rebel town appeared at a distance, in the form of an amphitheatre, sheltered from the sun by the foliage of a few lofty trees, the whole presenting a *coup-d'œil* romantic and enchanting beyond conception. In this field the firing was kept up, like one continued peal of thunder, for above forty minutes, during which time our black warriors behaved with wonderful intrepidity and skill. The white soldiers were too eager and fired over one another at random, yet I could perceive a few of them act with the utmost coolness, and imitate the rangers with great effect.

This whole field of rice was surrounded and interspersed by the enemy with the large trunks and roots of heavy trees, in order to make our approach both difficult and dangerous; behind these temporary fortifications the rebels lay lurking, and firing upon us with deliberate aim, while their bulwarks certainly protected them in some measure from the effects of our fire, as we had vast numbers of these fallen trees to scramble over before we could reach the town. But we still advanced in defiance of every obstacle, and while I admired the masterly manoeuvres of their general, I could not help pitying them for their superstition. One poor fellow, in particular, trusting to his amulet or charm, fancied himself invulnerable; he mounted frequently upon one of the trees that lay near us, discharged his piece, descended to re-load, and then with equal confidence and the greatest deliberation returned to the charge in my full view, till at last a shot from one of my marines broke the bone of his thigh, and he fell crawling for shelter under the very same tree which had supported him just before. But the soldier instantly advancing, and putting the muzzle of his musket to the rebel's ear, blew out his brains, while several of his countrymen, in spite of their spells and charms, shared the same fate.

As we were now about to enter the town, a rebel captain, wearing a tarnished gold-laced hat and bearing in his hand a torch of flaming straw, seeing their ruin inevitable, had the resolution to stay and set the town on fire in our presence, which, by the dryness of the houses, instantly produced a general conflagration. This bold and masterly manoeuvre not only prevented that carnage to which the common soldiers in the heat of victory are but too prone, but also afforded the enemy an opportunity of retreating with their wives and children, and carrying off their most useful effects. Our pursuit, and seizing of the spoil, were at once frustrated both by the ascending flames, and the unfathomable marsh which we soon discovered on all sides to surround us.

I must indeed confess that within this last hour the continued noise of the firing, shouting, swearing and hallooing of black and white men mixed together; the groans of the wounded and the dying, all weltering in blood and in dust; the shrill sound of the negro horns from every quarter, and the crackling of the burning village, formed, on the whole, such an uncommon scene as I cannot describe, and would perhaps not have been unworthy of the pencil of Hogarth.

Having washed off the dust, sweat, and blood, and having refreshed ourselves with a dram and a bit of bread till the flames subsided, we next went to inspect the smoking ruins, and found the above town to have consisted of about one hundred houses or huts, some of which were two stories high. Among the glowing ashes we picked up several trifles that had escaped the flames, and likewise found three skulls fixed upon stakes, the mournful relics of some of our own brave people who had been formerly killed. What surprised us most, were the heads of two young negroes, which seemed as if fresh cut off; these we since learned had been executed during the night of the 17th, when we heard the hallooing and the firing, for speaking in *our* favour.

Having buried all these remains promiscuously in one pit, we returned to sling our hammocks under those beautiful and lofty trees which I have already mentioned. But here I am sorry to add, we found the rangers shockingly employed in playing at bowls with those very heads they had just chopped off from their enemies. To reprimand them for this inhuman diversion would have been useless, as they assured us it was the custom of their country, and they concluded the horrid sport by kicking and mangling the heads, cutting off the lips, cheeks, ears and noses; they even took out the jaw-bones, which they smoke-dried, together with the right hands, to carry home, as trophies of their victory, to their wives and relations. That this barbarous custom prevails among savages is a well-known fact, which originates from a motive of insatiable revenge. And though Colonel Fourgeoud might have prevented their inhumanity by his authority, in my opinion he wisely declined it, observing that as he could not do it by persuasion, to do it by power might break their native spirit and produce no other effect than alienating them from the service.

About three o'clock, while we were resting from our fatigue, we were once more surprised by an attack from a party of the enemy; but after exchanging a few shots they were repulsed. This unexpected visit, however, put us more upon our guard during the night, so that no fires were allowed to be lighted and double sentinels were placed around the camp. Thus situated, being overcome by excessive toil and heat, I leaped into my hammock after sun-set and soon fell fast asleep; but in less than two hours my faithful black boy Quaco roused me, in the midst of pitch darkness, crying, '*Masera, masera! boosee negro, boosee negro!*'—'Master, master! the enemy, the enemy!' Hearing at the same moment a brisk firing, with the balls whistling through the branches, I fully concluded that the rebels were in the very midst of our camp. Surprised, and not perfectly awake, I suddenly started up with my fusee cocked and (without knowing where I ran) first threw down Quaco and next fell down myself over two or three bodies that lay upon the ground, and which I imagined to be killed until one of them, d—ning me for a son of a b—ch, told me that if I moved I was a dead man. He went on that Colonel Fourgeoud had issued orders for the troops to lie flat on their bellies all the night, and not to fire, as most of their ammunition had been expended the preceding day. I therefore took his advice, and in this situation we lay prostrate on our arms until sun-rise. During this time a most abusive dialogue was carried on indeed between the rebels and the rangers, each party cursing and menacing the other at a very terrible rate. The former reproached the rangers as poltroons and traitors to their countrymen, and challenged them next day to single combat; they swore they only wished to lave their hands in the blood of such scoundrels, who had been the principal agents in destroying their flourishing settlement. The rangers d—n'd the rebels for a parcel of pitiful skulking rascals, whom they would fight one to two in the open field if they dared but to show their ugly faces, swearing they had only deserted their masters because they were too lazy to work. After this they insulted each other by a kind of war-whoop, sang victorious songs on both sides, and sounded their horns as signals of defiance. Then the firing commenced once more from the rebel negroes, and continued during the night.

At length poor Fourgeoud took a part in the conversation—myself and a sergeant acting as his interpreters—by hallooing, which created more mirth than I had been witness to for some time. He promised them life, liberty, victuals, drink and all they wanted. They replied, with a loud laugh, that they wanted nothing from him, characterized him as a half-starved Frenchman who had run away from his own country, and assured him that if he would venture to pay them a visit, he should return unhurt and not with an empty belly. They told us that we were to be pitied more than they, that we were white slaves hired to be shot at and starved for fourpence a day, that they scorned to expend much more of their powder upon such scarecrows, but should the planters or overseers dare to enter the woods not a soul of them should ever return, any more than the perfidious rangers, some of whom might depend upon being massacred that day, or the next. They concluded by declaring that Bonny should soon be the governor of the colony.

After this they tinkled their bill-hooks, fired a volley, and gave three cheers; which being answered by the rangers, the clamour ended and the rebels dispersed with the rising sun.

Our fatigue was great, yet, notwithstanding the length of the contest, our loss by the enemy's fire was very inconsiderable. This was explained when the surgeons, dressing the wounded, extracted very few leaden bullets, but many pebbles, coat-buttons and pieces of silver coin, which could do us little mischief as they penetrated scarcely more than skin deep. We were nevertheless not without a number of very dangerous scars and contusions.

The rebels of this settlement being apparently subdued and dispersed, Colonel Fourgeoud made it his next business to destroy the surrounding harvest, and I received orders to begin the devastation, with eighty marines and twenty rangers. In the afternoon Captain Hamel was detached, with fifty marines and thirty rangers, to reconnoitre behind the village, and to discover, if possible, how the rebels could pass to and fro through an unfathomable marsh, while we were unable to pursue them. This officer at length perceived a kind of floating bridge among the reeds, but so constructed that only one man abreast could pass it. On this were seated astride a few rebels to defend the communication, who instantly fired upon the party, but were soon repulsed by the rangers who shot one of them dead.

On the morning of the 22nd, our commander ordered a detachment to cross the bridge and go on discovery at all hazards. Of this party I led the van. We now took the pass without opposition and, having all marched or rather scrambled over this defile of floating trees, we found ourselves in a large oblong field of cassava and yams, in which were about thirty houses, now deserted, being the remains of the old settlement called Cosaay. In this field we separated into three divisions, the better to reconnoitre, one marching north, one northwest, and the third west. And here, to our astonishment, we discovered that the reason of the rebels shouting, singing and firing on the night of the 20th, was not only to cover the retreat of their friends by cutting off the pass, but by their unremitting noise to prevent us from discovering that they were employed, men, women and children, in preparing warimboes or hampers filled with the finest rice, yams and cassava, for subsistence during their escape, of which they had only left the chaff and refuse for our contemplation.

This was certainly such a masterly trait of generalship in a savage people whom we affected to despise, as would have done honour to any European commander, and has perhaps been seldom equalled by more civilized nations.

Colonel Fourgeoud, on finding himself thus foiled by a naked negro, was unable any longer to restrain his resentment, and swore aloud he would pursue Bonny to the world's end. His ammunition and provisions were however expended, and even had they not, it would have been in vain now to think of overtaking the enemy. To the surprise of most persons, our hero however persevered in this impracticable project, and dispatched Captain Bolts, with one hundred men and thirty rangers besides a number of slaves, to transport a quantity of shot and a week's provisions from Barbacoeba, and at the same time issued orders for the troops to subsist upon half allowance, desiring the men to supply the deficiency by picking rice, peas and cassava, and preparing them in the best way they could for their subsistence. This was also my lot, as well as most of the officers, and it was no bad scene to see ten or twenty of us with heavy wooden pestles, like so many apothecaries, beating the rice in a species of mortars, cut all along in the hard trunk of a levelled purper-heart-tree by the rebel negroes. For us, however, this was a most laborious business, the sweat running down our bodies as if we had been bathing, while water was at this time the only beverage in the camp.

The rangers having been out to reconnoitre, returned on the afternoon of the 23rd and reported that they had discovered and destroyed another field of rice to the north-east. This pleased Colonel Fourgeoud very well, but when in the dusk of the evening I observed to him that I saw several armed negroes advancing at a distance, he turned pale, exclaiming, '*Nous sommes perdus!*' and ordered the whole camp immediately under arms. In a few seconds these negroes were near enough to be discerned, and we now saw that several of them were carried upon poles, in hammocks. Fourgeoud then said, 'We still are ruined, though not the enemy: 'tis Captain Bolts, beaten back, with all his party.' This proved literally to be the fact, for that unfortunate officer (having delivered the wounded to the surgeons) reported that, having entered the fatal swamp where Captain Meyland had been defeated, he was attacked by the enemy from the opposite shore, who, without hurting a single European, had made a dreadful havoc among his rangers.

Our mighty leader now found his absurd scheme of pursuing the enemy completely frustrated, and himself in danger of total destruction. Cut off from every supply, he had neither ammunition nor provisions left in his camp, and very few men, except the sick and wounded, to defend it. Thus he at last began most seriously to consider how to secure a safe retreat, to which he was urged likewise by the general and incessant murmurings of the troops, who were not only almost starved, but indeed dreadfully harassed by daily fatigues and nightly watchings.

On the 24th, a detachment of one hundred and forty men, commanded by two field officers, were ordered to destroy the fields and the old settlement called Cosaay, and upon the return of the detachment in the afternoon, we immediately decamped, and began to retreat for Barbacoeba. That evening we encamped upon the same ground where we had passed the night before the engagement.

Early on the morning of the 25th, we again marched, and proceeded on our return, having now a beaten path before us. It will suffice to say that we reached our place of general rendezvous, Barbacoeba, on the afternoon of the following day, but in a most shocking condition, the whole of the detachment being mostly spent and wore out with fatigue, some nearly starved, others mortally wounded. All the slaves were employed in carrying the sick and lame in their hammocks on long poles, though these poor wretches were scarcely able to support themselves. However, if during this expedition we neither captured any of the rebels, nor gained booty, we nevertheless rendered the colony a very essential service by rooting out this concealed nest of enemies, who being thus discovered and driven away from their capital settlements, never think of returning to live near the same spot. I might, indeed, pronounce our victory *almost* decisive; I say almost, for if we except the demolishing of a few plantations for immediate subsistence and from a spirit of revenge, the rebels were, by being driven from this settlement, so disconcerted and panic-struck, that from the present period their depredations were certainly less. They soon afterwards retired to an inaccessible depth in the forest, where they could neither do any material injury, nor be joined by negro deserters.

I must now observe that Barbacoeba, instead of being in a state of sending us provisions, as our chief had expected, could scarcely afford daily subsistence to his emaciated troops on their arrival. They, having for many days lived on rice, yams, peas and Indian corn, were now most violently attacked by the flux, for although that kind of nourishment will keep the Indians and negroes strong as horses, the Europeans cannot long subsist without animal food. This was so very scarce, that even the Jew soldiers of the Society troops devoured salt pork as fast as they could catch it.

As for the miserable slaves, they were so starved that, having killed a Coata monkey, they broiled it, with skin, hair, intestines and all, then tore it to pieces with their teeth and devoured it like so many cannibals, before it was even half dressed. Of this animal they offered me a limb, but, hungry as I was, my stomach could not relish this kind of venison.

A good constitution, sterling health and spirits, now supported me, or I must have sunk under the load of misery and hardships, which were at this time become so intolerable that the rangers again forsook the camp, and Mr Vinsack, their conductor, as brave and active a man as ever entered the wood, threw up his commission.

Colonel Fourgeoud's inhumanity to the officers was now actually become such that he would not even permit those who were past recovery a marine to attend them, whatever price they offered. At length he was himself seized with this dreadful malady, and his beloved *ptisan* proved to be of no more avail; yet he soon recovered, by the plentiful use of claret and spices, which he seldom wanted, and which his colleague Seyburgh also employed as a preservative of his health, though by swallowing too copious doses he frequently lost the use of his reason. In such a situation, and in such a despicable encampment, our commander-in-chief had the vanity to expect a deputation from the court at Paramaribo, with congratulations on his victory: in consequence of which he had built an elegant shed and sent for sheep and hogs to entertain them—but the expected deputies never yet arrived.

On the 5th, therefore, the hogs and sheep were slaughtered, and, for the *first time* in his life, he ordered one pound per man, bones and all, to be distributed among the poor emaciated soldiers: indeed the number able to partake of this bounty was at present very small.

On the following day a reinforcement of one hundred men arrived from Magdenberg in Comewina; and from the Society post Vreedenburg in Cottica, nearly as many.

Intelligence arrived at the same time that the defeated rebels had actually crossed the river Cottica below Patamaca Creek, intent on immediate mischief, and that they were marching to the westward. In consequence of this information, a captain and fifty men were immediately detached, by water, to reconnoitre the banks near the Pinenburg Creek. This party returned upon the 8th, and confirmed the intelligence. Our indefatigable chief now again determined to pursue them; but the slaves who were to carry the ammunition and provisions had been sent home to their masters, nothing but skin and bones, to be exchanged for others, not yet arrived, and to be starved in their turn.

Fortunately, all the world did not possess our chieftain's insensibility, for this day the good Mrs Godefroy once more sent up a flat-bottomed barge, with a fat ox, oranges and plantains for the private soldiers, which was accordingly distributed among them. The same evening a small supply of provisions also arrived for me from Joanna, with a few bottles of port wine; and though part was stolen and part was damaged by the way, it made me very happy, and I gave *nothing* to Fourgeoud.

On the 12th, the fresh supply of slaves being arrived, the necessary preparations were made to pursue the rebels the next day, directing our first course towards the spot formerly called Jerusalem, and on the 13th we at last decamped and, bidding a final farewell to Barbacoeba, re-entered the woods, marching south and south-east the whole day, then passed the night on the opposite bank of the Casepoere Creek, where we encamped.

Nothing could be more diabolically cruel than the persecution of the new slaves during this march; not only were they overloaded and starved, but beaten like mules or asses by every ill-tempered individual. For instance, I saw Fourgeoud's black favourite, Gousary, knock down a poor negro slave for *not* taking up his load—and the chief himself knock him down for taking it up *too soon*; whereupon the wretch, not knowing what to do, exclaimed, in hopes of pity, '*O masera Jesus Christus!*' and was actually knocked down a third time by an enthusiast, for daring to utter a name with which he was so little acquainted.

On the 14th we marched south-west till about noon, and arrived at Jerusalem, which the van had reached about an hour before us, all thoroughly soaked with mud and heavy rains, and several men unhappily with ruptures in the groin, by falling over the roots of trees or over large stones. Here just arrived, we found, to my astonishment, the identical Mr Vinsack, with one hundred fresh rangers. He had heard, it seems, of the rebels passing Upper Cottica, and had been prevailed upon to resume his command by the governor; thus he now once more offered his service to Colonel Fourgeoud, who was very happy indeed to accept it.

On the 16th, having rested one day at this place, Colonel Fourgeoud detached two strong parties to reconnoitre; Lieutenant Colonel de Borgnes, with 100 men, was sent to the Wana Creek in Upper Cormoetibo, and Colonel Seyburgh, with an equal number, was ordered to the Creek Pinenburg, in Upper Cottica. The latter returned about midnight with two canoes, which he had found hauled ashore on the opposite side of the river, a little below the mouth of the Claas Creek. This convinced us that the rebels were gone westward to plunder and had brought their empty canoes down the Claas Creek from the rice country, in order to send them back loaded with booty from the estates they intended to pillage. In consequence, therefore, of this information, the proper preparations were immediately made to pursue them with alacrity. Never did the old warrior display more vigour than on this occasion, swearing aloud that he now would be revenged of them all, *coute qui coute*.

But how far his generalship on this occasion proved to be a match for that of Bonny, I must beg leave to reserve for the succeeding chapter.

Joanna

18

On the morning of the 19th of September 1775, just before sunrise, Colonel Seyburgh marching off with one hundred marines and forty rangers, did me the honour to fix upon me as one of the party, and was upon the whole so polite, and his behaviour so contrary to what it had lately been, that I knew not at all in what manner to account for it.

Having crossed the Cormoetibo Creek, we kept course south-west by south till we approached the river Cottica, where we encamped, having met with nothing on our first day's march worth describing. The following day we proceeded along the banks of the river Cottica, till we came near the Claas Creek and early slung our hammocks; from here I was detached, with a few rangers, to lay in ambuscade in the mouth of the creek till it was dark. I discovered nothing, however, except that the rangers were possessed of the same superstition as the rebels, with regard to their amulets or *obias* making them invulnerable. When I asked them, 'How came any of you, or of your invulnerable adversaries, to be shot?' I was answered, 'Because, like you, *Masera*, they had no faith in the amulet or *obia*.' This piece of policy, however, had the effect of making all their free countrymen so undauntedly brave, that I must confess their valour had often surprised me.

An express on the 21st arriving by water from Colonel Fourgeoud, informing us that the alarm-guns * had been fired in the river Perica, we instantly crossed to the opposite or west shore of the river Cottica, where the rangers, with a party of marines, were again ordered to lie in ambuscade or under cover, in hopes of cutting off the rebels on their retreat, when they returned to cross the Cottica river with their booty. And this very afternoon a rebel negro was seen with a green hamper, who, startled by the smell of tobacco (for some of the rangers were smoking) stopped short of his own accord. He was instantly fired at by me and one ranger; the warimbo or hamper dropped to the ground, but he himself escaped. This bundle we found stuffed with a dozen of the finest table linen, a cocked gold-laced hat, and a couple of superb India chintz petticoats, etc. the bulk of which I gave to my black companion, reserving only the chintzes for another friend at Paramaribo.

* By this is meant minute-guns, which are fired on the estates when in danger. These, being regularly answered by the neighbouring plantations, soon alarm the whole river, and bring assistance from every quarter.

The free negroes now rushing forward with unrestrained valour, I asked Colonel Seyburgh liberty to follow them. Calling for volunteers, a great number presented themselves, but the Colonel thought proper to reduce these to *four only*, with whom he sent me off. Having scrambled through thorns and briars woven together like a net or a mat—which tore one of my thighs in a terrible manner—I overtook them at one mile's distance from the camp. Shortly after we discovered thirteen fresh huts, where the rebels, we conjectured, had slept but a few nights before. In consequence of this, I now dispatched a ranger back to Colonel Seyburgh to give him intelligence, and ask permission for the rangers and myself to march forward to Perica without delay, in hopes to meet the enemy: but the answer was a peremptory order instantly to rejoin him with all hands.

Here we found a reinforcement just arrived from Jerusalem, consisting of sixty men, black and white, with positive orders for us to break up and march early the next morning for Perica River, while this whole night a strong party lay once more in ambush.

Accordingly at six o'clock, with the rising sun, all was in readiness, but by some unaccountable delay it was very late before we left the camp. We, nevertheless, all started at last, I having the van-guard with the rangers, and the poor marines loaded each man with nine days' provisions on his back. In this condition we had not proceeded long, when one of the rangers sounding his horn, they spread, and I among them, all instantly falling flat upon the ground, with our firelocks cocked and ready to engage; but this, however, proving to be a false alarm caused by a stag rushing out through the foliage, we soon rose, and after marching the whole day through water and mire, at three in the afternoon encamped on a high ridge. Here not a drop of water was to be found till we had dug a hole for that purpose, and this was so very thick and muddy that we were obliged to strain it through our neckcloths or shirtsleeves before we could drink it. Here I was once more accosted by the lieutenant colonel, who invited me to some supper in his hut, and again treated me upon the whole with very great civility.

On the succeeding day we marched again, keeping course west and north-west with very heavy rain, while I had the rearguard. Once more we entered on a quagmire, which cost me three hours time to bring up the rear to the beach, this march being particularly distressing as the negro slaves, with their burdens, broke through the surface every moment, while the loaded marines had enough to do to mind themselves. At last, approaching the beach, I perceived the dead bodies of several rebel negroes scattered on the ground, with their heads and right hands chopped off. These bodies being fresh, induced me to conclude, that they must have been very lately killed, in some engagement with the troops and rangers stationed on the Perica river. And here I must again remark, that had I been allowed to pursue, on the 21st, with the rangers, when I was ordered to march back, the enemy would have been between two fires; in which case few could have escaped, and all the plundered spoil must have been re-taken.

While my mind was engaged by these and similar remarks, many of my loaded slaves still remained entangled and struggling in the quagmire, while the commanding officer, with all the other troops, having got on a dry ridge, were quite out of sight and out of hearing—by which separation the rearguard not only ran the hazard of losing all the provisions and the baggage, but of being cut to pieces.

Having not a single European that had sufficient strength remaining to overtake the party which had proceeded, I resigned the command to my lieutenant, and ventured forward alone through the forest till, greatly fatigued, I overtook them. Reporting the situation of the rearguard to Colonel Seyburgh, I requested that he would slacken his pace till they were able to extricate themselves and come up from the bog, without which I could not be accountable for the consequences. To this the reply was, that he would form his camp when he met with good water. I instantly returned to the rear where, having struggled until it was quite dark in a most distressed and dangerous situation, the last man was dragged out of the mud at seven o'clock at night, when we slowly proceeded on till we entered the camp.

My solicitude for the people, powder and provisions, instead of procuring me commendation from the person under whose command I then happened to be, and who had lately been so very polite, brought me now into such difficulties, and produced a misunderstanding of such a serious nature and so very distressing to my feelings, that it had nearly terminated my existence. The reader may judge of my mortification when I inform him that, instead of receiving the approbation of my commander as I certainly deserved, I was immediately on my arrival in camp put under arrest, to be tried by a court-martial for disobedience of orders. Colonel Seyburgh and I had never been on amicable terms, and though, during the former part of this march, he had treated me with apparent civility, yet from this step it was evident that he was my mortal enemy. I must not omit that, though a prisoner (strange to tell!), I was ordered to carry my own arms and accoutrements till further orders.

On the 24th, we took our departure very early, and directed our course south and south by west when we passed close by Pinenburg, a forsaken rebel village formerly mentioned—I still a prisoner, in the most dejected spirits.

On the following day our course was south-west through a matakey or trumpeter morass, which was very deep and which we entered when we were all in a violent sweat by advancing too fast while upon the hard ground.

Having got again upon a ridge, an accident had now nearly befallen me incomparably greater than all my former misfortunes put together. This was no less than, having fallen into a deep reverie while I followed the rearguard, I imperceptibly wandered away from the troops till I was entirely lost and by myself in an unbounded wilderness. Quaco no sooner had missed me than, poor fellow, at every hazard he rushed through the wood to recover his master, and by a miracle saw me as I was sitting under a tree in the most dejected state of mind that it is possible to conceive, immersed in grief and abandoned to despair. I had this morning thought myself perfectly unhappy, but now would have given the world once more to have been in the same situation. Good God! entirely cut off from society, in a forest, surrounded by relentless savages! while a deluge of rain poured from the heavens, and tigers, famine, with every woe and every danger, stared me in the face. Such was the picture of my mind when, on discovering the boy, I started up from the ground and a new life instantly diffused itself through my whole frame. Having now straggled backwards and forwards together for some time, I called to the lad that I saw a pool through which the troops seemed to have passed, the water being fresh clouded with mud; but to my utter disappointment, he observed that this puddle was only occasioned by a *tapira*,* and showed me the print of the animal's foot in the surrounding mire. In the midst, however, of this distress, I recollected that, by the map, the river Perica was due west from us, and determined to lose no more time, but to set forward without delay. Thus having fresh primed my fuzee, I ordered Quaco to follow me; but again to no purpose, my compass being with the troops, and not a glimpse of sunshine owing to the heavy rain. Then the black boy put me in mind that on the fourth side the bark of the trees was usually most smooth, and on this fortunate hint we proceeded through thick and thin, till, overcome by fatigue and hunger, we both sat down and looked at each other, exactly like two victims doomed to execution. During this last mournful silence, we heard a sound like coughing and the rustling of arms, which, thank Heaven! soon proved to be our own troops, luckily for us resting near an old encampment. Having now been heartily welcomed by the other officers, I partook of some cold beef and bread, and a gourd full of grog, as did also my poor boy. After this regale the party rose, and pursuing our march, we once more entered a quagmire, or rather a mud-pool, the surface being too thin to carry us; through which having waded till it was pitch dark, we were obliged to encamp in the very middle of it, the troops by

* By some called the hippopotamus of South America.

slinging their hammocks in the trees one above another, and the slaves on temporary rafts made above the surface of the water, on which were also placed the powder, the victuals, etc.

On the 26th, the good Colonel having now drank his coffee in his hammock, while he kept the troops standing round it in water above their middle a whole hour before daylight, we again scrambled forward, keeping our course, first west and afterwards north-west when the road was so excessively bad that many slaves let fall their burdens, breaking, wetting and spoiling everything that was in them. At last, having passed through a second deserted camp, we halted on the old path of communication on which I formerly discovered the track of the rebels, when I commanded in Cottica river. Here, having erected slight sheds, we passed the night—I still a prisoner.

On the 27th we again broke up, and finally arrived in the forenoon, and in a forlorn condition, at the estate Soribo, on the river Perica, to defend the plantations against Bonny and his rebel negroes.

The river Pirica by its many windings is thought to extend about three-score miles. It is very deep but narrow, and has its banks, like all the others, lined with fine coffee and sugar plantations; its general course is from south-east to north-west. We were scarcely arrived at this post, than I was accosted by several deputies from Colonel Seyburgh, who earnestly intreated that I would only acknowledge myself to have been in fault, assuring me that I should then be set at liberty and all would be forgotten. As I was conscious, however, of my own innocence, I could not in common justice criminate myself in an instance where even my alleged crime amounted to no more than an anxious solicitude for the poor men and the provisions who were entrusted to my care. I was, therefore, placed under the guard of a sentinel—for what my commander was pleased to term unpliant stubbornness—and disarmed. In the meantime the marines caused me fresh uneasiness of the most poignant kind, by loudly threatening to mutiny in my behalf; nor could anything have prevented them but my decisive declaration that, as no cause could justify military disobedience, and rebellion, I should be under the necessity myself (however injurious to my feelings) of taking an active part against them, and seeing the ringleaders brought to condign punishment.

The day after our arrival in this station, we received the particulars of the Perica news, which were, that on the 20th the estates Schoonhoove and Altona had been pillaged by the rebels whom we had routed at Gado Saby, but that at the plantation Poelwyk they had been beaten back by the slaves; that the rangers stationed at an estate called Hagenbos had pursued them on the 21st, overtaken them on the 23rd, killed several, and brought back most of the booty; that on the same day another party of the rebels had made an attempt to seize the powder magazine at Hagenbos (which was no bad plan) but that (while the rangers were in pursuit of their associates) they had been repulsed by the manly behaviour of a few armed slaves, one of whom, belonging to the estate Timotibo, took an armed rebel himself, and next discovered their camp at the back of his master's plantations—for which he was handsomely rewarded. From all which intelligence, there was now no doubt remaining that if Seyburgh's detached party on the 16th had marched forward instead of backward by his orders, the above mischief might have been prevented and the enterprise of the rebels entirely frustrated.

On the morning of the 30th of September, having nothing more to do in the neighbourhood of the Perica river, we left it, and on the 1st of October came to Devil's Harwar much fatigued, nothing remarkable having happened on our march. I had written on the preceding day to Colonel Fourgeoud, informing him that I was weary of existence in my present state, and requesting that a court-martial might be *immediately* called; and this letter I had sent by a slave to the commander-in-chief. On our arrival at this station, I indeed found every hard means employed to bring me to terms; and such was the severe usage I experienced, that one of the rangers exclaimed, 'If in this manner these Europeans treat one another, is it to be wondered at that they should take a pleasure in torturing us poor Africans?'

At Devil's Harwar, however, my stormy voyage drew to a conclusion. Colonel Seyburgh was evidently convinced that he was wrong, and knowing what must follow, now only wished for a handsome opportunity of extricating himself from the effects of his unmanly passion. On the 2nd of October, therefore, he asked me with a smile, if I had a heart to forget and forgive? To which I sternly answered, 'No!' He repeated the question. I then said that I venerated truth, and would never confess myself in an error unless my heart coincided in the acknowledgment—that this was a concession I would make to no man living and least of all to him. He here grasped my hand, begged me to be pacified, and declared that he would make peace on any terms. But I again drew back with contempt, and decidedly avowed that I could not agree to any compromise, unless he owned his fault in the presence of all the officers, with his own hands tearing from his journal every sentence that could reflect upon my character. The journals were immediately produced, my arms were returned me, and my triumph was attended with every circumstance that could add to my full satisfaction. I then frankly and sincerely gave my hand to Colonel Seyburgh, who gave a feast in honour of our reconciliation. After dinner, to my utter surprise, he produced the letter which I had written to Colonel Fourgeoud, and acknowledged that he had intercepted it to prevent the affair proceeding to extremities: at the same time he acquainted me that Fourgeoud was encamped at the Wana Creek instead of Lieutenant Colonel de Borgnes, who had fallen sick, and was gone to Paramaribo. A perfect reconciliation having taken place, and the troops having had some rest, we set out once more on the 4th for the headquarters at Jerusalem; but I was obliged to leave poor Quaco, who was very ill, at Devil's Harwar, under care of the surgeon. That evening we encamped opposite the mouth of the Cormoetibo Creek. On the following morning early, having crossed the river Cottica, the troops marched back to Jerusalem.

19

On the 9th of October, 1775, Colonel Fourgeoud broke up the encampment at the Wana Creek to join us at Jerusalem, having sent down the half of his party sick in barges; and their number being greatly augmented by the invalids from this place, they were all together transported to receive the *coup-de-grâce* in the hospital at Devil's Harwar. The rangers also took their leave, and marched, with Mr Vinsack their conductor, to guard the Perica River.

Fourgeoud, during his last cruise, had discovered a hundred empty houses and seen some straggling rebels, but he had taken none.

On the 13th my black boy, Quaco, being perfectly recovered, arrived, to my great satisfaction as his fidelity to me was so steady and unshaken. At the same time we received an account that Captain Stoelman, with some rangers, had discovered a fresh settlement of the rebels by a great smoke appearing at a distance in the forest, but had not yet attacked them; that Captain Fredericy, with a party of black volunteers, was scouring the seaside below Paramaribo; that the two men we had lost on the 18th of August had miraculously escaped and found their way to the post at the river Marawina; and that no less than twelve fine negro slaves had just deserted from the Gold Mine estate to join the rebels.

This news so much exasperated Colonel Fourgeoud, that the indefatigable man again determined to persevere in pursuing his enemies. We accordingly entered the woods very early on the morning of the 15th, although he and his little army were at this time greatly reduced. I must not omit that, a little before our departure, seven more of our negro slaves did desert us, who went home to their masters perfectly broken-hearted, emaciated, and nearly starved. However, we proceeded and marched directly north-east during which nothing happened, except my box with all my bottles being dashed to pieces; and in the evening we encamped, though *then* unknown to us, near the Casepoere Creek, where the dry season having commenced, we dug a pit for water. Orders were also issued to the troops no more to build huts and sheds, as the rains were now less violent.

On the 16th we continued our route, marching north-east as before, and towards the evening arrived at the houses which Colonel Fourgeoud had lately discovered, which proved since to be only a temporary settlement, erected by the rebels as a shelter or asylum in their expected retreat, before they were dislodged from Gado Saby; and to this little settlement they had given the name of Boossy Cry, that is, 'the woods lament'. Here we encamped, and took much notice of Bonny's house in particular, which was built like a watering machine, being elevated from the ground, with two doors, so that he might the better observe all around him and prevent his being taken by surprise. It also had more air and, of course, was better calculated for his health, he having in some late action received a very dangerous wound in the groin, as we afterwards learned from a rebel negro prisoner. Near to Bonny's house were the private baths, where his women washed themselves morning and evening, there being no river near this settlement.

On the 17th we continued our march north and north-east in hopes of more discoveries, but without success. We this day passed some ant-hillocks above six feet high, and, without exaggeration, above one hundred feet in circumference. We also saw great quantities of valuable timber, and, among the rest, the black-cabbage tree, the wood of which is of a deep brown, and is in high estimation among carpenters and joiners.

On the 18th we continued the same course for a few hours longer, when we found a beaten path which, though circuitous, seemed to be a communication between Gado Saby and Boossy Cry. We followed this path, which led us due west for a few hours, when a poor rebel negro was found by men covered with branches of the manicole-tree, and indeed barely alive, being in appearance nothing but skin and bone, with one of his eyes almost beaten out of the socket. Fourgeoud ordered this man to be carried with us in a hammock, and we soon afterwards encamped near a biree-biree swamp or quagmire. I ought not to forget that this day we saw some very fine locust-trees, being eighty or a hundred feet high, and prodigiously thick. Innumerable indeed are the various fine trees that this country produces, and which may be had for the cutting; yet, when we consider the distance they usually grow from navigable rivers, the great labour in felling and working them, the vast number of slaves required to drag them through the forest where no horses can be employed, besides the danger and loss of time, we may easily account for the enormous price generally paid for the best timber in Guiana.

This march undoubtedly afforded us the most enchanting prospects that can be imagined, in a luxuriant and evergreen forest, while the dry season contributed greatly to beautify the scene and simple nature by far outshone the most strenuous endeavours of art. Here we met with immense savannahs of the most lovely verdure interspersed with meandering brooks of water, cool and clear as rock crystal, their borders adorned with flowers of every lively hue and fragrance. In some places we observed small clumps of elegant shrubs, or perhaps a single tree, whose beauty would almost induce one to think they had been designedly left growing to enrich the scene.

On the 19th we again marched, and fell in with our old path leading directly to the fields of Gado Saby, where quantities of rice once more appeared in full bloom, which we cut down and burned to ashes. On the 20th, we marched to visit Cosaay, with the unhappy negro captive still carried along with us; but the slaves, being discontented with such a load, took every opportunity, in my absence, of torturing him, by knocking him against roots and stones and dragging him through mud and water as they went along. Different patrols were now ordered out to reconnoitre the grounds, while the remainder of the troops encamped in the west part of Cosaay; and these patrols discovered no less than four beautiful fields in one chain, situated due west from Cosaay, well stocked with cassava, yams, plantains, pistachio nuts, with maize and pigeon peas. There were also several human carcases, the relics of our late engagements in August.

On the morning of the 21st, all these and every useful vegetable were cut down, and again destroyed by fire; after which, returning to our last night's camp, we found it also in flames, and were obliged to sling our hammocks in the east skirts of the woods. Here, recollecting that the poor disabled rebel was left alone, I ran back west to the burning camp to afford him assistance; but after seeking him in vain through clouds of smoke and darkness, I was forced to consult my own safety by hastily returning to my companions; some blaming me much for my temerity, others damning the *skeleton*, whether dead or alive.

The devastation being now completed, we marched back to Jerusalem, where on the 24th we arrived perfectly exhausted, and Fourgeoud at last so ill with a fever, that he was confined to his hammock with small hopes of surviving the night. But he however still continued to command, and the next morning ordered a marine to be bastinadoed for asking shoes, although he was bare-footed and his feet tore to pieces. Another, who had a feverish cold, was flogged for coughing; a captain was dismissed from actual service and confined in Fort Zelandia, for having dared to marry without his consent. Sickness and death now raged through the camp, and everything was in the utmost confusion.

To complete the whole, on the 1st of November twenty-five more negro slaves ran away; and on the 3rd we received intelligence that no less than fifty armed rebels had been seen swimming across the River Cottica, about a musket-shot above Barbacoeba.

In consequence of this information, Colonel Seyburgh was detached, with the few men that remained able to carry arms. Through distress and famine these were now almost ready to attack their own officers, and being unsupplied with their favourite luxury, tobacco, sat smoking grey paper, and chewing leaves and leather as a substitute for the want of it. Few men, however, were worse off than I was at this time. Having neither provisions nor clothes, I was almost naked as well as starved, with a running ulcer in my left foot; nor had I a friend in the camp who could give me the smallest assistance. To complete my misery, the little blood I had remaining was in two successive nights nearly sucked away by the vampire-bat, or spectre; thus I fainted away in my hammock, and was almost sorry to recover, particularly upon being informed by a letter that Joanna and her boy were dying with a putrid fever at Paramaribo.

On the 14th Colonel Fourgeoud was so dangerously ill that he at length was obliged to relinquish his command and proceed to town for his recovery. Accordingly on the 15th, he set out by water for Paramaribo: thus, after having sacrificed all his troops, he became himself a victim to his unbounded ambition and obstinate perseverance in this worst of all climates, while by toiling less and living better both he and his soldiers might have rendered the colony, if not a superior, at least an equal service. A barge loaded with sick and dying was at the same time once more sent to the hospital at Devil's Harwar.

The command of the remaining scarecrows now devolved upon the Lieutenant Colonel, who (strange to tell!) that very evening inherited the same distemper, as well as the chief command. Several officers would have before now thrown up their military commissions, could they with decency have taken such a measure during an expedition on actual service. I could myself have wished to go for some time to Paramaribo, but as this favour was not offered me, while all the others, and even the slaves, were relieved, I scorned to petition for it while I was able to stand.

On the 19th, however, my foot became so bad that the surgeon reported me unfit for duty; yet I still remained in the camp, where I could be to none of any service.

A supply of fresh troops, slaves, and provisions being arrived on the 20th, Major Medlar, with 150 men, was detached to make new discoveries.

Among other plagues, the whole camp at this time swarmed with locusts, which appeared everywhere in most formidable troops, devouring everything that lay in their way. Indeed the curse of Heaven seemed to visit us here in various shapes, and vermin were so plentiful at this time, that no exertion could keep us perfectly free.

On the 3rd of December, Major Medlar's party returned, after fourteen days' absence, with a captive rebel woman and her boy about eight years old, taken in a small field of bitter cassava. The poor woman was pregnant and under great alarms, but was tenderly treated by Medlar, who was always a humane and well-disposed gentleman. He had, however, unluckily lost two of his best men, who, having inadvertently eaten a few roots of the above bitter cassava, were poisoned and died during the same night with the most excruciating pain and convulsions.

The black woman confirmed the account that Bonny had been wounded; also that the poor starved negro we had found was called Isaac, and had been left for dead. Bonny, she assured us, maintained the strictest discipline among his troops: he was, she said, absolutely despotic, and none of his people were trusted with arms until they had first served him some years as slaves and given him unquestionable proofs of fidelity and resolution. But these, she observed, were but few in number, when compared to his numerous vassals, who were bound to do without murmuring whatever he thought proper to command them; yet that he *still* was more beloved than he was feared, on account of his inflexible justice and manly courage.

On the 4th December, this poor woman and her boy were sent to Paramaribo. It being proved at the court that she had been forcibly carried off by the rebels, though many years before, the poor creature was pardoned, and joyfully returned with her child to her master's plantation.

I have just mentioned, that, on account of a very bad foot, I had been returned unfit for duty by the surgeon, on the 19th of November; yet this day, December 5th, another surgeon, with two captains and the adjutant, were sent to inspect both me and Captain Perret, who was also sick. The surgeon gave his declaration *upon oath* that we were incapable of walking without danger, much more of undergoing fatigue; but Seyburgh, who was still in his fever, declared we should instantly enter the woods, though he should see us carried in two wheelbarrows. Poor Captain Perret complied to turn out, though he looked like a ghost and could scarcely stand; but I solemnly swore that I would blow out the first man's brains who dared *disrespectfully* to touch me. In consequence I was close guarded by a sentinel, while the whole camp, upon my soul, now seemed to be composed of none but madmen.

On the 11th we received intelligence that a number of armed rebels had been just seen opposite to Devil's Harwar, and were afterwards informed that they were upon their retreat from the Comewina River, where on the 5th they had burnt to ashes the dwelling-house of the estate Killestyn Nova, with Mr Slighter the overseer in it, ransacked the whole plantation, killed and carried off thirty-three women, and chopped off the limb of a male mulatto child, to be revenged of its father. The Perica rangers were in pursuit of them. Captain Fredericy also arrived this day, having exchanged from the Society troops into Colonel Fourgeoud's regiment of marines, and confirmed to us the above unhappy news.

About this time, after having starved four months, my remaining stores arrived at last, but three-fourths rotted and destroyed by the cockroaches: the remaining part I distributed among the sick people. But what proved truly acceptable, was the cheering account that Joanna and Johnny were past danger and recovering at Paramaribo. This intelligence indeed so elevated my spirits that the next morning I reported myself fit for duty, though God knows that I was not. To this I was the more induced by the want of fresh air, of which I was perfectly debarred in my confinement, and stood so much in need.

Eight days later, the 20th of December, being actually recovered of the wound in my foot and Seyburgh of his phrenetic fever, another officer and I played him the following trick for his bad usage. Having invited this gentleman, with his adjutant and a few more, to see us act a farce by candlelight, we affected to quarrel, and beating out the candle, the door being well secured, laid on in the dark with such success upon a certain somebody's shoulders that, calling out 'Murder!' he leaped out at the window. Nothing ever gave me greater entertainment than to perceive his agility, but Colonel Seyburgh declared he would never more be a spectator to our play.

At this time orders arrived from Colonel Fourgeoud, who was also better, to break up our camp at Jerusalem and march once more to the Wana Creek. On the 22nd, at six o'clock in the morning, we all decamped and scrambled up along the banks of the Cormoetibo Creek through a perfect bog, while one poor negro, who had his head fractured, was left behind, and another knocked overboard and drowned.

This march was peculiarly disagreeable upon account of the heavy rains, which now began to fall down in torrents, overflowing the banks of all the rivers; and so cold were the damps in the morning, contrasted with the late warm days, that we frequently lay shivering in our hammocks as in frost, especially when sleeping in wet clothes. This inconvenience, however, I obviated by marching half naked, like the rangers, and putting my shirt in one of the reversed kettles. Thus my skin soon drying after a shower, I again put on my linen and found myself much more comfortable than any of my trembling ghastly looking companions.

On the evening of the 23rd, we encamped near a rivulet called the Caymans or Alligator Creek; on the 24th we slung our hammocks in the evening, near a brook called Yorica, or the Devil's Creek, and on the following day, having once more laboured through deep mud and water in very heavy rains, we encamped at another small brook, called the Java Creek, three miles below the Wana.

On the 26th I was selected, with a small party, to reconnoitre the old camps at Wana Creek. In the evening we returned, half swimming through mud and water, having literally seen nothing except some birds and curious trees.

On the 27th, another patrol was sent out, but to no better purpose than the first. I have mentioned that my foot was recovered, and so it was, but I had now extracted out of my right arm two dreadful insects, which left behind them very deep ulcers.

My heart now began to sink with accumulated disasters; my mind was agitated and depressed with a constant train of tortures to which I could see no end, and I became weary of life. In this dreadful situation I fell upon my naked knees, and invoked the malediction of Heaven to fall on me, if I did not separate myself from my present commanders and this service at the first honourable opportunity that should offer itself.

The place of our present encampment was now intolerable beyond every description, being constantly overflowed, so that the ammunition and provisions were stowed for preservation on wooden rafts; nor could we step out of our hammocks without being up to the knees in mud and water, while the gnats and other insects devoured us alive. The consequence of all which was, that another barge full of dying wretches was sent down the Cormoetibo Creek, bound for the hospital at Devil's Harwar. This floating charnel-house weighed anchor on the last day of the year 1775.

20

To what good star I was obliged, in the midst of all our confusion and distress, I know not, but certain it is that Colonel Seyburgh having sent for me on the first day of the new year, not only solicited my future friendship, but declared he was sorry for all the ill-treatment he had ever occasioned me. Then, taking me by the hand, he permitted me as a proof of his real regard, from that moment to go to Paramaribo or wherever I pleased, to refresh and refit until further orders. This had such an effect on me, that having instantly converted every drop of my rum into grog, we sat down, together with two other officers, and drowned all former animosity in oblivion, till we could hardly see each other. In this condition I took my leave that very evening of my *new* friend and the camp at Java Creek, and rowed down in the best spirits for Paramaribo.

On the 3rd I arrived at the fortress Amsterdam, where I was entertained with an excellent fish dinner, and in the evening at six o'clock I arrived once more at Paramaribo. There I found Joanna with her little boy perfectly well, after having both been blind for above three weeks. Being now invited to lodge with them, at the house of my friend Mr de Graaf, I was completely happy.

The following day I dined with Colonel Fourgeoud, who now also was as sound as ever, and who gave me a very indifferent meal of salt provisions,* but an *uncommonly* hearty welcome. He acquainted me that two new companies of free mulattoes and two of free negroes, all volunteers, had just been raised; that the Seramica and Ouca negroes encouraged and favoured the rebels and were deceitful rascals; that a few rebels had been killed in the Cassivinica Creek; that Bonny, with his people, was almost starving in the forest, notwithstanding their late depredations, and that he was fully determined, if he should lose his last man, to make *this* rebel surrender, or harass him till he and his gang, through hunger and distress, should be obliged to quit the colony.

The Colonel, in a word, was now quite the reverse of what he had been before, and upon the whole so very agreeable in his manners, that I would never wish to spend my time in better company; but how I should become at once the favourite of both these rival commanders, was a secret I could never yet discover, unless it might

* This he absolutely held as the best regimen for health, notwithstanding he had brought three cooks from Europe.

proceed from a desire of gaining me from each other, as they still continued mutual enemies. Be that as it may, I resolved to preserve the most inflexible neutrality, as I also did between them and the governor, where I was invited next day, and dined not on salt-beef but found as usual a truly magnificent entertainment.

I was present too at a mulatto ball, composed however not of slaves, but of free independent settlers. Here the music, the lights, the country dances, the supper, and, above all, the dresses were so superb, and their behaviour so decent and genteel, that the whole might serve as a model for decorum and etiquette to some of the fairer and more polished inhabitants.

On the 25th I was seized with a fever and blooded in the foot, in which the orifice being struck too deep—for struck it was as they bleed the horses—I again became lame; during which time Colonel Seyburgh arrived from the Java Creek to recover, he being at last also taken very ill.

In the meantime Colonel Fourgeoud, ready to renew his operations and having already sent a small detachment to the Jew Savannah for intelligence, received letters from the Hague with express orders to abandon the expedition immediately, and with his few remaining troops to sail for Holland without delay.

In consequence of these commands, the transport ships were put in commission, and all the officers and privates received their clearance, which made them very happy; and indeed all at Paramaribo were alive with joy, except some of the inhabitants and myself.

On the 14th of February, ill as I was with a bad foot, a sore arm, the prickly heat, and all my teeth loose with the scurvy, I found means to scramble out on crutches, with a thousand florins in my pocket, which having divided between Fourgeoud and Mrs Godefroy for the redemption of the black boy Quaco and my mulatto, I returned home without a shilling in my purse; yet for this small sum of 500 florins, so inadequate to 1800 which I owed that lady, she was induced generously to renew her persuasions of carrying Joanna and the boy with me to Holland. This, however, Joanna as nobly as firmly refused.

On the 15th, however, by letters from Holland to our chief, our return was again countermanded for six months. My companions were therefore suddenly cast down with disappointment, while I was as suddenly revived, and now determined to save all my pay until Joanna's redemption should be fully accomplished.

On the 18th of Feburary, the poor dispirited men were again sent up to Magdenberg, a large party still remaining at the Java Creek. The temper of the officers was now so ruffled that a Mr Fisher of our corps fought no less than two duels in two succeeding days, danger-

Marching through a swamp

ously wounding both his antagonists, who were both officers of the Society regiment.

As I was not yet recovered, I stayed some time longer at Paramaribo. On the 21st of February, Mr Reynsdorp, the son-in-law of Mrs Godefroy, took me in his sail barge for change of air to Nuten-Schadelyk, one of his own coffee estates. The following day, sailing up Comewina River, we proceeded to the delightful cacao plantation Alkmaar, the property of the above lady, where the negro slaves are treated like children by the mistress, to whom they all look up as to their common parent. Here were no groans to be heard, no fetters to be met with, nor any marks of severity to be seen—but all was harmony and content.

On the 27th we returned to town where, the day before, a Society soldier had been shot for mutiny, and the day following a ship was burnt in the roads. This being the period for the sessions, another negro's leg was cut off for skulking from a task to which he was unequal, while two more were condemned to be hanged for running away altogether. The heroic behaviour of one of these men before the court deserves particularly to be noticed. He begged only to be heard for a few moments, which being granted, he proceeded thus:

'I was born in Africa, where, defending my prince during an engagement, I was made a captive and sold for a slave on the coast of Guinea by my own countrymen. One of your countrymen, who is now to be one of my judges, became my purchaser, in whose service I was treated so cruelly by his overseer that I deserted and joined the rebels in the woods. Here again I was condemned to be a slave to Bonny, their chief, who treated me with even more severity than I had experienced from the Europeans, till I was once more forced to elope, determined to shun mankind for ever and inoffensively to end my days by myself in the forest. Two years had I persevered in this manner quite alone, undergoing the greatest hardships and anxiety of mind, preserving life only for the possibility of once more seeing my dear family, who were perhaps starving on my account in my own country. I say two miserable years had just elapsed, when I was discovered by the rangers, taken, and brought before this tribunal, who are now acquainted with the history of my wretched life, and from whom the only favour I have to ask is that I may be executed next Saturday, or as soon as it may possibly be convenient.'

This speech was uttered with the utmost moderation, by one of the finest-looking negroes that was perhaps ever seen. His former master, who, as he observed, was now one of the judges, made the following laconic reply: 'Rascal! that is not what we want to know; but the torture this moment shall make you confess crimes as black as yourself, as well as those of your hateful accomplices.' To which the negro, who now swelled in every vein with indignation and ineffable contempt, said: '*Masera*, the tigers have trembled for these hands,' holding them up; 'and dare you think to threaten me with your wretched instrument? No, I despise the utmost tortures you can now invent, as much as I do the pitiful wretch who is going to inflict them.' Saying which, he threw himself down on the rack, where amidst the most excruciating torments he remained with a smile, without uttering a syllable; nor did he ever speak again, until he ended his unhappy days at the gallows.

Having dined with Colonel Fourgeoud on the 8th of March, when we celebrated the Prince of Orange's birthday while Mr Reyndorp gave a treat to all the soldiers, he acquainted me that the rangers were now alone encamped at the Wana Creek, that the pestilential spot Devil's Harwar was at last entirely forsaken, and that the two lately raised companies of sable volunteers had taken a few prisoners and killed others on the Wanica path, behind Paramaribo. I was at this time a good deal better, but still, not being quite recovered, he who had formerly treated me so severely, now even insisted on my staying some longer time at Paramaribo: nay, gave me an offer to return to Europe, which I absolutely refused. In short, about the middle of the month, I was as well as ever I was in my life. At this time Colonel Fourgeoud and myself were daily visitors of the ladies, in whose company no man could behave better, while I could often not avoid disgust; indeed so languid were many in their looks, and so unrestrained were some in their conversation, that one even asked me, *sans ceremonie*, to supply the place of her husband. She might as well have asked me to drink, for a relish, a tumbler of salts.

On the 17th, however, my eyes were better feasted, when, going to dine with Colonel Texier of the Society troops, I first took a walk in the orange grove and the governor's gardens. Here, peeping through the foliage, I soon discovered two most elegant female figures after bathing, the one a fine young Samboe, the other a blooming Quadroon, which last was so very fair complexioned, that she might have passed for a native of Greece, while the roses that glowed in her cheek were equal to those that blossomed in the shrubbery. They were walking hand in hand, and conversing with smiles near a flowery bank that adorned the side of a crystal brook, in which they plunged the instant they heard me rustling among the verdure.

Leaving them to enjoy their innocent amusement of bathing, I spent the remaining hour before dinner among the shady fruit-trees, blooming bowers and serpentine gravel walks, where I saw a greater variety of European plants than I imagined were produced in a tropical climate.

At this time Captains Van Geurick and Fredericy, with Sergeant

Fowler, were sent on an embassy to the Ouca and Saramica free negroes, if possible to procure their assistance against the rebels, which they always continued to promise (while Colonel Fourgeoud gave them presents) but never yet performed. A few of the other officers still stayed with us gallanting at Paramaribo, among whom were Major Medlar and Captain Hemmet. It was no small change of appearance for us, who had so little a time before appeared like wild men, now to strut through Paramaribo dressed like so many French marquises.

Having on the 26th once more saved a poor black girl from receiving some hundred lashes, by replacing a dozen of china which she had broken by accident—while another was stabbed by a Frenchman, who immediately cut his own throat from remorse, and his companion, an overseer, hanged himself—and having visited the poor negro whose leg had lately been cut off by law, I packed my boxes to set out next morning on my sixth campaign, once more to take the command of the River Comewina.

On the 30th, a little before we landed at the Hope, I discovered that all my sugar, with the greatest part of my rum, was gone, and detected the thief by the following laughable stratagem (though not my own invention). I told the negroes, six in number, that a parrot's feather would grow within six minutes upon the tip of the nose of the guilty one. At the same time, pronouncing a few incoherent words and making two or three circles with my sabre, I shut myself within the tilt. Here, peeping through the keyhole, and observing the rowers with great attention, without their perceiving me, I soon saw one of them, at every stroke of the oar, put up his hand and feel the tip of his nose. I instantly ran up to him, and cried, 'I see the parrot's feather! Thou art the thief, thou rascal!' To which the poor superstitious fellow instantly answered, '*Yaw, me masera!*' then kneeling to the *sorcerer* for mercy, and the others also intreating me to spare him, I pardoned the credulous thief and his accomplices, who by their candid confession obtained a piece of salt beef for their dinner, and a gourd full of good grog in the bargain.

Immediately on my arrival I took the command of the whole river, and now was once more the Prince of Comewina. I also built an elevated palace, in imitation of Prince Bonny's at Boossy Cry, on twelve strong stakes; which aerial habitation I found very necessary, the whole post being almost under water by the inundations, and by neglect become a perfect mire-pool, while of my former cottage not a vestige was to be seen. Here I found the marines in perfect misery, being almost naked, and having sold their very shoes for a mouthful of fresh provisions. These grievances, however, by my labour and intercession with Colonel Fourgeoud, whose favourite I now became more and more, were speedily redressed, and the Hope, in a little time, appeared like a paradise when compared with its former state.

Shooting was now, as formerly, my favourite diversion, while swimming was another of my favourite amusements, which contributed to make me more healthy, and stronger than most of my companions. On the 14th I shot an alligator, but returning from this excursion in a boat, a packet of letters from Colonel Fourgeoud unfortunately fell overboard into the water and sank immediately. Some officers, however, the next day coming to the Hope, informed me of the principal contents; that Colonel Fourgeoud, being determined once more to scour the woods, had ordered me to send up all my spare men and provisions, as also the Society troops who were now at Oranjebo, the former to Magdenberg and the latter to the river Perica. This I performed, retaining only twelve crippled soldiers at the Hope, and as many at Clarenbeek, without either surgeon or medicines; nevertheless, with this small number, I made daily patrols by land and water.

Colonel Fourgeoud, though he himself remained at Paramaribo, continued attentively to command. Thus, on the 23rd, he ordered a detachment of one hundred men to reconnoitre from Magdenberg to the Wana Creek and Marawina river; but they returned without any new discoveries.

As I was now likely to continue at the Hope for some time, I sent for my sheep and poultry, from the estate where I had left them, and I found with joy that my flocks had considerably increased in numbers.

On the 28th I paid a visit to Thomas Palmer, late King's counsellor at Massachusett's Bay, at his estate called Fairfield. Here both the master and his slaves were perfectly happy and contented, chiefly owing to Mr Palmer's just and equitable administration to all around him; and such were the consequences of his wise government, that few plantations in the West Indies could boast of greater prosperity, either in point of produce or population, while the courtesy and hospitality of the gentleman-like proprietor to strangers, completed his happy character, which shone conspicuously throughout the colony.

Upon my return to the Hope I received a letter from the commander in chief, informing me that Mr Vinsack with his rangers had killed several rebels and taken eleven prisoners, but that another party of the rangers had been surprised by the enemy and several of them shot dead while asleep in their hammocks.

During these skirmishes, an instance of presence of mind was exhibited by a rebel negro, I think but seldom equalled. A ranger having levelled his piece was just going to fire at him, when the man called out, holding up his hand, 'What, Sir, do you mean to kill one of your own party?' The ranger, believing him, replied, 'God forbid!' and dropping the muzzle of his piece, instantly received a ball through the body from his adversary. Having thus saved himself, he disappeared like a flash of lightning.

On the 6th of May it blew a violent hurricane, accompanied with thunder and lightning, so that many trees were torn up by the roots, and most of the houses on the Hope blown down or unroofed. My aerial palace, however, by good fortune, withstood this gale, and upon the 8th, Joanna, with her boy, arriving at this place, I promised myself a scene of happiness equal to that I experienced in 1774, especially as my family, my sheep, and my poultry, were now doubled. Besides, I had at this time a beautiful garden, and if I could not with propriety be called a planter, I might at least claim, with some degree of justice, the name of a little farmer.

Colonel Fourgeoud now sending a proper supply of men, with a surgeon and medicines, the Hope wore a more pleasing aspect, and health and content began to be visible in every countenance. It was now truly a charming habitation, being perfectly dry even in spring-tides and washed by pleasing canals that let in the fresh water every tide, while the hedges surrounding the fields and gardens were neatly cut, and produced fruit and vegetables of many species for our use. The houses and bridges were also all repaired, while the strictest adherence to cleanliness was recommended and enforced among the men. By these means not one sick person out of fifty was now to be found, where sloth, stench and disease had so lately spread their destructive influence, and to which the land and sea-scurvy had given the most fatal assistance.

I now enjoyed the greatest flow of health and spirits, while most of my old shipmates were either dead or returned to Europe. Not a single officer at this time was in rank above me, except only such as had been formerly inured to the West India climate.

But to return to my garden—this at present exhibited carrots, cabbages, onions, cucumbers, lettuces, radishes, pepper and cresses, all thriving as well as in Europe, besides sorrel of two kinds, the common and the red. The jessamine also was found here of different species, that growing on a small tree being most admired: it is of a pale but beautiful red colour, and a most agreeable smell. A species of sensitive shrub they call *shame-shame*, grew here also as did the sleeping-plant, so called from its leaves, which are set in pairs, clapping close together from sunset to sunrise, and appearing as if the two were but one; but as soon as the sun is up they again open, and resume their double form. The above-mentioned shrubs were all dispersed through my hedges, besides pomegranates and Indian roses, which blow every day; while a few elegant red-lilies, which also grow wild in the savannahs, adorned the banks of my canals.

My soldiers, and even negroes, seemed now completely happy, among whom the most perfect harmony subsisted, while I frequently indulged them with a merry evening, and a grey-beard of rum. One night, in the midst of this festivity, I secretly ordered the sentinel to fire his piece and cause a false alarm, as if the enemy were on the estate. I then had the satisfaction to see them seize their arms, and rush out with the utmost order and intrepidity. This experiment I was the more inclined to put in practice, as it was reported that the rebels intended soon to pay a visit to the River Comewina. But we soon experienced that no scene of perfect felicity can be lasting, for the dry season now suddenly setting-in, disease and mortality once more began to rage among us, ten or twelve men dying daily at the Java Creek and Magdenberg, while those under my command at the Hope diminished hourly.

On the 4th of June, the spring-flood broke down my dams while we were drinking the king's health, and laid the whole post under water, which created vast confusion. In this distress the overseer Blenderman refused to lend me any assistance, which occasioned so violent a quarrel that he was glad to take to his heels and make his escape from the plantation. I shall never have done mentioning the insolence of these savage brutes, who mostly are the refuse of the earth, brought up in Germany or elsewhere, under the cane of a corporal. 'Well,' said one of these miscreants ironically to an old *free* negro, 'don't you believe that the monkeys are a race of damn'd Christians, who have been thus transformed for showing so much lenity to such as you?' 'No, sir,' replied the black man, 'we do not think that the monkeys are damn'd Christians, but I, and all of us, believe that many who call themselves Christians are a pack of damn'd monkeys.' Which pointed repartee afforded me infinite satisfaction.

On the 7th, Mr Moryn, administrator of the Hope, being in a piece of newly-cultivated ground on the opposite shore, I rowed over to obtain satisfaction of the impertinent Blenderman who was along with him. But this fellow's cowardice being equal to his insolence and barbarity, he made every concession, and promised likewise to repair my dams, rather than run the risk of broken bones. Thus a reconciliation was established.

On the 16th I was visited by a neighbouring gentleman, whom I conducted up my ladder; but he had no sooner entered my aerial dwelling, than he leapt down from the top to the ground, roaring like a madman with agony and pain, after which he instantly plunged his head into the river. Looking up, I soon discovered the cause of his distress to be an enormous nest of wild bees in the thatch, directly above my head as I stood within my door. I immediately took to my heels as he had done, and ordered them to be demolished by my slaves without delay. A tar mop was now brought, and the devastation just going to commence, when an old negro stepped up, and offered to receive any punishment I should decree if ever one of these bees should sting *me in person*. '*Masera*,' said he, 'they would have stung you long ere now had you been a stranger to them; but they being your tenants, and having been gradually allowed to build upon your premises, they assuredly know both you and yours, and will never hurt either you or them.' I instantly assented to the proposition, and tying the old black man to a tree, ordered my boy Quaco to ascend the ladder quite naked, which he did and was not stung. I then ventured to follow, and I declare upon my honour that, even after shaking the nest which made its inhabitants buzz about my ears, not a single bee attempted to sting me. I next released the old negro, and rewarded him with a gallon of rum and five shillings for the discovery. This swarm of bees I since kept unhurt as my bodyguards, and they have made many overseers take a desperate leap for my amusement, as I generally sent them up my ladder upon some frivolous message, when I wished to punish them for injustice and cruelty.

The above negro assured me, that on his master's estate was an ancient tree, in which had been lodged ever since he could remember, a society of *birds*, and another of *bees*, who lived in the greatest harmony together. But should any strange birds come to disturb or feed upon the bees, they were instantly repulsed by their feathered allies, and if strange bees dared to venture near the birds' nests, the native swarm attacked the invaders, and stung them to death. His master and family had so much respect for the above association, that the tree was considered as sacred, and was not to be touched by an axe until it should yield to all-destroying time.

On the 22nd, a patrol arrived from Rietwyk, in Perica, who informed me that a party of our troops were just returned to Java Creek from a cruise to Vredenburg, at the Marawina. In conjunction with the rangers, they had during this campaign destroyed many fields of provisions belonging to the rebels and, for their faithful services, our sable allies had been complimented by the Society with new arms and, for the first time, clothed in green uniform jackets. I further learned that the ambassadors to the Ouca and Seramica negroes were returned after a fruitless journey, as neither of these associations would lend the smallest assistance. In consequence of this refusal, Colonel Fourgeoud, being wearied himself and having exhausted his troops in destroying most of the rebel settlements, at length determined to relinquish the whole expedition. This resolution he communicated to his Serene Highness the Prince of Orange at the Hague.

On the 23rd I received positive orders to prepare and be ready on the 15th of July to break up, and with all the troops under my command to leave the River Comewina and row down to Paramaribo, where the transport ships were put in commission to convey us back to Holland. This order I instantly read before the front to all my men, who received it with unbounded joy and three cheers—but I alone sighed bitterly. Oh my Joanna! Oh my boy! At this time both were dangerously ill, the one with a fever, the other with convulsions, so that neither were expected to survive. Add to this, that I ran a nail quite through my foot—thus was I completely miserable.

An old Indian woman of Joanna's acquaintance being now sent for to the Hope, I myself was soon cured by her skill and attention, but my little family continued so very unwell that I thought it right to send them to Paramaribo before it was too late. On the 10th of July I sent all my sheep and poultry to Fauconberg, one couple of fat ewes excepted, which I killed and with which, by the addition of fish and venison, I entertained for two days following twenty-four of the most respectable inhabitants in the river, while the white bread, fruit and Spanish wines to help out the feast, I received as a present from my very worthy friend, Mr James Gourlay, at Berghoven.

On the 13th I ordered down the troops from Clarenbeek, where a hospital had been a second time erected, and they this evening anchored off the Hope. On the 14th, an officer of the Honourable Society troops arrived to relieve me in the command of the river, and his men from that moment began to perform the duty. I now removed my flag from the Hope to the barges, and in the evening took my last farewell of Joanna's relations on the Fauconberg estate. They crowded round me, expressed their sorrow aloud for my departure, and with tears invoked the protection of Heaven for my safe and prosperous voyage.

On the 15th we finally left the Hope, having marched my troops on board the barges at ten o'clock. At noon I fired my pistol as a signal to weigh anchor, and we immediately proceeded down the River Comewina for the roads of Paramaribo, to be embarked on board the transport ships for Europe.

21

On the evening of the 15th of July, we anchored off the estate Berghoven, where I spent the night ashore with my friend Gourley; and in the morning we continued to row down the river, when I took my last farewell of Mr Palmer. I passed the evening of the 17th with Captain MacNeyl, and, on the 18th, the whole fleet, consisting of my own barges together with three from Magdenberg and those from the River Cottica, arrived safe at anchor in the roads of Paramaribo, where three transports lay ready to receive us, on board of which vessels I immediately embarked all the troops that had come down under my command.

This service being accomplished, I went ashore and made my report to Colonel Fourgeoud; after which I went to visit Joanna and her boy, whom, to my great joy, I found very much recovered.

The following day I was again sent on board to make the necessary arrangements for the voyage. On the 20th I dined with Colonel Fourgeoud, and on the 21st we once more received our clearance, but in card money, by which we all lost very considerably. However, I instantly went to Mrs Godefroy, and again gave her all the money that was in my pocket, being no more than £40. This excellent woman now renewed her entreaties that I should carry my boy and his mother with me to Holland, but to no purpose; Joanna was perfectly immoveable, even to a degree of heroism, and no persuasion could make the least impression upon her, until her redemption should be made complete by the payment of the very last farthing. In this situation we affected to bear our fate with perfect resignation, though what each of us felt in particular may much more easily be imagined than described.

The regiment's colours were now carried on board in great state on the 23rd, but without receiving any honours from Fort Zelandia, not a single gun being fired, nor even the flag hoisted on the occasion, to the great mortification of Colonel Fourgeoud—though in effect it was chiefly owing to his own neglect, as he had never given the Governor *official* notice of his intended departure. The baggage was also sent on board the ships, and a gentleman of the name of Van Heyst entertained the marines at his private expense with three hundred bottles of wine, fruit, etc.

I have often remarked the hospitality and generosity of these people, which I now also once more experienced, receiving various presents of fruits and preserves from my numerous friends, to refresh me at sea while on the voyage.

On the 24th of July, the sails being bent to the yards, we *at last* proceeded to take leave of His Excellency the Governor of the colony, who, while he still received us with the greatest politeness, yet gave our hero to understand that were his colours *now* to be sent on board, they should most certainly be saluted with those honours which indisputably were their due. After which he sent the whole corps of Society officers in state to the headquarters, to wish us a prosperous voyage to Holland. In this contest of etiquette His Excellency most assuredly led the van; for hinting so, however, to some of Fourgeoud's favourites, I nearly engaged myself once more in a serious quarrel. Our men, who had been on board since the 18th, being now joined by their officers, the poor remains of this fine regiment were thus finally embarked and, in the highest flow of spirits, expected to set sail the following day for Europe. Every countenance (one alone excepted) wore the appearance of happiness and joy; and nothing indeed could equal the exultation of the few surviving troops, when the next morning the orders were issued for the ships to weigh anchor and put to sea.

But it was by fate ordained that their eager hopes and expectations once more should be blasted; for on the very moment of departure, a ship entered the river with dispatches, enclosing an order for the regiment immediately to *re-enter the woods* and remain in the colony until relieved by fresh troops to be sent out from Holland for that purpose. The *sincere thanks* of His Serene Highness the Prince of Orange were now read to the men from the quarter-deck of each vessel, 'for the manly and spirited conduct they had displayed during so long a trial, and so many great and unprecedented hardships'. But as they concluded with orders for the troops to *disembark*, and remain in this dreadful service, I never saw dejection, disappointment and despair so strongly marked. At this moment I, who but just before had been completely miserable, was now in turn the only one who was not depressed with sorrow.

In the midst of this gloomy scene, the men were ordered to give three cheers, which the marines on board one of the vessels absolutely refused to comply with. Colonel Seyburgh, and unluckily myself, were in consequence ordered to compel them, which he undertook with a cane in one hand and a loaded pistol cocked in the other. Knowing his temper to be fiery and irascible, what did I not feel at this moment? I suddenly leapt into the boat that lay alongside, where, after haranguing those few that leaned over the gunwale, I promised the ship's crew twenty gallons of Holland's gin if they would only begin the melancholy chorus. Then mounting again the quarter-deck, I acquainted the Colonel that all were *now* ready and willing to obey his commands. We then re-entered the boat, and in shoving off had the satisfaction to receive three hearty cheers from the sailors, in which joined a few marines, but with such languid looks and heavy hearts as cannot be described.

At this time however the Prince of Orange's goodness of heart appeared in a conspicuous light, as he ordered all private accounts due by the troops to surgeons and physicians to be paid by the treasury, which was no trifle to many of the officers, and evinced an attention in His Serene Highness which is not always to be found in princes.

If our disembarkation distressed the troops, it afforded joy to most of the colonists. Indeed a petition, signed by the principal inhabitants, had been presented to Colonel Fourgeoud but two days before, 'praying that our regiment might stay some time longer, and give the finishing stroke to the rebels, as we had so gloriously begun and persevered in routing and harassing them'. This indeed was certainly true, for our regiment, in conjunction with the Society and rangers, had demolished most settlements the rebels possessed in the colony, and had driven them to so considerable a distance, that their depredations, and the desertion of slaves, were incomparably less than upon our arrival. Assuredly this was much better than the Dutch making a shameful peace with them, as had been done with the rebels of the Ouca and Seramica settlements before, yet which would probably again have been the consequence had we not landed in Guiana.

Though we continued in Surinam some time longer, our future services could add but very little to its prosperity, as our numbers were now so very few, and out of this number, small as it was, nine officers and above one hundred and sixty privates, all sick and incurable, embarked again for Holland on the 1st of August. I was ill with an ague at this time, and had the offer of making one of the party, but declined it, being determined to see the end of the expedition if I could.

Major Medlar being quite emaciated with fatigue and hardships, now also sailed for Holland. Thus, during his absence acting as major, I began to entertain an expectation that I should one day carry home the regiment myself, so very rapidly were our officers daily diminishing.

Everything now being peaceable and quiet, I recovered my strength so far as on the 10th to walk to Mrs Godefroy, when I acquainted her that I wished much to emancipate at least Johnny Stedman, and requested her to become bail before the court, for the usual sum of £300, as he should never be any charge to the colony of Surinam. But this she peremptorily declined, though there was no risk, it being only a matter of form; at which I could not help feeling some astonishment, till I was acquainted that she had actually refused the same favour to her own son.

The mention of slavery reminds me that I have not been sufficiently full upon this subject, and I am the more disposed to bring forward all the information that I have gained concerning the negroes, because I flatter myself that I shall be able to bring some truths to light that have hitherto been unobserved or imperfectly related, at least to the generality of Europeans.

With respect to the shape of the African negroes, it is from head to foot certainly different from the European mould, though not, in my opinion, in any degree inferior, prejudice being laid aside. Their strong features, flat noses, thick lips and high cheek bones, may appear deformities to us, and yet among themselves may be esteemed the reverse; their bright black eyes and fine white teeth, we are forced to admire; and one decided advantage in a black complexion is that all those languid pale sickly-looking countenances, so common in Europe, are never exhibited among them, nor are the wrinkles and ravages of age equally conspicuous, though I must confess that when a negro is very ill, his black changes to a very disagreeable sallow olive.

For exertion and activity, their shape is assuredly preferable to ours, being generally strong and muscular near the trunk, and slender towards the extremities; they have mostly a remarkable fine chest, but are small about the hips; their buttocks are more prominent, and their necks are thicker than ours; the thighs are strong, as also the arms above the elbow, but the wrists and lower part of the legs are very slender. As to the crookedness of their limbs, it is to be accounted for by the manner in which they are carried while infants upon the mother's back, their tender legs being tied close round each side of her waist, which occasions that unnatural bent with which they are not born; nor are their children ever taught to walk, but left to creep among the sand and grass until they gradually acquire strength and inclination to erect themselves, which they do very soon. By this custom, however, the position of their feet is much neglected, yet by exercise and daily bathing, they acquire that strength and agility for which they are so remarkable.

Another custom which, in their opinion, conduces much to their health and vigour is that, during the two years in which the mothers suckle their children, they frequently make them swallow large quantities of water, after which they shake them twice a day with much violence; they are then taken by a leg or an arm, and tossed into the river, to be well scoured outwardly; nor are the females exempt from this mode of rearing youth, which renders them not inferior to the men.

These hardy daughters of the Torrid Zone are no less remarkable for propagation. I knew a female servant who actually bore *nine* children in the course of three years, the first year four, the next two, and the third three. They bring their offspring into the world without pain and, like the Indian women, resume their domestic employments even the same day. During the first week their infants are as fair as any Europeans, except that in the males there is a little appearance of black in a *certain part*, and the whole body becomes gradually of that colour. Their females arrive early at the age of puberty; but, as in the fruits of this climate, this early maturity is succeeded by a sudden decay. Many of the negroes, however, live to a very considerable age: I have seen one or two that were above one hundred, and the London Chronicle makes mention of a negro woman in South America, still living at the surprising age of one hundred and seventy-five years.

In the constitution of the negroes I have still observed this singularity, that while they bear the fatigue of labour in the hottest days, they can also bear the cold and damp better than a European, at least better than I could—sleeping all night on the wet grass, perfectly naked, without any injury to their health, while I have been glad, especially early in the morning, to have a fire lit under my hammock, and while the marines for want of it lay in a shiver. They also bear hunger and thirst, and pain or sickness, with the greatest patience and resolution.

With the languages of the African negroes I am but little acquainted, but as to that spoken by the black people in Surinam, I consider myself a perfect master, it being a compound of Dutch, French, Spanish, Portuguese and English.

Their vocal music is like that of the birds, melodious but without time, one person constantly pronouncing a sentence extempore, which he next hums or whistles, and then all the others repeat the same in chorus; another sentence is then spoken, and the chorus is a second time renewed, and so on. This kind of singing is much practised by the barge rowers or boat negroes on the water, especially during the night in a clear moonshine; it is to them peculiarly animating, and may, together with the sound of their oars, be heard at a considerable distance.

All negroes firmly believe the being of a God, upon whose goodness they rely, and whose power they adore, while they have no fear of death, and never taste food without offering a libation. In the rivers Gambia and Senegal they are mostly Mahometans, but generally the worship and religious ceremonies of the Africans vary, as do the numberless superstitious practices of all savages, and indeed of too many Europeans.

No people can be more superstitious than the generality of negroes; and their pretended prophets find their interest in encouraging this superstition by selling them *obias* or amulets, as I have already mentioned. These people have also among them a kind of *sibyls*, who deal in oracles; these sage matrons dance and whirl round in the middle of an assembly with amazing rapidity, until they foam at the mouth and drop down as convulsed. Whatever the prophetess orders to be done during this paroxysm, is most sacredly performed by the surrounding multitude. This renders these meetings extremely dangerous, as she frequently enjoins them to murder their masters, or desert to the woods. For this reason this scene of excessive fanaticism is forbidden by law in the colony of Surinam, upon pain of the most rigorous punishment; yet it is often practised in private places, and is very common among the Ouca and Seramica negroes.

However ridiculous some of their rites may appear, yet among the African blacks they are certainly necessary to keep the rabble in subjection; and their priests know this as well as the infallible Pontiff of the Roman church. These illiterate mortals differ, however, in this respect from the modern Europeans, that whatever they believe, they do it firmly, and are never staggered by the doubts of scepticism, nor troubled with the qualms of conscience; but whether they are, upon this account, better or worse, I will not pretend to determine. I however think that they are a happy people, and possess so much friendship for one another, that they need not be told to 'love their neighbour as themselves'. The poorest negro, having only an egg, scorns to eat it alone, but were a dozen present, and every one a stranger, he would cut or break it into just as many shares; or were there one single dram of rum, he would divide it among the same number.

Nothing can exceed the fidelity and attachment the negroes have for those masters who use them well, which proves that their affection is as strong as their hatred. They are also susceptible of the tender passion, and jealousy in their breasts has produced the most dreadful effects. The delicacy of these people deserves likewise to be noticed: I do not remember, among the many thousands I have seen during several years' residence among them, ever to have observed even an offer to kiss a woman in public. Maternal tenderness for their children is also natural to the females, for in general, during the two years which they usually suckle them, they never cohabit with their husbands; this they consider as unnatural, and prejudicial to the infants. The cleanliness of the negro nation is peculiarly remarkable, as they bathe above three times a day.

The negroes are likewise spirited and brave, patient in adversity, meeting death and torture with the most undaunted fortitude. Their conduct, in the most trying situations, approaches even to heroism; no negro sighs, groans, or complains, though expiring in the midst of surrounding flames. Nor do I remember, upon any occasion whatever, to have seen an African shed a tear, though they beg for mercy with the greatest earnestness when ordered to be flogged for offences which they are conscious deserve to be punished; but if they think their punishment unmerited, immediate suicide is too often the fatal consequence, especially among the Coromantyn negroes, who frequently, during the act of flagellation, throw back their heads and *swallow their tongue*, which chokes them upon the spot, and they drop dead in the presence of their masters. But when negroes are sensible of having deserved correction, no people can be more humble, or bear their unhappy fate with greater resignation. The swallowing of the tongue, which they only practise during moments of severe discipline, has of late been prevented in Surinam by the *humane* method of holding a fire-brand to the victim's mouth, which answers the double purpose of burning his face, and diverting his attention from the execution of his fatal determination. Some have a practice of eating common earth, by which the stomach is prevented from performing its ordinary functions, and thus dispatch themselves without any immediate pain, but linger perhaps for a twelvemonth in the most debilitated and shocking condition. Against these ground-eaters the severest punishments are decreed by the laws, but without much effect, as they are seldom detected in this act of desperation.

In Surinam the slaves are kept nearly naked, and their daily food consists of little more than a few yams and plantains; perhaps twice a year they may receive a scanty allowance of salt-fish, with a few leaves of tobacco, and this is all. But what is peculiarly provoking to them is that, if a negro and his wife have ever so great an attachment for each other, the woman, if handsome, must yield to the loathsome embrace of an adulterous and licentious manager, or see her husband cut to pieces for endeavouring to prevent it.

By such inhuman usage this unhappy race of men are sometimes driven to such a height of desperation, that to finish their days and be relieved from worse than Egyptian bondage, some even have leaped into the cauldrons of boiling sugar, thus at once depriving the tyrant of his crop and of his servant.

From these sketches can it be a matter of surprise, that armies of rebels are assembled in the forest, at every opportunity thirsting for revenge?

On the other hand, however, there are those negro families who know that state of tranquil happiness which they always enjoy under a humane and indulgent master. Under a mild master and an honest overseer, a negro's labour is no more than a healthy exercise which ends at the setting sun. The remaining time is his own, which he employs in hunting, fishing, cultivating his garden, or making baskets and fish-nets for sale; with this money he buys a hog or two, sometimes fowls or ducks, all which he fattens upon the spontaneous growth of the soil, without expense, and very little trouble, and, in the end, they afford him considerable profit. Thus pleasantly situated, he is exempt from every anxiety, and pays no taxes, but looks up to his master as the only protector of him and his family. He adores him, not from fear, but from a conviction that he is indebted to his goodness for all the comforts he enjoys. He never lives with a wife he does not love, exchanging for another the moment either he or she becomes tired, though this separation happens less frequently here than divorces do in Europe.

No people can more esteem or have a greater friendship for one another than the negro slaves; they appear to have unbounded enjoyment in each other's company, and are not destitute of social amusements, such as the *soesa*, which consists in footing it opposite each other, and clapping with their hands upon their sides to keep in time. So very eager are they at this animating play, in which sometimes six or eight couples are engaged at once, that, as the violent exercise has been known to kill some of the negroes, it is forbidden by the magistrates at Paramaribo. *Awaree* is an innocent amusement, consisting in pitching with a large kind of marbles, in defect of which they use the awaree nuts or large pebbles.

The men also cudgel and wrestle, but swimming is their favourite diversion, which they practise every day at least twice or thrice, promiscuously, in groups of boys and girls, and both sexes exhibit astonishing feats of courage, strength and activity. I have not only seen a negro girl beat a hardy youth in swimming across the River Comewina (while I was one of the party) but on landing challenge him to run a two mile race, and beat him again, naked as they were; while all ideas of shame on the one side, and of insult on the other, are totally unknown.

Every Saturday evening, the slaves who are well treated close the week with an entertainment, and generally once a quarter are indulged with a grand ball, to which the neighbouring slaves are invited; the master often contributing to their happiness by his presence, or at least by sending them a present of a few jugs of new rum.

At these grand balls the slaves are remarkably neat, the women appearing in their best chintz petticoats, and many of the men in fine Holland trousers. So indefatigable are they at this diversion, that I have known the drums continue beating without intermission from six o'clock on Saturday night till the sun made its appearance on the Monday morning; thus had passed thirty-six hours in dancing, cheering, hallooing, and clapping of hands. The negroes dance always

A rebel negro

in couples, the men figuring and footing, while the women turn round like a top, their petticoats expanding like an umbrella; and this they call *waey-cotto*. During this, the by-standing youths pass the liquor round, while the girls encourage the performance and wipe the sweat from the brows and sides of the unwearied musicians.

Such is indeed the love and confidence of some planters for their slaves, that they often entrust their infants to a negro wet-nurse, in preference to a European, where both may be had; and such the attachment of some slaves to their masters, that I have known many refuse to accept of their emancipation, and even some, who had their liberty, voluntarily return to dependence.

22

NOTWITHSTANDING the successive defeats and repeated distresses of the rebels, news was brought to Paramaribo, on the 12th of August, that they had fallen upon the estate Bergendal, which is also called Mount Parnassus, situated in the higher parts of the River Surinam, and carried away all the black women, but without committing any kind of cruelty, as too generally had been their custom. Upon this intelligence a party of the rangers was instantly detached thither to assist in pursuing them; and about this same time the cutting of the long-projected *cordon*, or path of circumvallation round the colony, was also begun by seven hundred negro slaves. This path was henceforth to be manned with military piquets at proper distances, to defend the estates against any further invasions from without, and to prevent desertion to the enemy from within.

The 24th, being the Prince of Orange's birthday, the whole corps of officers were entertained with salt beef, salt pork, barley puddings and hard pease, by Colonel Fourgeoud. And this day (poor Joanna being inflexible in her resolutions) I ratified the agreement with the good Mrs Godefroy, in presence of her mother and other relations, whereby the above lady bound herself never to part with her, except to myself alone, as long as she lived; and that upon her death, not only her full liberty, but a spot of ground for cultivation, besides a neat house built upon it, should be her portion for ever, to dispose of as she pleased. After this she returned my remaining bond of 900 florins, and gave Joanna a purse with gold containing near twenty ducats besides a couple of pieces of East India chintz, advising me at the same time to give in a request to the court for little Johnny's immediate manumission.

Having both of us thanked this most excellent woman, I went to sup with the governor, where being transported with joy, I gave him my request in full form, which he coolly put in his pocket with one hand, while he gave me a hearty squeeze with the other. Shaking his head, he told me frankly that he would lay it before the court, but at the same time was perfectly convinced my boy must die a slave, unless I could find the necessary bail. Thus, after spending so much time and labour, besides the expense of above a hundred guineas already paid, I had still the inexpressible mortification to see this dear little fellow, of whom I was both the father and the master, exposed to perhaps eternal servitude.

One consolation, however, in the midst of this disappointment, most opportunely presented itself. The famous negro, Graman-Qwacy, who was just returned from Holland, brought the news that partly by *his* interest a new law was there enacted, by which all slaves were to be free six months after their landing at the Texel. This, on application of their masters, might be extended to twelve, but not a single day longer on any account whatsoever. Thus being persuaded that I should *one day* joyfully carry both him and his mother over the Atlantic, my heart was greatly relieved.

On the 25th, the governor of the colony gave a very sumptuous feast to several of his friends at his indigo-plantation, situated but a few miles from his palace, and I had the honour to be invited as one of the party.

When dinner was over I departed in His Excellency's coach to the water-side, where a tent-barge and eight oars lay in waiting to row me down to the estate Catwyk, in the River Comewina, whither I was invited by Mr Goetzee, a Dutch naval officer, who was the proprietor of this beautiful country seat. In this charming situation, no amusements were wanting. There were carriages, saddle-horses, sail-boats, billiard-tables, etc. all ready for immediate use. But what embittered the pleasure was the inhuman disposition of Mr Goetzee's lady, who flogged her negro slaves for every little trifle. For instance, one of the foot-boys called Jacky, not having rinsed the glasses according to her mind, she ordered him to be whipped the next morning. But the unfortunate youth soon put himself beyond the reach of her resentment, for, having taken farewell of the other negroes on the estate, he went upstairs, laid himself down upon his master's own bed and, placing the muzzle of a loaded fowling-piece in his mouth, by the help of his toe he drew the trigger and put an end to his existence. A couple of stout negroes were now sent up to see what was the matter. Finding the bed all over bespattered with blood and brains, they got orders to throw the body out of the window to the dogs, while the master and mistress were so very much alarmed, that they never got the better of it;* nor would any person consent to lie in the same apartment, till I chose it in preference to any other, as it was assuredly the most pleasant room with the very best bed in the house. What added much to the alarm of the family, was the circumstance of a favourite child lying fast asleep in the same apartment where this shocking catastrophe happened. They were, however, relieved from their alarms on this score, by being informed that it had not received the smallest injury. Disgusted with this barbarity, I left the estate Catwyk, determined never more to return to it.

* The above unhappy people were poisoned by their slaves about six years after this happened.

I have already stated that on the 24th of August I gave in a hopeless request to the governor for my boy's emancipation; and on the 8th of October I saw with equal joy and surprise the following advertisement posted up, 'That if anyone could give in a lawful objection why *John Stedman*, a Quadroon infant, the son of Captain Stedman, should not be presented with the blessing of freedom, such person or persons to appear before January 1st, 1777.' I no sooner read it, than I ran with the good news to my good friend, Mr Palmer, who assured me that the above was no more than a form, put in practice on the supposition of my producing the bail required, which undoubtedly they expected from my having so boldly given in my request to the governor of the colony. Without being able to utter one syllable in reply, I retired to the company of Joanna, who, with a smile, bid me never to despair, that Johnny certainly one day would be free.

About this time we were informed, that in the Utrecht paper an impertinent libel had appeared against the good Fourgeoud, ridiculing him for his embassy to the Ouca and Seramica negroes. This gentleman, though he had no assistance from these *allies* to expect, and his troops now melted down almost to nothing, nevertheless scorned to keep those that could stand upon their feet inactive. Thus, having provided the few remaining privates with new clothes (the first they had received since 1772) besides new sabres, bill-hooks, etc. he sent them all once more, accompanied only by the subalterns, to be encamped at the mouth of the Casepoere Creek, in the upper parts of the Cottica river. The staff officers and captains were ordered soon to follow, and on the 7th *we* were treated by our commander, for the *first* time, with a sirloin of good roast beef.

Having now prepared myself once more for actual service, and again received a profusion of wine, spirits, and refreshments of every kind to carry with me to the woods, from different friends at Paramaribo, I left my dear mulatto and her boy to the care of that excellent woman Mrs Godefroy, in order to set out on my seventh campaign, and help, if possible, to complete that business we had so long and so ardently undertaken for the safety and welfare of this valuable colony.

23

On the 10th of November, in company with several other gentlemen, I set out in a tent barge for the encampment at the Casepoere Creek. On our passage we met Colonel Texier, who assured us that since the blow we gave to the rebels at Gado Saby, they were mostly fled to the other side of that great river, where they found refuge among the French who were settled in Cayenne. Thus everything promised fair to crown our endeavours with success, and finally to re-establish safety and tranquillity in the colony.

We arrived safe in the encampment at the Casepoere Creek, in Cottica river, on the 13th, but, in stepping ashore without shoes and stockings, I narrowly escaped being bitten by a land-scorpion.

Almost the first accidents that I saw here was a poor fellow, a marine, going to bathe in the river, who was instantly snapped away by a large alligator. I no sooner beheld him sink and disappear, than having stripped, I actually dived after the poor man, by the help of a long oar, which a negro held perpendicular under water for the purpose, constantly taking care to keep all my limbs in motion. However I found him not, and tugging the oar as a signal to pull it up, the fellow, by miscomprehension, pushed both it and myself down with such violence that we did not rise again to the surface till near the middle of the stream, which carried down the oar, while I regained the shore by swimming and very great exertion.

On the 20th, being now once more ordered to march on discovery to Gado Saby, I set out at six o'clock in the morning, with two subaltern officers, three sergeants, seven corporals, and fifty privates, besides a surgeon, and the noted free negro Gousary (whom we lost for three or four hours) and encamped near the banks of the same creek, not having been able to advance above six miles due west from its mouth.

On the 21st we marched north for about seven or eight miles, without meeting with one drop of water to alleviate our burning thirst, it being at this time in the very heart of the dry season, which this year was more scorching than I ever remembered it before.

Having now changed my course to the north-east, and passed the quagmire, about noon the following day we marched *dry* through the late fatal marsh, and an hour after we kept due west. Falling in with a large field of yams, we demolished it, then proceeding forward, I encamped in the old settlement Cosaay almost choked for want of water, not having met with anything like it from the moment we set out. Here, however, the negro slaves found means to procure us some, which, though stagnant and stinking like a kennel, we drank, straining it through our shirtsleeves.

On the 23rd I marched east from Cosaay, with a view of obtaining some fresh accounts of the rebels, and proceeded by a path of communication through cultivated fields. But we fell in with nothing, some delightful views and a large herd of *warree* hogs excepted, which from the gnashing of their teeth and their stamping the ground before we saw them, we had actually mistaken for a straggling party of the enemy, and had consequently fresh-primed, and prepared to engage them.

About noon we returned to Gado Saby, where, sitting down to rest from our fatigue, a tall old rebel negro appeared suddenly in the very midst of us, with a long white beard, a white cotton sheet tied about his shoulders, and a broken cutlass in his hand. Seeing this venerable apparition, I instantly started up, and forbidding my people to fire at him, I civilly desired him to approach me, pledging myself that no person under my command should dare to hurt him, but that he should have everything for his relief that I could afford. He answered, 'No, no, *masera!*' with the utmost deliberation, and in an instant disappeared. Two of my men (contrary to my orders) fired after him at the distance of perhaps six paces only, yet both missed their object, to my great satisfaction, he being a poor forsaken creature that had been left behind the rest, gleaning a precarious subsistence from his own deserted fields which we had formerly destroyed. What renders the negroes so difficult to hit with a ball is this, that they never run straight forward, but zig-zag, like the forked lightning in the elements.

I now, to fulfil my orders, once more ransacked Cosaay with its adjoining plains, though with a sore heart on account of the poor lonely old rebel. Here, having cut down several cotton and plantain-trees, pigeon-pease, maize, and some rice, most of which had spontaneously sprung up again since our last devastation, I could not help leaving, before a little shed where was some fresh ashes and banana shells, a few rusk biscuits and a good piece of salt beef, as also a bottle of new rum, for the unfortunate solitary old man. After this we once more encamped in the fields of Cosaay.

Having now fully completed my commission, I, with my detachment, marched back for the Casepoere Creek, directing my course through the ruined fields of Gado Saby, which were at present choked up to a perfect wildneress. Hence we kept first to the south-west, and then due south, after which we slung our hammocks near a former encampment. It is to be observed that at this time all the marshes were nearly dry, on account of the hottest season I ever remember;

while the foetid smell occasioned by the quantities of dead warrapa fish, that had been deserted by the water, was an intolerable nuisance. From among these putrid fishes, our negro slaves nevertheless selected the most tolerable, which, fried in the evening, served them for a delicate morsel.

The morning following we again marched south-west by west, when we slung our hammocks not above four miles from the Casepoere Creek; and on the 26th (keeping south-south-west) we arrived in the grand camp, much fatigued and emaciated.

A detachment of fifty men was next sent out to reconnoitre at Jerusalem, and on the 6th of December the long-expected relief, consisting of three hundred and fifty men, arrived in the river Surinam from Holland, after a voyage of nine weeks and three days, of which they spent a fortnight at Plymouth.

By these the unfortunate account was brought that Captain Jochem Meyer (who had on board a considerable sum of money for our troops) was taken by the Moors and carried with his crew to Morocco, where they were condemned to be slaves to the emperor;* and that the ship *Paramaribo*, Captain Spruyt (being one of the vessels that carried over the sick in the beginning of August) was wrecked and entirely lost in the channel, on the rocks of Ushant. By the exertions of some French fishing-boats, the crew and troops had all been saved and carried into Brest, whence they had taken a fresh passage for the Texel. After the Prince of Orange (who was ever distinguished for benevolence, and doing good and humane actions) ordered the officers and private men, above one hundred in number, to receive the following sums by way of defraying their loss: each marine received about four, the subalterns thirty, the captains forty, and Major Medlar, who commanded, fifty pounds sterling. However, by this shipwreck, I lost all my three chests of sweetmeats and pickles, besides parrots, butterflies and monkeys, intended as presents to my friends in Europe.

Having now for above a month been lodged in a paltry hut, beaten by the wind and showers of rain (which began to set in unexpectedly), and being informed that, notwithstanding the arrival of the relief, we were still to stay some time longer in the woods—which broke many hearts—I, on the 12th of December, earnestly set about building for myself a comfortable house, which was finished, without either nail or hammer, in less than six days. It had two rooms, a piazza with rails and a small kitchen, besides a garden, in which I sowed, in pepper-cresses, the names of Joanna and John. My next-door neighbour, who was my friend Captain Bolts, made shift to keep a goat, and thus

* The above captain and his crew were since set at liberty, having been ransomed by the Dutch.

we lived not altogether uncomfortably. Others kept hens and ducks, but not a cock was to be seen in the camp, for these, having first had all their tongues cut out to prevent their crowing (though to no purpose) had been since condemned to lose their heads. In short, our gentlemen built a row of very curious houses indeed, all projecting from the beach; while, on the opposite side, above a hundred green huts being constructed to receive the newly arrived troops, the whole together formed no contemptible street, though it must be confessed its inhabitants were little better than scarecrows.

What was most remarkable in my own habitation, however, was its entry, which was not by the door, nor yet by the window, but only by the roof, where I crept in and out, allowing absolutely no other admittance; and by this contrivance alone I was effectually guarded from those frequent visitors who smelt my pancakes, and used to make too free with my eggs and bacon, besides interrupting me while I was drawing, writing, or reading. Upon the whole, I must acknowledge that this encampment was agreeable enough (more so as being on elevated ground), had it not been for the pestilential damps and mephitic vapours that exhale constantly from the earth, and had already sent numbers to the other world.

The troops of the Society of Surinam, who had been encamped at the Wana Creek (the rainy season prematurely setting in) now wisely broke up, and on the 26th passing by us, rowed down the River Cottica on their way to the plantations in the Perica Creek; but as for us, we were as usual condemned to linger in the Casepoere camp, while Fourgeoud still kept snug at Paramaribo. With the above officers we received intelligence that a few more rebels had been taken at the Marawina, while we ourselves daily continued to send out patrols to the right and left, but met with nothing to capture.

At last, on the 29th, six barges came to an anchor before our encampment, with part of the fresh troops that were arrived from Holland for our relief. I could not help viewing them with compassion, and not without a cause, for many of them had been already attacked with the scurvy and other loathsome diseases. We however sent for bricks, built an oven to bake fresh bread, and did all that was in our power to comfort them. Having received also a supply of wine for my own use, I gave a hearty welcome to all the officers to cheer their spirits; but this ill-fated liquor had an effect far different from what I intended on one of our captains, who, from some misunderstanding, challenged me to fight him instantly. Having retired to some distance from the camp, and drawing our sabres, he burst out into an immoderate fit of laughter and, throwing away his weapon, desired me to cut away, but that for his part he had such a real regard for me, that he felt it was impossible for him to make any resistance.

After which, catching me in both his arms, he gave me so hearty an embrace, that he had nearly stifled me, and I could not without the greatest difficulty get disentangled. Being recovered from my surprise, I could not help smiling in my turn and, after a friendly reprimand, re-conducted my valiant opponent to the company, where we closed the year with the greatest mirth and conviviality.

A confounded tumble through my hammock having ushered in the morning of 1777, we went to the commanding officer of the camp, to pay him the compliments of the season.

On the 3rd, six more barges with troops came up from Paramaribo, which completed the number of three hundred and fifty men arrived from Holland. Among these, being informed there was a Captain Charles Small, come from the Scots Brigade, I instantly sculled down the river alone in a canoe to meet him and offer him my assistance. I had no sooner got on board his barge than I found him suspended in a hammock with a burning fever. He, not knowing me on account of my dress which was no better than that of the most ragged sailor, asked me what I wanted; but when he saw in me his poor friend Stedman, changed from a stout sprightly young fellow to a miserable debilitated tatterdemallion, he grasped me by the hand, without uttering a word, and burst into tears. This agitation, while it increased his illness, showed the goodness of his heart to me, more than anything he could have uttered on the subject. 'D—n your blubbering, Charles!' said I; 'turn out of this stinking cockleshell. I'll presently cure thee.' Getting him hoisted into my canoe, I brought him on shore to my own habitation, but with the greatest difficulty, being obliged to thrust him through a crevice made on purpose, as the hole in the roof was not calculated even for any healthy person's admittance, myself excepted. Having here slung his hammock near to my own, and boiled some water, I treated him with warm grog and a toasted biscuit, and he became much better from that very moment. He now acquainted me that one of his men was drowned on the passage, and that Colonel Fourgeoud having entertained the officers with a ball after their landing, he concluded his illness to be the consequence of too much dancing. A little after this, Colonel Fourgeoud himself appeared in person in the camp and entertained us with music of a different kind. This was no less than the discouraging news that by the newly-arrived corps of officers several of us had lost our rank (both in the regiment and in the army) after parching above four years in a burning sun, toiling ourselves almost to death, and subsisting upon stinking meat and black rusk. To add to this grievance, while the above gentlemen usurped our preferment, we were, instead of being relieved, ordered to continue in the woods in order to teach them their duty.

During the above unpleasing probation, the major's duty again fell to my share. This was at the time extremely disagreeable, as I was obliged to chastise the men, many of whom pilfered the magazine to alleviate hunger, having been without the article of bread for seven days, since the oven had dropped to pieces. Among others, one poor fellow was nearly flogged to death for having borrowed one of the colonel's Bologna sausages; for, let it be remembered, that our commander-in-chief, whatever might be the distress and hardships of the rest, never forgot to support his own dignity by at least half a dozen of stout negroes loaded with bacon hams, Bologna sausages, bullocks' tongues, tea, coffee, sugar, Madeira wine, Holland's gin, etc.

At length, on the 8th, a barge arrived, not only with a supply of salt beef and rusk, but a bullock and two hogs, as a present from Mr Felman, who, accompanied by his lady, came actually on a visit to Fourgeoud, in this very strange encampment. The above animals being immediately killed, they were distributed among four hundred people, so that it may well be conceived the shares, though sweet, were not very large. Afterwards the company walked about to view our different habitations. Being arrived at my dwelling, Fourgeoud led them round and round, but seeing no door to get in, he called out, 'Nobody at home?' I instantly thrust my head through the thatch, with a pancake in my hand, and offered to haul in the ladies; but this they civilly declined. I never saw Fourgeoud laugh so much in my life. As soon, however, as he was able to recover his gravity, he exclaimed, '*Sacré Dieu! Il faut être Stedman—il faut être original comme lui*'; and re-conducted the company to his own apartment.

Whenever Captain Small and I went out, we generally spent our time in a beautiful savannah where we had erected a green shed and called it Ranelagh; here we caroused and cracked a bottle in private, till we could crack no longer, having lived so well that in a little time more than a week my cheese and bacon hams quite disappeared, and not a drop of wine or rum was left in the flasks. After this he, as well as I, were obliged to live on short allowance. Small had the satisfaction, however, to see his shipmates do the same for, not being acquainted with the economy necessary in a forest, they had made all their flour into plum-pudding, and were already obliged to break their teeth on a piece of rye rusk.

As early as the 12th, one hundred and fifty of these newly-arrived people were ordered to march, and, by the way of seasoning them, each man, besides heavy accoutrements and a hammock, had orders to carry a stuffed knapsack on his back. Of this party, my friend Small happened to be one; being as corpulent as Sir John Falstaff, and I having accoutred him in the above manner, the poor fellow could hardly walk at all. By declaring to Fourgeoud that I must roll him along like a hogshead, he got leave to be disengaged from a part of his unwieldly encumbrances.

Everything being ready, this loaded detachment now faced to the right and set out, with Colonel Fourgeoud at their head, for the river Marawina. While I must here acknowledge that this chief was now become to myself as civil as I could expect or desire, yet justice compels me to add that to all others he remained just as inflexible a tyrant as ever I had known him.

At this time the discipline was peculiarly strict in the camp, so that whoever made the very least noise was most severely punished, nay, threatened to be shot; and even the sentinels were ordered to challenge rounds and patrols by no other sound than whistling, which was answered in the same manner.

On the 18th, one of these being condemned to be flogged for speaking loud, I however found means (Fourgeoud not being yet returned) to get him pardoned, after he was already stripped. The following day, nevertheless, evinced that I could punish when things were carried too far. Seeing a large piece of boiled pork (about two pounds weight) flying past me with great velocity, and finding it was thrown by one marine to another, in the course of a quarrel, I instantly ordered them to pick it up, and (having cut it in two) I stood over them myself till they swallowed every morsel of it in my presence, sand and all, without either bread or drink. This they since declared was such a punishment as surpassed my conception, and they should remember it to the end of their lives.

On the 23rd, I received from town a well-timed supply of wine and fresh provisions; and the same day Colonel Fourgeoud, with his detachment, arrived from the Marawina. During this trip, our active commander had again discovered and destroyed fifty-nine houses, besides three fields of provisions. This certainly gave the finishing blow to the rebel negroes, since, having no further supply on this side of the water, they entirely abandoned it and went to settle in the French colony Cayenne. In this hard though necessary service the men had suffered prodigiously, especially those newly arrived; numbers of them were carried in hammocks on poles, while near thirty were left sick at the Marawina, and my friend Small was at least one stone lighter.

At this time, in the camp hospital, above one hundred were also dangerously ill. Nothing was heard but sighs and the shrieking of the Guiana owl, which for ever kept them company during the dismal nights. Cramps, so common in Surinam, also infested those that were able to do duty, and there reigned a general melancholy all around.

Here one man was to be seen covered over with bloody boils from head to foot; there another led along by two of his comrades in a deep lethargy, who, in spite of pinching and pricking, dosed into eternity; a third, swelled by the dropsy, and imploring the surgeon in vain to tap off the water (who generally answered that it was too late), was left to expire by suffocation. In the hospital some were observed clasping their hands and praying aloud to God to be relieved, while others lay at their side in a frenzy fever, tearing their hair, blaspheming Providence, and cursing the day that they were born. In short, all was dreadful beyond description.

From day to day mortality now gained ground, while by some accident, to complete the distress, part of the camp got on fire; but this was fortunately extinguished without any material ill consequences, by the activity and exertions of the poor negroes.

On the 26th my misery, however, drew towards an end, when, to my astonishment, and without my asking it, Colonel Fourgeoud gave me a leave of absence, if I chose it, to accompany him and stay henceforth at Paramaribo. Without hesitation, I most joyfully accepted. Thus, having made my friend Captain Small a present of my house, my Ranelagh, and all my fresh provisions, besides entertained him and some other officers, I took my last adieu from them all and at midnight, with Colonel Fourgeoud, rowed down the River Cottica in an elegant barge with ten oars, in company with two more of his officers.

As the boat shoved off, Colonel Fourgeoud declared to us that, having ransacked the forest in every direction and driven the rebels over the Marawina in to Cayenne, he was determined no more to return to the woods, but in a few weeks to draw the long and painful expedition to a conclusion.

The celebrated Gramman Quacy

24

BEING now once more arrived in town, and wishing to be no longer troublesome to anybody, I hired a very neat small house by the water-side, in which we lived nearly as happy as we had done at the Hope.

Having been waited on by a number of planters and others with congratulations on our success against the rebels, among the rest appeared the celebrated Gramman Quacy, who came to show me his fine coat and gold medal which he had received as a present from the Prince of Orange, in Holland. This man, being one of the most extraordinary characters of all the negroes in Surinam, or perhaps in the world, I cannot proceed without giving some account of him. This African (for he was born on the coast of Guinea) by his insinuating temper and industry, not only obtained his freedom from a state of slavery, but by his wonderful ingenuity and artful conduct found the means of procuring a very competent subsistence.

Having got the name of a lockoman, or sorcerer, among the lower slaves, no crime of any consequence was committed, especially at the plantations, but Gramman Quacy, which signifies Great-man Quacy, was instantly sent for to discover the perpetrators. This he so very seldom missed, owing to their faith in his sorceries added to his penetrating look and authority among them, that he has often prevented further mischief to their masters. For these services he occasionally received very capital rewards. The corps of rangers, and all fighting free negroes, are under his influence; to them he sells his *obias* or amulets, in order to make them invulnerable. By this deceit he has most certainly done much good to the colony, and at the same time filled his pockets with no inconsiderable profit to himself, while his person is adored and respected by the blacks like a God. The trash of which his amulets are made costs him in reality nothing, being neither more nor less than a collection of small pebbles, sea-shells, cut hair, fish-bones, feathers, etc. the whole sewed up together in small packets, which are tied with a string of cotton round the neck or some other part of the bodies of his credulous votaries.

But besides these, and many other artful contrivances, he had the good fortune, in 1730, to find out the valuable root known by the name of *quaciae bitter*, of which he was actually the first discoverer, and by this drug alone he might have amassed riches, were he not entirely abandoned to indolence and dissipation. Nevertheless his age,

Q

though he could not exactly ascertain it, must have been very great, since he used frequently to repeat that he acted as drummer, and beat the alarm on his master's estate, when the French commodore, Jacques Cassard, put the colony under contribution, in the year 1712.

In returning the visits of my friends, I paid one to Mr Andrew Reynsdorp, who showed me the loop and button of his hat, which being diamond, had cost him two hundred guineas—such is the luxury of Surinam. But even this is exceeded by the magnificence of M. d'Albergh, who, when I waited on him, besides a gold snuff-box set with brilliants, value six hundred pounds sterling, made me remark two silver bits (small pieces of money) set in gold, and surrounded with diamonds, and declared to me that they were all the money he had in the world when he first came to Surinam from his own country, Sweden. 'Did you work?' said I. 'No.' 'Did you beg?' 'No.' 'You did not steal, sir?' 'No: but, *entre nous*, I whined and acted the enthusiast, which sometimes is very necessary, and I found it preferable to the other three.' One instance more of the extravagance and folly of the inhabitants of this colony, and I have done. Two of them disputing about a most elegant and expensive carriage that was imported from Holland, a law-suit immediately ensued to determine who was to possess it, during which time the coach was left uncovered in the street till it fell to pieces and was totally destroyed.

On the 10th of February, most of our officers being now arrived at Paramaribo from the camp, Colonel Fourgeoud entertained the whole with a feast, as he was pleased to call it, at the headquarters. Here he acquainted us, with evident marks of satisfaction, that he had at last put a final end to the expedition, having—notwithstanding there was so little bloodshed—perfectly accomplished his aim in rooting out the rebels, by destroying twenty-one towns or villages, and demolishing two hundred fields with vegetables of every kind, on which they depended for subsistence: also, that the intelligence was now confirmed, that the negroes were to a man fled over the River Marawina, where they and their friends were settled and protected by the French colony of Cayenne, who not only gave them shelter, but supplied them with everything they wanted. On which good news we all heartily congratulated him, and drank further prosperity to the colony of Surinam, the future safety of which now depended on the new cordon or path of circumvalation, defended by the troops of the Society and the corps of black soldiers or rangers.

What cannot but redound to his honour is that, at the time he imposed such hardships on his own troops, he never deliberately put a rebel negro captive to death, nor even, if he could avoid it, delivered them into the hands of justice, well knowing that, while it was his duty to expel them, nothing but the most barbarous usage and tyranny had driven these poor people to this last extremity. Indeed I myself, whom during the first three years he persecuted with unremitting severity, must do him the justice to say that he was indefatigable in doing his duty, and that, though confused, I believe him at bottom to have been an undaunted and very brave officer.

He further acquainted us that the vessels, with a fresh supply of provisions from Holland, had been cast on the lee-shore in the Texel Roads, one of them having her upper cabin stove away, with the second mate and three of her men washed overboard. He added, however, that part of the stores had been saved and loaded on board two bilanders, which were this very day arrived in the River Surinam. And now, so much in particular was I become his favourite, that he even made me his confidant and declared that he proposed keeping the last arrived troops, however fast they were dying away, encamped for many months after our departure. He then began to tell me what officers he meant, if possible, to ruin on their return, and which, by his recommendation, he intended to promote. But here I took the liberty to stop him short by declaring, upon my honour, that those very gentlemen should be apprised by myself of their impending danger, if he persisted in carrying this cruel plan in execution.

On the 16th, being invited to dine with His Excellency the Governor, I laid before him my collection of drawings, and remarks on the colony of Surinam, which I had the satisfaction to see him honour with the highest approbation. I then returned him my thanks, not only for the material assistance he had afforded me in completing this work, but for the unlimited marks of regard and distinction with which he had treated me from first to last, during the whole time I resided in Guiana.

Availing myself of his friendship, I ventured, two days after, to give him the following very uncommon request, praying him to lay it before the court; this, with a smile on his countenance, and a hearty shake by the hand, he actually promised me to perform.

I, the under-subscribed, do pledge my *word of honour* (being all I possess in the world besides my pay) as *bail*, that if my late ardent request to the court for the emancipation of my dear boy JOHNNY STEDMAN be granted, the said boy shall never to the end of his life become a charge to the colony of Surinam.

(Signed) JOHN G. STEDMAN

Paramaribo,
Feb. 18th, 1777

Having now done the utmost that lay in my power, I for several days waited the result with anxiety, but without meeting with the smallest hopes of success. Thus, with a broken heart, I was obliged at last to give him (sweet fellow) over for lost, or take him with me to Europe, which must have been plunging a dagger in the bosom of his mother.

While I remained in this situation, the transport ships were put in commission on the 26th for our departure, and I myself ordered as one of the commissaries to see them wooded and watered. The officers were also cleared their arrears, and thirteen men discharged at their own desire, to push their fortune at Paramaribo.

On the 3rd of March my friend de Graaf sailed for Holland, and to my great satisfaction took with him Joanna's youngest brother, Henry, for whom he has since obtained his freedom. I sailed with them down the river as far as Braam's Point, and wished them a successful voyage. As I here went ashore in a fishing-boat, I was tempted to leap into the sea, and enjoy the cooling and healthy pleasure of swimming in the Atlantic ocean.

The 8th of March, being the Prince of Orange's birthday, it was celebrated at the headquarters. After dinner, hearing Captain Bolts in an undeserved manner censured by the colonel's adjutant for recommending one of the young volunteers of an excellent character, but who had no friends to support him, I broke through the ring that surrounded them in a passion and, not being able to restrain myself, publicly reproved the aggressor, even in Fourgeoud's presence. A furious altercation and very high words immediately ensued, the consequence of which was that next morning at sunrise, without seconds, we walked to the savannah where, near the gallows, we drew our small swords. After making a few passes at each other, Captain Van Geurick's point met my shell; having nearly pierced it, his blade snapped in two pieces, and the fortune of war put him entirely in my power. Disdaining, however, to take a mean advantage, I instantly dropped my small sword, and desired him to step home and replace his own, in order to renew the battle; but this proposal he was pleased to call so generous that, taking me by the hand, he requested a renewal of friendship. Thus, acknowledging we had been too hasty on both sides, we went to visit poor Bolts, who knew nothing of our morning's walk, and was (though not without difficulty) persuaded also to enter into the amicable treaty, and a general reconciliation took place.

On the 10th, having spent most of the day with the governor, in the evening I went on board the ships with Captain Bolts, to inspect the preparations for the voyage. There we found that the mice and rats had made such havoc among our provision, with which we were now very well stocked, that I was under the necessity of procuring half a dozen cats to destroy them, which useful animals are in Surinam neither so plenty, nor so good, as in Europe, being lazy and indolent on account of the climate.

The following day I was surprised with a polite message from the governor and the court, acquainting me that, 'having taken my former services into consideration, together with my humanity and gallantry in offering my honour as bail to see my child, before I left him, made a free citizen of the world, they had unanimously decreed, without further ceremony or expense, to compliment me with a letter, which was at the same time officially presented to me, containing his emancipation from that day for ever after'.

No man could be more suddenly transported from woe to happiness than I was at this moment, while his poor mother shed tears for joy and gratitude—the more so as we had left all hopes, and the favour came perfectly unexpected, while near forty beautiful boys and girls were left to perpetual slavery by their parents of my acquaintance, and many of them without being so much as once enquired after at all.

What is most extraordinary indeed is that, while the well-thinking few highly applauded my sensibility, many not only blamed, but publicly derided me for my paternal affection, which was called a weakness, a whim. So extravagant was my joy on this day, that I became like one frantic with pleasure. I not only made my will in his favour (though, God knows, I had little to dispose of) but I appointed my friends Mr Robert Gordon and Mr James Gourlay to be my executors and his guardians during my absence. In their hands I left all my papers sealed, till I should demand them again or they should be informed of my death. I then ordered all my sheep and poultry, which had prodigiously increased, to be transported and put under their care and, making a new suit of clothes for the occasion—which cost me twenty guineas—I waited on a Mr Snyderhans, one of the clergymen at Paramaribo, to appoint a day when my boy, my Johnny Stedman, should be made a Christian.*

On the 18th Colonel Fourgeoud's remaining troops at last came down from the encampments at Casepoere Creek, and every preparation was made for our departure. At the same time, the ecstasy of the few surviving marines at their quitting this country was so

* I should not here omit to mention that in the colony of Surinam all emancipated slaves are (if males) bound to help in defending the settlement against all home and foreign enemies, and no emancipated slave, male or female, can ever go to law at all against their former master or mistress. Finally, if any emancipated slave, male or female, dies in the colony and leaves behind any possessions whatever, in that case one quarter of the property also goes to his former owners.

great, that such intemperance, riot, and disorder ensued as produced the most formidable quarrels between them and the troops of the Society, till, some being wounded and some being flogged, peace was finally, though with difficulty, re-established.

The day of our departure now approached fast, and I gave up my house and, at Mrs Godefroy's pressing invitation, I spent the few remaining moments in that which she had prepared for the reception of Joanna and her boy, in her beautiful garden, charmingly situated under the shade of tamarind and orange-trees. The house she also had nearly furnished with every accommodation that could be desired, besides allowing Joanna a negro woman and a girl to attend on her for life. Thus situated, how blest should I have been in this spot to end my days! But fate ordained it otherwise.

On the 22nd, I made it my business with Captain Small (who was come down with leave of absence) to wait on the Reverend Mr Snyderhans, according to appointment. But he, to both our great surprise, peremptorily refused to christen the boy, alleging for his reason, that as I was going to Holland, I could not answer for his *christian* education. We replied, that he was under two very proper guardians. The blacksmith's son (for such was this divine) persisted, and we remonstrated, but to no purpose, for he was just as deaf as his father's anvil, and I believe, upon my soul, quite as empty as his bellows. At length, wearied out with his fanatical impertinence, I swore that I would sooner see the boy die a heathen, than christened by such a blockhead. My friend Small could not help bestowing on him a hearty curse, and, slapping the door with a vengeance, we departed.

Feasting and conviviality now prevailed once more at Paramaribo, as on our first arrival. Grand dinners, suppers, and balls were heard of in every quarter. But I only visited a few of my select friends, among which number had constantly been Governor Nepveu. There, for the last time, I made one of the company at a truly magnificent entertainment, a scene of liberality and hospitality for which the inhabitants of Surinam are so justly conspicuous; and on the 25th the baggage was shipped on board the vessels.

On the 26th, we took our last leave of His Excellency the Governor, *en corps*, as assuredly was his due; after which all the officers of the Society troops waited on Colonel Fourgeoud, at the headquarters, to wish us a prosperous voyage to Holland. I believe that now a hundred times Fourgeoud shook me by the hand, declaring that there was not a young man he loved better in the world, that had he commanded me to march through fire as well as water, he was convinced I should never have left it without accomplishing his orders, with many other fine compliments. But I must candidly acknowledge, that though I had a heart to *forgive*, my mind would never permit me to *forget* the many and unnecessary difficulties and miseries to which I had been too wantonly exposed. At the same time he informed me that he did not propose to depart with us, but intended to follow the regiment very soon, with the remains of the last-come relief, when he would render me every service in his power. Whatever were his *real* motives for such a sudden change in his disposition towards me, suffice it to say that few people at this time were better friends than were the old Colonel Fourgeoud and Captain Stedman.

In the evening I went to take a short farewell of my most valuable acquaintances, but my soul was too full of a friend that was still dearer, to be impressed with that sensibility on separating from them, that it must have felt on another occasion. And here I cannot in justice omit remarking that while I gave the most impetuous vent to my feelings, not the smallest expression of poignant sorrow, or even of dejection, escaped from Joanna's lips, while her good sense and fortitude even restrained the tear from starting in my afflicted presence. I now once more earnestly pressed her to accompany me, in which I was seconded by the inestimable Mrs Godefroy and all her friends; but she remained equally inflexible. What could I say or do? Not knowing how to answer, or how sufficiently to admire her firmness and resignation—which so greatly exceeded my own—I determined, if possible, to imitate her conduct, and calmly to resign myself to my fate, preparing for the fatal moment when my heart forebode me we were to pronounce the last adieu, and separate for ever.

The whole corps being ordered, at seven o'clock on the morning of the 27th, to wait on Colonel Fourgeoud at the headquarters, I tore myself away from all that was dear to me in this world without disturbing them, in order to prevent the tender scene of parting. He then conducted us to the water-side where the boats lay in waiting, and we were immediately embarked under a general salute from the fortress and the vessels in the roads. The whole corps now having dined on board the staff-ship with Lieutenant Colonel de Borgnes, Colonel Fourgeoud politely invited me to accompany him back to town till next morning, but, with a broken heart, I thought best to decline. He then took his final leave, and wishing us all a safe and prosperous voyage to Europe, he returned, under a salute of nine guns and three cheers, back to Paramaribo.

On the 29th of March, at midnight, the signal-gun being fired, the two ships got under way, and dropped down till before Fort Amsterdam, where they once more came to an anchor.

Here my friends Gordon and Gourlay, the guardians of my boy, affectionately coming to visit me, did no less than actually prevail on me to accompany them back to Paramaribo. My soul could not resist this second invitation of once more beholding what was so dear to me. I went and found Joanna, who had displayed so much fortitude in my presence, now bathed in tears and scarcely alive, so much was she become the victim of melancholy and despair. Nor had she partaken of food, or sleep, since my departure, nor spoken to any living creature, indeed not stirred from the spot where I had left her on the morning of the 27th.

The ships not being quite ready to go to sea till two days after, I was prevailed upon to stay on shore a little longer, with poor Joanna and her boy, which seemed to cheer her. But few hours had elapsed, however, when a sailor abruptly came in with the message that the ship's boat lay in waiting that minute to carry me on board. Joanna's mother took the infant from her arms, but the unfortunate Joanna (now but nineteen) gazing on me and holding me by the hand, with a look ten thousand times more dejected than Sterne's Maria, was unable to utter one word. The power of speech also forsook me, and my heart tacitly invoked the protection of Providence to befriend them. Joanna now shut her beauteous eyes—her lips turned the pale colour of death—she bowed her head, and sank motionless in the arms of her adopted mother. Here I roused all my remaining fortitude and, leaving them surrounded by every care and attention, departed and bid God bless them.

25

EVERYTHING being at last perfectly adjusted for our departure, both vessels, under the command of Lieutenant Colonel des Borgnes, weighed anchor on the morning of the 1st of April, 1777, when, with a fresh breeze, we put to sea and kept course north and north-west. Motionless and speechless, I hung over the ship's stern till the land quite disappeared. After some days, however, by considerable exertions, I got the better of my melancholy, though not of my affection, and my mind became once more composed and calm. What chiefly contributed to the restoring of my peace, was the comfortable reflection that if I had in some measure injured myself, I had at least done good to a few others, by relieving three innocent and deserving young people from a state of bondage. Yet, for this action, I was assuredly most amply rewarded by the preservation of my life, principally owing to their unremitting care and attention, while such numbers fell all around me, the victims of the climate and the service, some having lost the use of their limbs, and some of their memory. Nay, one or two were entirely deprived of their mental faculties, and continued in a state of incurable insanity for ever.

In short, out of the number of near twelve hundred able-bodied men, not one hundred returned to their friends and their country, and perhaps not twenty among these were to be found in perfect health. So very destructive is the service to Europeans in such a climate, that such must ever be the result of the most successful operations in the unwholesome atmosphere of woods and marshes.

About the 14th of April, having passed the Tropics, and changed course to north-north-east and north-east we were becalmed for some days. By the 19th, the calm still continuing, we were daily entertained by swarms of flying fish, and several doradoes and grampusses swimming and tumbling before and after the ships, as if delighting to keep us company.

About the 22nd, the weather began to change considerably, and the whole ship's company were attacked with a severe cold and cough, and many also with the ague. On the 30th, the crew was so weak as to be hardly able to do their duty; two of them indeed, and one marine, were already dead and overboard. Colonel de Borgnes was also at this time so much indisposed that the command devolved upon me for a few days during his illness.

On the 1st of May, being exactly one month at sea—during which time, by way of making a trial, I had continued bare-footed and bare-headed, without catching cold—I, for the first time, not only dressed like my shipmates, but wore everything double, and some things triple, which I found exceedingly comfortable.

On the 13th, in the morning-watch, being not far from the Azores, the vessel was nearly laid on her beam-ends, though then under double-reefed topsails, by a sudden squall. At this time a broken top-gallant-mast a new hand-spike, etc. floated past the ship, the melancholy remains of a shipwreck, which we since were informed to be a Dutch homeward-bound East Indiaman, that had foundered with all the crew near the island of Terceira.

On the 14th the wind was violent, carrying away our fore-top-gallant-mast, and splitting the mainsail. On the evening of the 15th it blew a perfect storm, accompanied with thunder and lightning and very heavy rain, which continued during the night and brought our main-top-mast by the board, while the ship's crew were so very much reduced as to be hardly able to clear the wreck by cutting away with a hatchet.

The two following days we continued scudding before the wind, with a reef in the foresail, the sea running mountains high, and constantly breaking over the vessel—pumps going day and night. Soon after this we saluted the *Alarm* frigate from Holland, which compliment they returned.

At length, the weather becoming fair, we were carried within soundings on the 19th, when we hove the lead in ninety fathom water. But the wind shifting to the north-east with foul weather, we beat about in the chops of the Channel till the morning of the 21st, when at half past one we saw the light off Scilly, and at four o'clock got the pilot on board.

Having been becalmed two days off Dover, it was the 27th before we first saw the Dutch coast. Having kept off shore during the night, we at last doubled Keykduyn and the Helder, and on the 28th, at three o'clock p.m., under a discharge of nine guns, dropped anchor in the Texel roads.

On the 30th, having passed the small island of Urk, in the Zuyder Zee, and running before the wind with a fine breeze, we premeditatedly stuck fast upon the Pampus—a large bank of soft mire, covered with shoal water, not far from Amsterdam, which it naturally protects like a barrier from all foreign invaders. All ships whatever must either be lifted over or dragged through this bank of mud.

On the morning of the 31st, having been becalmed all night, a fresh breeze again sprang up, when we fired a gun as a signal, and five or six water-manakins instantly came off, by the help of which we were dragged over the Pampus, not at the rate of fourteen knots an hour, but at that of fourteen hours a knot, since we did not get clear of it in less than three days sailing, though not four miles in length. However, I must confess, that the last day we had scarcely any wind at all.

During this tedious passage, it was no bad entertainment, to observe the contrast between some newly-arrived Norwegians and us; those people sitting upon deck in their shirts, and wiping off the perspiration, while we were strutting in great coats and fur caps, like so many Muscovites, to keep us from the cold.

Having at this time received a considerable present of refreshments, sent by the city of Amsterdam to the deliverers of their favourite colony, and being so near revisiting their old friends and acquaintances, all on board were in the highest flow of spirits and exulting with gladness—excepting one, from whose mind every happiness was banished.

On the 3rd of June, everything being in readiness, the troops were put on board six lighters appointed to transport them to Bois-le-Duc, in which town they were next to be completed, and do the duty as part of the garrison. As we passed in the lighters through the inland towns, such as Saardam, Haarlem and Tergow, I thought them truly magnificent, particularly the glass painting in the great church of the latter; but their inhabitants, who crowded about us from curiosity to see us, appeared but a disgusting assemblage of ill-formed and ill-dressed rabble, so much had my prejudices been changed by living among the Indians and blacks. Their eyes seemed to resemble those of a pig, their complexions were like the colour of foul linen; they seemed to have no teeth, and to be covered over with rags and dirt. This prejudice, however, was not against these people only, but against all Europeans in general, when compared to the sparkling eyes, ivory teeth, shining skin, and remarkable cleanliness of those I had left behind me. But the most ludicrous circumstance was that during all this we never once considered the truly extraordinary figure that we made ourselves, being so much sunburnt and so pale that we were nearly the colour of dried parchment, and so thin that we looked like moving skeletons; to which I may add, that having lived so long in the woods, we had perfectly the appearance of wild people; and I in particular, very deservedly, obtained the characteristic title of *le Sauvage Anglais*, or the English savage.

In this state we arrived, on the 9th, at the town of Bois-le-Duc, where the troops were finally disembarked. Thus ended, perhaps, one of the most extraordinary expeditions that was ever undertaken by European troops; and to which only the exploits of the American buccaneers have any, and even that a very distant, resemblance.

Now came the time to keep my long-made resolution of bidding a lasting farewell to Colonel Fourgeoud's regiment, from which, on the 10th day of August, I obtained my free dismission, having requested it immediately after my debarkation from the Prince of Orange. He, at the same time, honoured me with a fresh Captain's commission in the Honourable General Stuart's regiment, which I had left in September 1772.

Having now exchanged my blue coat for a scarlet one, bought a very handsome horse, and put Quaco in a brilliant livery, I for the last time entertained my shipmates, with whom, without exception, I drank an everlasting friendship. Then taking my final farewell of them all, I the next morning set out to rejoin the old Scots regiment, where I was received with the strongest marks of joy and unfeigned friendship by the corps.

About the latter end of October, I was offered by the directors of the settlement to be sent over as a lieutenant governor to the colony of Berbice, situated next to Surinam. In consequence, I immediately went to Amsterdam, to wait on them and hear the proposals, in which they indeed offered me a higher salary and greater advantages than they had ever offered to any other gentleman in that situation. But I insisted on having either the government if I survived, or a decent pension after a certain number of years at my return. This being out of their power, they said, to grant, I declined accepting of the offer altogether, judging it more prudent to recover my health and vigour in Europe with a Scottish company, than to parch any longer under the Torrid Zone, without a prospect of settling at home with honour and a competent fortune. Nor was it long before I perfectly recovered, and became as stout and healthy as I had ever been in all my life—a happiness of which not one among one hundred of my late shipmates could boast.

I must now draw this narrative to a conclusion, by once more mentioning the name of Joanna, and acquaint the reader, that, alas!—Joanna is no more!!

In the month of August 1783, I received the melancholy tidings from Mr Gourlay that on the fatal fifth of November this virtuous young woman departed this life, as some suspected by poison,* administered by the hand of jealousy and envy, on account of her prosperity and the marks of distinction which her superior merit had so justly attracted from the respectable part of the colony.

Her adopted mother, Mrs Godefroy, who bedewed her beauteous body with tears, ordered it to be interred with every mark of respect, under the grove of orange-trees where she had lived. Her lovely boy was sent to me, with a bill of near two hundred pounds, his private property, by inheritance from his mother.

This charming youth, having made a most commendable progress

* Her emancipated brother Henry underwent the same melancholy fate.

in his education in Devon, went two West India voyages, with the highest character as a sailor, and during the Spanish troubles served with honour as a midshipman on board his Majesty's ships *Southampton* and *Lizard*, ever ready to engage in any service that the advantage of his king and country called for. But he also is no more, having since perished at sea off the island of Jamaica.

And now, farewell my friends, who have been pleased to peruse this narrative of my distresses with sympathetic sensibility; particularly those whose goodness of heart can forgive my inaccuracies and foibles. I say farewell, claiming no other merit whatever throughout these pages, than that of having spoke the simple truth; which, if I wilfully have violated, may these chapters perish, and be forgotten with their author! But should this treasure, truth, so rarely to be met with, be found in this performance:

Let one poor sprig of bays around my head
Bloom while I live; and point me out when dead.

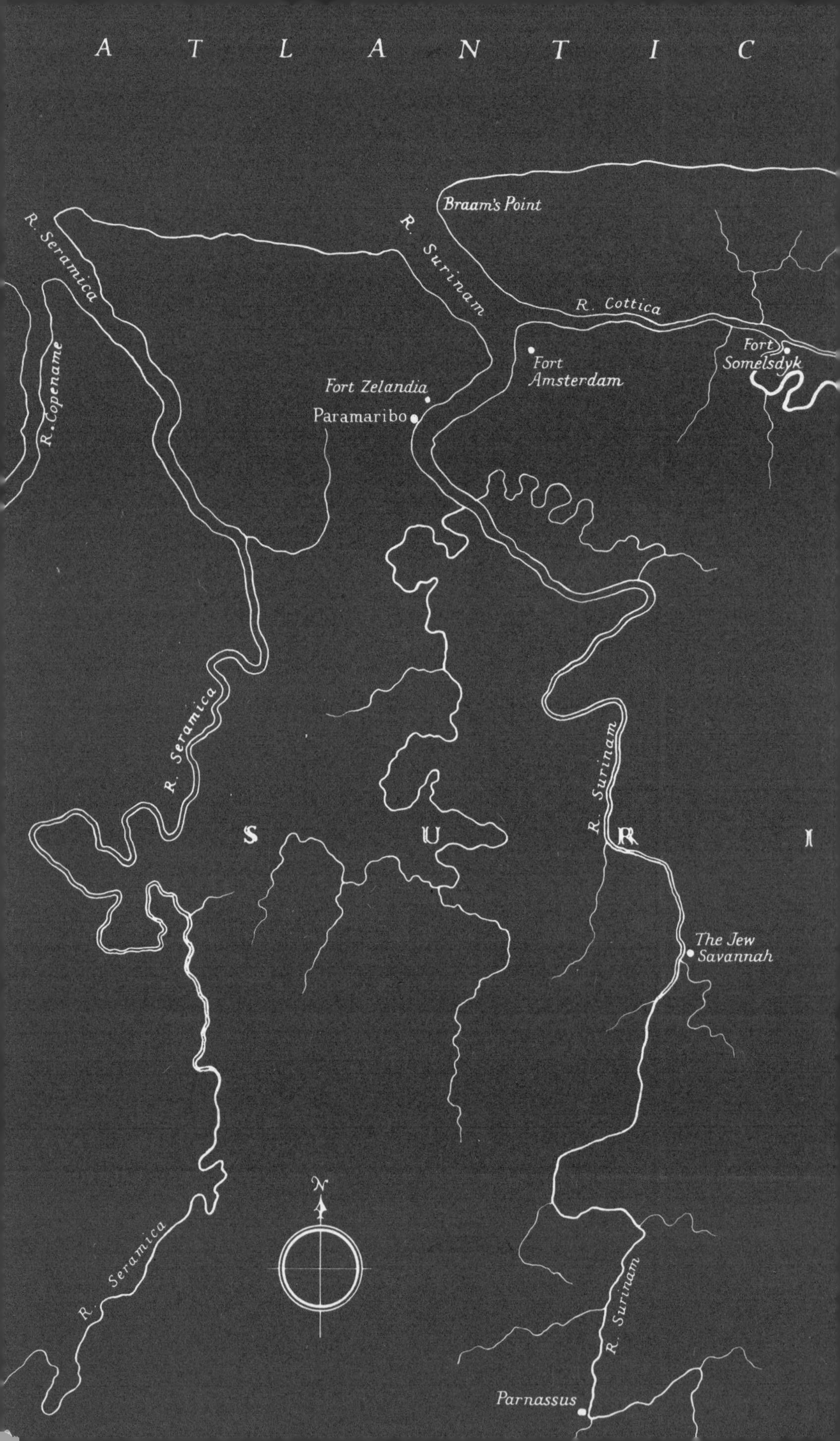

A T L A N T I C

Braam's Point

R. Seramica

R. Surinam

R. Copename

R. Cottica

Fort Somelsdyk

Fort Amsterdam

Fort Zelandia

Paramaribo

R. Seramica

S U R I

R. Surinam

The Jew Savannah

N

R. Seramica

R. Surinam

Parnassus